HARDY'S USE OF ALLUSION

HARDY'S USE OF ALLUSION

Marlene Springer

University Press of Kansas

First published in the United Kingdom 1983 by
THE MACMILLAN PRESS LTD

First published in the United States of America 1983 by the
UNIVERSITY PRESS OF KANSAS
*(Lawrence, Kansas 66045), which was organized by the Kansas
Board of Regents and is operated and funded by Emporia State
University, Fort Hays State University, Kansas State University,
Pittsburg State University, the University of Kansas, and
Wichita State University*

Library of Congress Cataloging in Publication Data

Springer, Marlene.
   Hardy's use of allusion.

   Bibliography: p. 189
   Includes index.
   1. Hardy, Thomas, 1840–1928—Style.   2. Hardy,
Thomas, 1840–1928—Characters.   I. Title.
PR4757.S8S67   1983   823'.8   82–21977
ISBN 0–7006–0231–3

Printed in Hong Kong

For
Haskell, Ann, and Rebecca

Contents

Acknowledgements

I should like to thank Professors Allan Hollingsworth, Paul Zietlow, Peter Casagrande and the late J. O. Bailey for their careful reading and useful suggestions during the development of the manuscript, as well as Professor Harold Orel for his valuable advice during its last stages. The librarians of the Berg Collection in the New York Public Library, the Fitzwilliam Museum in Cambridge, England, the British Library and the Dorset County Museum (especially Mr R. N. R. Peers) were helpful during my study of Hardy's manuscripts. I am also indebted to the University of Missouri—Kansas City Research Council for its financial support of my manuscript work in England. And finally my deepest thanks to Haskell Springer for his undeviating support, fine critical suggestions and willingness to share his life with Thomas Hardy.

Part of Chapter 2 of this book has appeared in the *Colby Library Quarterly*, and Chapter 5 in *Inscape*.

Introductory Textual Note

All references, unless otherwise stated, are to the New Wessex Edition, paperback printing (London, Macmillan), based on the text of 1912 Wessex Edition. Since Hardy did revise parts of the earlier novels for his Wessex Edition, whenever there is a question of stylistic development and evidence that he revised his allusions to accord with a new concept of the novel, a comparison between the manuscript or the first edition, depending on which is extant, and the 1912 Wessex, the last authorised version, is included.[1] Such revisions fall within the scope of this study of Hardy's allusive technique in that they support the thesis that he increasingly improved his literary talents, and that his allusive method was stylistically intentional.

1   Style and Thomas Hardy

Even a cursory survey of style in major Victorian writers reveals
that, in contrast to the eighteenth century, the nineteenth is
remarkable for its diversity: Carlyle is recognised for involved
negatives, Pater his affectation, Ruskin his imperatives, Eliot her
didacticism and detachment, Dickens his labelling, Scott his legal-
istic distance and Hardy for his study of the London *Times*. Even
within this diversity, however, many fiction writers of the period
share a common stylistic trait — the abundant use of literary allusions. George Eliot even felt called to warn against them in a letter
of 22 April 1873: 'As to quotations, please — please to be very
moderate, whether they come from Shakespeare or any other servant of the Muses. A quotation often makes a fine summit to a
climax. . . . But I hate a style speckled with quotations.' Hated or
not, she used them herself, speckling her fiction, her essays, even
her letters with literary references. Hardy was decidedly of his age
in this respect in that he out-alluded virtually every allusionist —
not only in substance, but in skill as well.

Hardy's style in general has long been the subject of debate.
Even so fine a novel as *Far From the Madding Crowd* was attacked
by the *Saturday Review* (9 January 1875, p. 57) for its 'clumsy and
inelegant metaphors', and Hardy was admonished that 'eccen-
tricities of style are not characteristic of genius, nor of original
thinking'. More recently Robert Heilman, while admitting that
Hardy's style has compensatory virtues, lists his rhetorical faults as
'disorderly heaps of modifiers, relative clauses with unclear
antecedents, upsidedown *when* clauses, excess of participial con-
structions, awkward absolute and gerund construction, dangling
modifiers of various kinds, faulty parallelism, clumsy passives,
separation of related elements, confused pronoun references'.[1]
Critics and readers alike, then, concede that Hardy, like Shakespeare, was sometimes cavalier about grammar.

However, most critics now agree that Hardy's occasional lapses
in form are far outweighed by his more comprehensive stylistic

talent. Countering his intermittent defects are his brilliant manipulation of characters, his mastery of set description and his ability
to maintain a balanced and formal structure even as he explores
questions of cosmic range. These stylistic skills, guided by his
profound understanding of the intricacies of human emotions,
helped him to make the English novel a fit vehicle for tragedy —
his major contribution to the genre.

There is little question that Hardy, in spite of an avowed preference for poetry, was deeply concerned about the craft of fiction. In
'The Profitable Reading of Fiction' he defined prose style:

> Style, as far as the word is meant to express something more
> than literary finish, can only be treatment, and treatment
> depends upon the mental attitude of the novelist; thus entering
> into the very substance of a narrative, as into that of any other
> kind of literature. A writer who is not a mere imitator looks
> upon the world with his personal eyes, and in his peculiar
> moods; thence grows up his style, in the full sense of the term.

He undertook a formal study of what he considered to be exem-
plary prose, and in turn drew the method, and often the content,
of his fiction from innumerable sources. His acquaintance with
gothic fiction, and especially Wilkie Collins, taught him to crystal-
ise a particular scene with one image, and, more important, to
probe abnormal states of consciousness.[2] His interest in painting
helped him develop his manipulation of physical point of view,
sharpened his attention to perspective and was germinal to his
masterful technique of looking from a great distance at his
characters in a vast landscape.[3] From his architectural training he
drew some of his concern for form. His interest in science is mani-
fest in his use of technical language — occasionally a deficit rather
than an asset — and in the attention his characters pay to scientific
discoveries. All of these influences, when cemented by Hardy's
philosophy, become parts of a mosaic portrait of the writer as
stylist. But perhaps the most striking piece of the mosaic is Hardy's
intricate use of abundant allusion.

Hardy's profuse use of allusion and his occasional dependence
on a secondary source for plot give unusual value to a catalogue of
his reading.[4] Though it is of course impossible to ascertain all of
what he read, Hardy's major interests can be easily traced. From
the first book of his acquaintance, the Authorized Version of the

Bible, he selected as his favourite parts Genesis, Job, Psalms and Ecclesiastes. He also liked the narratives, especially those of the prophets and those in the Gospels. He read the Bible in Latin, at least the New Testament in Greek, and further used his Greek to do a close study of Sophocles and Aeschylus and peruse Euripides. His interest in English, Continental and American literature focused on poetry, and in fact Mrs Hardy records, with some obvious exaggeration, that he read no prose at all, except *The Times*, during the years 1865–7. Though his poetic knowledge was extensive, it particularly emphasised Shakespeare. There are few clues to the total range of Hardy's knowledge of fiction, though *Tom Jones*, *The Bride of Lammermoor*, *Kenilworth*, *Tristram Shandy*, *Vanity Fair*, *Clarissa* and *Pelham* are among the titles he mentioned as early reading.[5] In the recently published literary notebooks we see that especially in the last part of the 1870s he was extremely interested in extending his literary studies.[6] He obviously, for example, read extensively in Arnold (stimulated by the advice of Leslie Stephen to look at Sainte-Beuve and Arnold as the only modern critics worth reading), a study that was to prove especially fruitful for *Jude the Obscure*. And, in an article contributed to a symposium in the *Fortnightly Review* of August 1887, Hardy gives more clues to his literary taste: he lists the best English prose as some passages in Carlyle's *The French Revolution: A History*, especially those sections on the silent growth of the oak, and his sentences on night in a city. The best narrative prose Hardy deemed to be in the Bible: 2 Samuel 18 on the death of Absalom.

However, his first love remained poetry; he even regretted Scott's switch from poetry to prose. In the *Fortnightly Review* he listed Byron and Shelley as his favourite poets. After 1882 he owned the complete Shelley, in which *The Revolt of Islam* and *Prometheus Unbound* are exceptionally well marked.[7] Shelley's 'A Lament', 'O world! O life! O time'! he considered to be the most beautiful of English lyrics, and Byron's *Childe Harold*, especially Canto III, stanzas 85–6, the best English descriptive poetry.

References from this extensive reading were an integral part of Hardy's style from his first to his last published novel: *Desperate Remedies* has at least forty poetic allusions plus the Biblical allusions which always abound in Hardy; Jude dies alluding to Job. Even his titles mirror the device: *Under the Greenwood Tree* is indebted to *As You Like It*, II. v. 1; *Far From the Madding Crowd* is easily recognisable as a line from one of the poems most quoted in the nineteenth century, Gray's 'Elegy written in a Country Churchyard'. The unusual breadth of his reading becomes strikingly clear when one notes the diversity in the works from which he takes his references. The Bible, the Greek and Latin classics and English and American literature, past and present, are all represented. He admitted debts to such obscure authors as William Barnes and George Crabbe, but he drew more extensively from the famous. Carl Weber has gleaned 153 references to Shakespeare from the Hardy canon, and others have been quick to add to Weber's list.[8] Hardy's admiration of Shelley and Byron is almost as evident, but he also drew extensively from Keats, Milton, Coleridge, Tennyson and Browning (though Hardy criticised them for their optimism), Rossetti (Hardy did not approve of his Preraphaelite excesses of expression), Virgil (his favourite Latin classic was *The Aeneid*), Aeschylus, Sophocles and a host of minor figures.[9] In fact, the only notable classical omission in Hardy's artistic borrowing is Euripides, who is represented only in Jude's reading list, though Hardy was familiar with the plays and had annotated his copy of *The Trojan Women*.

That Hardy would seek this affinity with the greatness of tradition is not surprising in view of his definition of good fiction as 'that kind of imaginative writing which lies nearest to the epic, dramatic, or narrative masterpieces of the past'. Hardy, being a laborious writer, must have wrestled with what linguists see as the common weaknesses of language itself: vagueness, ambiguity, deceptive morphological and etymological structures and misleading figures of speech. He attempted to surmount these by borrowing from the literature of the past, to clarify his intention and to manipulate the responses of the educated reader.

On the most obvious level Hardy uses allusions for all the traditional reasons: to evoke in the reader the pleasure of recognition; to impress a learned audience; to illustrate his own remarks; to buttress an opinion; or to give an air of universality to the literature at hand — in Hardy's case to raise his novels from the level of pastoral romance to the realm of the masterpieces he so admired. Even the staunchest of his partisans will admit that Hardy occasionally loses control of this device and that his novels become 'too literary'. At times the allusions appear to be used *merely* to impress the learned audience he hoped to reach, and he becomes a prime example of the self-educated man attempting to prove himself to the English Establishment: some critics, such as S. F. Johnson and Michael Millgate, go as far as to contend that the majority of Hardy's allusions are more showy than functional; Johnson uses as one illustration of his point the pedantic reference in *The Return of the Native* to Dante as 'the sublime Florentine'.[10] In his earliest attempts some of these allusions are so crudely incorporated that they can only be called unfortunate. However, Hardy did master the allusive technique already evident in *Desperate Remedies*, developing it into an extremely useful device influencing tone, theme and character development. Ultimately his allusions become intricately polyvalent within his fictional world as they afford comic relief, endow his rustics with universal significance and allow Hardy to comment ironically on his characters.

A study of Hardy's practice reveals that his allusions are predominantly attached to character rather than to action. A sizable number are relegated to group characters, the 'rustics' of the novels, and perform several important functions. Often in the serious novels these country folk are used intermittently as comic relief, as in *Far From the Madding Crowd* and *The Return of the Native*. *Under the Greenwood Tree* is centred on such people, however, and the entire tone of the novel is analogous to its title's reference to a comedy. In the sombre novels' periodic sections of rustic comedy, and throughout *Under the Greenwood Tree*, the allusions distinctly heighten the comic tone and give a touch of ironic comedy, always a rarity in Hardy. In the graver parts of the darker novels the allusions attached to the rustics are used for their evocative value, adding verisimilitude to the choric pronouncements of these subordinate figures.

The allusions applied to principal figures and major events are also more than mere pedantry. Patently, in Victorian novels the author continually acted as a master of ceremonies, cicerone or annotator. Hardy was of his age in this respect, and did not hesitate to intervene between his characters and the reader. Even when he set a scene he rendered it as he saw it rather than as his people saw it. Moreover Hardy practised a type of editorial omniscience in which he not only reported what went on within his characters, but also commented upon it — in contrast to the more objective, neutral omniscience in vogue earlier in the century, when the author merely described and explained.[11] Much of Hardy's authorial intervention takes the form of overt, unambiguous statement, a fact which surely pleased the mass audience courted by the

Victorian magazines which serialised his stories. But the more sophisticated segments of his audience could see additional levels of meaning by detecting the authorial judgment evidenced through allusive subtlety. Hardy elevates, undermines, even degrades his own people by means of the allusions he attaches to them. And by applying a specific allusive pattern to particular characters he wields a stylistic tool to work the mine of irony that the universe presents to him.

To view Hardy's allusions as comic elements, elevating devices and, most important, as ironic comments is to open up a major new approach to the intricacies of his style. Since he attained his mature style by 1878 and *The Return of the Native*, a close study encompassing his earlier five novels – *Desperate Remedies* (1871), *Under the Greenwood Tree* (1872), *A Pair of Blue Eyes* (1873), *Far From the Madding Crowd* (1874), *The Hand of Ethelberta* (1876) – and culminating in *The Return of the Native* presents some salient theses about this relatively unexplored branch of Hardy's method. My final chapter, focusing on *Tess of the d'Urbervilles* and *Jude the Obscure*, sets out to prove Hardy's perfection of these techniques. But a convincing analysis of his allusive technique requires a review in some depth, at the risk of stating the obvious to readers familiar with Hardy scholarship, of the philosophical structure that provides the motivation for his allusions. Necessary, too, are an exploration of the meaning and implications of 'irony' with specific regard to Hardy, and the establishment of a common critical vocabulary for discussing Hardy's multi-levelled use of the ironic mode.

To be successful in a shrewd allusive technique Hardy had to assume in his more refined audience a reading background as eclectic as his own: 'A perspicacious reader will see what his author is aiming at, and by affording full scope to his own insight, catch the vision which the writer has in his eye, and is endeavouring to project upon the paper, even while it half eludes him' ('The Profitable Reading of Fiction'). However, Hardy does not spare the artist:

> A story must be exceptional enough to justify its telling. We tale-tellers are all Ancient Mariners, and none of us is warranted in stopping Wedding Guests (in other words, the hurrying public) unless he has something more unusual to relate than the ordinary experience of every average man and woman.

The whole secret of fiction and the drama — in the construc-
tional part — lies in the adjustment of things unusual to things
external and universal. The writer who knows exactly how
exceptional, and how nonexceptional, his events should be
made, possesses the key to the art.[12]

Some critics have questioned Hardy's possession of the key, supporting their charges by pointing out that he considered too many
incredible coincidences as 'nonexceptional' events. While it is true
that one is often amazed at the almost malign timing of some of
Hardy's contrivances, this use of coincidence, and especially perverse coincidence, is not merely a superimposed device, nor is it
evidence of amateurish artistic judgment. Rather it is the result of
Hardy's personal philosophy, which saturates the novels and
moulds his style. Buffon's famous aphorism contends that 'le style
est l'homme même'. And Stephen Ullmann in turn convincingly
supports the reflection theory of style when he asserts that there
can be 'habits peculiar to a given writer and that this individual
style is closely bound up with the writer's mind and experience and
bears the stamp of his personality'.[13] The alliance between Hardy's
philosophical assumptions and his style testifies to the validity of
these observations.

Hardy maintained in his often quoted introductions to the
Wessex novels and poems that his work was never intended to
advance a homogeneous philosophy or a 'coherent scientific theory
of the universe'. Countless studies have been written to prove that
Hardy succeeded in spite of himself. Obviously, whether it was
homogeneous or not, during most of his long career Hardy was
consistently burdened with a bleak world-view that undeniably
coloured his work. As a youth he seemed to have a fairly optimistic
and orthodox outlook. He taught Sunday School, and at one time
began reading for Cambridge — still planning as late as 1865 to
take orders. His early interests reflect this optimism, for he read
the romances of Ainsworth, G. P. R. James and Dumas, who held
the view that poetic justice prevailed in this somewhat paradisial
life.[14] But his reading in philosophy and, Robert Gittings maintains, his personal problems, slowly eroded his faith in the established church and a benevolent Godhead.[15] Gradually he became
torn between the High Church indoctrination of his youth and the
scepticism inflicted upon him by his time. Two books in particular
had a profound influence on his thinking: Darwin's *Origin of*

Species and *Esssays and Reviews*, published in 1860 by a group known as the 'Seven Against Christ'. Hardy read in Frederick Temple's chapter in *Essays and Reviews* that the Bible could be considered primarily as a history book recording the significant religious events of the time. C. W. Goodwin's essay in the same book discusses the conflict between modern science and the Mosaic cosmology, while Baden Powell's 'Evidence of Christianity' advocates judging the miracles by the rules of modern science and says that Darwin has proved the narrative of Genesis to be untenable.[16] The pricks of scepticism continued to irritate Hardy and Darwin did not soothe them. He was quick to accept Darwin's thesis, but, unlike Meredith, he derived no consolation from it; nature gave him no indication that it would improve the human race, and he morosely reflected in 1888:

A woeful fact − that the human race is too extremely developed for its corporeal conditions, the nerves being evolved to an activity abnormal in such an environment. Even the higher animals are in excess in this respect. It may be questioned if Nature, or what we call Nature, so far back as when she crossed the line from invertebrates to vertebrates, did not exceed her mission. This planet does not supply the materials for happiness to higher existences. Other planets may, though one can hardly see how.[17]

As his faith in the church was supplanted by the new concerns of evolution, he continued to read Biblical scholars and philosophers in an attempt to clarify and substantiate his own speculation. He studied and absorbed, for example, Spencer and Comte, as well as Spinoza, Von Hartmann and of course Schopenhauer − though the extent of the German philosopher's important influence on him has long been a subject of critical debate. There was some talk of Schopenhauer in England in the 1870s, but the first English translation of *Die Welt Als Wille und Vorstellung* did not appear until 1883. Hardy owned this book, but there is little proof that he read it thoroughly.[18] However, Hardy's copy of Schopenhauer's *Fourfold Root of the Principle of Sufficient Reason* contains evidence that he did read it conscientiously.[19] *The Dynasts* was obviously influenced by his acquaintance with Schopenhauer, but prior to that Hardy relied as much on the

German philosopher's terms as on the theory behind them, and continued to collect his assumptions about existence from a wide variety of sources.

The cumulative result of Hardy's study and experience was more an incurably curious habit of mind than a rigid, comprehensive system, and he always retained reservations about all men's systems.[20] In an attempt to define his attitude, many have called him a pessimist; some have labelled him a corrective sceptic. Hardy deemed himself an evolutionary meliorist, while noting in his preface to *Poems of the Past and the Present* that 'the road to a true philosophy of life seems to lie in humbly recording diverse readings of its phenomena as they are forced upon us by change'.[21] None the less, by the 1890s Hardy had at least settled on the belief that any supreme power must be indifferent to or ignorant of human life. The world, and human destiny, were controlled by the Schopenhauer-derived Immanent Will − a force that he describes in a letter to Alfred Noyes as 'neither moral or immoral, but *un*moral: "loveless and hateless" I have called it, "which neither good nor evil knows" . . .' The human effects of the Universal Will Hardy equates with the workings of Chance. Since people can seldom escape this force, coincidence plays a prime role in existence. In turn, because he believed fiction should include a precise transcript of ordinary life, coincidence became an increasingly evident factor in Hardy's plots, with pure chance gradually giving way to a much more fatalistic determinism. *Desperate Remedies* still evidences some immaturity and ambiguity in its philosophic bias; in *A Pair of Blue Eyes* his attitude begins to mature, with chance and determinism holding almost equal sway; by *Far From the Madding Crowd* and *The Return of the Native* chance increasingly gives way. In *Tess of the d'Urbervilles* he first mentions Schopenhauer, and haphazard chance has become malign determinism − an unrelenting Fate which crushes the human will to enjoy. This view of the nature of things suffuses *Jude the Obscure*, and by the time he writes *The Dynasts* (1903−8), he can retrospectively label this aspect of his system.[22]

Yet Hardy disliked being forced into any one mould. He periodically protested the public view of him as a gloomy man whose gaze was limited to the dark shadows of existence, and reacted vehemently to the charge that he was a pessimist. None the less, he is dishearteningly consistent in his bleak outlook, and when momentarily resigned to the tag, he defended his view with Pascalian logic:

> Pessimism (or rather what is called such) is, in brief, playing the sure game. You cannot lose at it; you may gain. It is the only view of life in which you can never be disappointed. Having reckoned what to do in the worst possible circumstances, when better arise, as they may, life becomes child's play.[23]

The 'better' rarely arises − nor does his statement promise that it ever will. In the later novels Fate seems squarely aligned against mankind, with no hope of poetic justice; human beings rarely receive the happiness they deserve. Yet to deem humanity worthy of happiness is a modicum of optimism, and one that Hardy struggled successfully to retain in his novels. Sadly, by the time of the First World War that too was lost, and he could no longer be even guardedly hopeful. Harold Orel summarises the matter: 'Thomas Hardy, who so violently and so often reacted against charges that he was a pessimist in his art, finally became one in his study at Max Gate, and . . . did so largely as a consequence of reflections on the "barbaric age" in which men and women lived as "the slaves of gross superstition".'[24]

But Hardy capitulated to his very darkest fears only a decade before his death. And, in spite of the concentrated gloom that obviously pervades his work, it is easy to see in his novels his deep sympathy for the indomitable human spirit and his profound respect for human endeavour. Much of his fictional world reflects his belief that the innocent suffer and the noble are ruined simply because they are noble and incapable of paltry compromise.[25] He depicts his admiration for mankind's attempt to cope with an inflexible fate in two rather disparate types: his active heroes, and his passive, stalwart ones. His aggressive figures struggle with predestined futility to change the scheme of things. They are isolated by their very sensitivity; their force makes them superior to their material circumstances, and they are often greater than their fate.[26] They are usually victims − and always so in the late novels − but they are allowed either to remain ignorant of the extent of their failure or to be admirable even in defeat. Their tragedy lies in the fact that they search intensely for happiness in a world that merely tantalises through dreams. Life promises, only to deny.

As any reader of Hardy learns, some of his most sympathetic

characters are people who, though strong and courageous, do not take arms against their troubles; rather, they stoically accept their parts in life. At times he goes as far as to suggest that people can only have even the smallest portion of happiness by nullifying their will and suppressing all desires – a Schopenhauerian view. In these heroes – for example, Gabriel Oak – the reader is taught to admire simplicity and passivity. In fact in much of Hardy's fiction the complicated person often verges on insanity, and single-mindedness is depicted as a virtue. Oak, Giles Winterborne and their ilk numbly accept reversal and patiently strive to recoup their losses. Sometimes they are successful, as in Oak's case, but more often their steadfastness is rewarded only with more adversity; *Far From the Madding Crowd* is the only Wessex novel which ends with a possibility for happiness. None the less, the reader is persuaded to admire perseverance rather than achievement, for Hardy presents uncomplaining acceptance of maltreatment as noble, rather than cowardly or masochistic. In this group of Hardy heroes quiescence supersedes defiance.

But be his fictional heroes active or passive, they are consistently drawn from obscure, middle- or lower-class folk; the most successfully portrayed are the country people. Hardy advocated that fiction should be a reflection of the truths of the human heart. By concentrating on the more primitive layers of society, he could let his men and women yield to universal human instincts while he avoided distorting his portraits with the frills and furbelows of manners. On the more metaphysical level, the natural world provides a successful environment for Hardy's fiction partially because he portrays it as an organic, living whole, capable of great influence. It is exceedingly complex and varied, but displays an overall unity through time and space, its heterogeneous intricacies integrated in a system of rigid and undeviating law.[27] Yet he also sees the natural world as full of unexpected events. As we have seen, in his fiction Hardy synchronises these two aspects of his world view – the multiplicity of unexpected events and undeviating natural law – in his lavish use of coincidence which is not simply indefinable chance nor entirely the result of cause and effect, but rather is evidence of the workings of the Immanent Will. Thus, by linking with the universal the coincidences which act upon his characters, and in turn joining the universal with the natural, Hardy ties his situations and his people to the land. He minutely studies landscapes, bringing both the trivial and the cosmic into his ken — but his landscapes are always peopled. The forces which govern the land regulate his characters, and the two are inextricably united. Cliffs, storms, heaths become instruments of fate that influence both extrinsic and intrinsic action, their timing or their presence either aiding or thwarting human desires.

Clearly, Hardy's speculation revealed several contradictions in man's relation to the universe. Modern science implies determinism, but humanity still nurtures the idea of free will. The indifference of the cosmos, as evidenced by the laws of nature, conflicts with the sensitivity and aspirations of human beings.[28] Superior forces demand acquiescence, while the human spirit fosters rebellion. Hardy saw no resolution for these conflicts, and was consequently haunted by the discrepancy between what seems and what is — the traditional ironic contradiction. He added to this view his own idiosyncratic idealism: if this world was not made for happiness, it should have been. The ironic contradiction therefore includes not only the difference between what seems and what is, but also the dichotomy between what is and what ought to be.

Because Hardy's ironic vision is the focal point of his philosophical outlook, it too inevitably invades his fictional world. Irony as a literary device is at least as old as the Hellenistic rhetoricians. Historians of irony such as Norman Knox, A. R. Thompson and G. G. Sedgewick agree that two general patterns of meaning for 'irony' have finally evolved.[29] One is rhetorical, dealing with specific speech and writing patterns, and is now recognised under the familiar rubric of Socratic irony, or feigned ignorance. The second ironic pattern is figurative, concentrating on an entire philosophic outlook. Its labelling is more modern, for Bishop Connop Thirlwall's 1833 essay 'On the Irony of Sophocles', and the studies it instigated, have since produced the commonly accepted definition of the irony of fate; Sophoclean, or dramatic, irony has become the critical catch-all for describing that situation wherein certain characters are unconscious of the trend of events known to the reader.[30] From these two broad areas, in turn, the various categories have emerged — romantic irony, cynical irony, dismissive irony, formal irony — many of which Hardy incorporated, as his speculation and his temperament demanded that he deal thematically with the contradiction between one's desires and performance, between one's rational will and compulsive emotion, and between the illusions fostered by pride and real self-ignorance.[31]

Haakon Chevalier contends in his *Ironic Temper* that irony 'is the product of certain radical insufficiencies of character and a mode of escape from the fundamental problems and responsibilities of life'.[32] Hardy directly refutes this thesis, for it is his concern for the victim, and not his escapism, that so distinctively directs his art towards irony. His empathy with the tragedy of human life caused him to stop short of satire, or militant irony, and he preferred to write instead in the ironic perspective cogently summarised by Northrop Frye when he traces the phases of tragedy in its gradations from the heroic to the ironic. Hardy's work falls into what Frye terms the fourth phase, where tragedy has moved into the ironic mode. In this phase the viewpoint is from the 'moral and realistic perspective of the state of experience. It stresses the humanity of its heroes, minimises the sense of ritual inevitability in tragedy, supplies social and psychological explanations for catastrophe, and makes as much as possible of human misery seem, in Thoreau's phrase, "superfluous and evitable".'[33] For Hardy, though, the 'as much as possible' was severely limited. Because of his tragic, ironic vision, even Hardy's worst characters are mixtures of good and evil; he has almost no unredeemed villains in his work. But this is not to say that he is blinded by his compassion; he does make value judgments of his characters, and guides his readers into agreeing with his decisions.

Hardy's varied use of irony was an important tool in other areas as well. Often it is irony (Sophoclean, for the most part) which points the significance of a situation, as it does in Eustacia's relationship with Mrs Yeobright in *The Return of the Native*. Irony also clarifies the conflict of the dramatic forces — for example, in the confrontation of Gabriel and Troy before the storm scene in *Far From the Madding Crowd*, where Gabriel's competence is clearly pitted against Troy's irresponsibility, and the reader is unalterably convinced that Troy not only will never be a farmer, but is also selfishly unconcerned about Bathsheba's interests. Or it is a device which heightens the sense of Burkean pity and terror in a scene, as in Fanny Robin's painful trip to the Casterbridge Union house, and the consequent stoning away of the dog that helped her there, in *Far From the Madding Crowd*.[34]

This facet of Hardy's ironic vision, then, his comprehensive concept of the irony of fate, was a potent factor in his work. It shaped his characterisations by limiting him to mere men and women: there are no supermen or double-dyed villains. It shaped

the action by its emphasis on coincidence. It influenced his choice
of scene and social class, for he saw all of life as a collage of ironies,
and to represent the democracy of his vision he created average
figures in an uncomplicated environment. It accentuates the
dramatic conflict of the novels by underscoring the antagonism
between humans and an inflexible fate which steadily follows its
immutable, insensitive track. And it contributes to the atmosphere, for pity, terror and isolation are all natural elements of a
world controlled by such a fate. It influences tone in the novels, for
Hardy's concern about the tragedy of man's fate prodded him to
intrude upon his story and defend his characters; and certainly his
ironic mode develops a unity of effect that not only binds together
the diverse personalities evident in his characters, but also gives all
of his major novels a common sober mien.

Thus, an understanding of Hardy's view of the irony of fate is of
great importance when approaching one of his novels. In the relationship between the author, the reader and the work the reader is
often aware of a Sophoclean ironic situation wherein he is cogni-
sant of fateful events that are unknown to the fictional characters.
However, Hardy augments his dramatic irony with the more
complex rhetorical irony.[35] It is this basically Socratic method that
Hardy is using when he enters into the novel through his choice of
allusion and comments ironically on his characters.

These allusive comments can become ironic in an entangled
variety of ways. The allusion can be so through its relationship
with plot or character within the novel itself, or by an extrinsic
comparison with its original context which reveals a currently sympathetic individual connected through allusion to a base character
or situation — or, conversely, a base character similarly connected
to a noble one. Irony is also developed by allusively linking a sympathetic figure to a noble character or situation whose nobility is
beyond approximation by the Hardy figure. Consequently when
the allusions used are interpreted in terms of their sources, or, on
occasion, through the context of the novel itself, they become a
subtle guide to the author's intention.

Hardy, then, uses allusions as a deliberate device in creating a
style. A chronological treatment of the early novels focusing on
these allusions reveals a steady progression towards the masterful
selection that is to mark his late masterpieces, such as *Tess* and
Jude. Even more important, however, is the fact that the ways in
which he employs these references prove to be as various as the

fictional modes he attempts, with the allusions always playing an augmentive, and often determining, role in both the development of characters and the tone of the novels. *Desperate Remedies*, its roots unfortunately entangled in the traditions of melodrama, primarily exemplifies Hardy's use of adumbrative allusions and contains enough allusive clues to events to satisfy the most Holmesian of mystery readers. Though somewhat crudely inserted, the references in this novel also elevate and undercut the characters, as well as intensify plot action, contributing the sense of exaggeration which melodrama requires. *Under the Greenwood Tree*, in turn, dwells with exaggerated seriousness on an insignificant courtship, with the allusions now informing the reader of the light tone of the novel. And, in the same story, where the message is more serious, the allusions help regulate the change; Hardy does not joke about the sad disappearance of the traditional church musicians, one of whom was his own grandfather.

When Hardy next turns, irrevocably, from the world of fancy into first the mundane and then the grave and passionate, his allusive techniques keep pace with his developing intensity. In *A Pair of Blue Eyes*, in fact, Hardy appears to be blindly infatuated with his own method, and loads his 'romance' with such a welter of allusions that he almost destroys the stylistic rewards of his approach. None the less, the allusive chapter titles, the references attached to the principal characters and those used miscellaneously all make major contributions to the novel as they enlarge character, foreshadow events and provide humour.

With *Far From the Madding Crowd* we encounter Hardy at his first major stylistic plateau. Analysis verifies that once again the allusions are primarily employed to manipulate our response to the major characters; but we also now find allusions being used to establish setting and to increase the importance of the rustic chorus by adding to their common-sense judgments an air of universal truth. This novel, moreover, will move us much deeper into Hardy's tragic vision. Allusions contribute to this tone of high seriousness, yet they also acquire the added duty of being an integral part of the novel's comic relief; the rustics mitigate the pathos by making us laugh at 'King Noah' and the 'horned man in the smokey house' — even though we are quickly brought back to Fanny's coffin waiting outside in the inimical rain.

The Hand of Ethelberta is largely a failure, and the allusions suggest little to counter this judgment. The book will be considered

briefly, but only to illustrate this relapse. This novel and its powerful successor illustrate that even a talent as strong as Hardy's can
be limited to a particular environment, and that certain locales
and classes proved to be closed to him.

The clumsiness of *The Hand of Ethelberta*, and the rather
maladroit way in which Hardy employs allusions in this, his fifth
book, are easily forgotten when one examines his progress in his
next novel, *The Return of the Native*, where he at last attains his
mature style. He is still to have failures, but obviously also more
successes, as a survey of the last two novels, *Tess of the d'Urbervilles* and *Jude the Obscure*, will demonstrate. But it is with his
sixth novel that we see him clearly showing the sustained power
that has established him as a great writer. His allusions are a neatly
polished facet of the style here, as references evoke the Hebraic–
Hellenic dichotomy that was a token of the age while intricately
and subtly judging the players of Egdon Heath. Eustacia, Wildeve, Clym, even the more minor Mrs Yeobright receive allusive
treatment which expands their personalities and exposes their
weaknesses. The rustics, too, are of prime import, and their part,
that of chorus-plus-characters, is given credibility and humour
through the Biblical phrases they commonly use. Nor is setting
ignored, as Hardy shows himself to be unsurpassed in describing
the wilds of England by means of allusions which serve to make of
the all-important locale a personified and universal entity.

And finally, as the Hardy canon becomes steadily bleaker and
more tragic, the pervasive irony Hardy saw in the universe moves
to centre stage, with allusions playing the part of prompter. Irony
is part of every early Hardy novel, and references contribute to it
from the beginning; by *The Return of the Native* the ironic
allusions have developed a devastating edge which Hardy wields as
he goes on to demonstrate his contention that no one escapes the
blows of the Immanent Will – least of all Tess, Angel, Sue and
Jude. As the tragedy seems to deepen with each succeeding master-
piece, so do the references gain in importance and power. The
Hebraic–Hellenic split used in *The Return* continues in *Tess* and
is dominant in *Jude*, with the allusions sharply flavouring the
tragic results.

It took Hardy eight years of intermittent progress to surmount
his early desperate stylistic remedies, to learn to discard melodrama and the societal novel and to concentrate on novels of
character set in the environment he knew best. That Hardy was a

conscious artificer, eventually successful in his search for a comfortable stylistic mantle, becomes graphically apparent through a study of his allusive practices. For through his increasingly adroit manipulation of references he not only helps transform the prosaic into the complex, but also gains an unusually strong control over the total effect of his fiction.

2 Three Experiments in Form

Hardy's first published work of fiction, *Desperate Remedies*, was issued anonymously by Tinsley Brothers in 1871 and was paid for by Hardy himself. The story was the direct result of his following George Meredith's advice to 'attempt a novel with a purely artistic purpose', and to give it more plot than his previous attempt at fiction, the unsuccessful *The Poor Man and the Lady*. When Hardy wrote his second story, he zealously followed Meredith's suggestions, turning out an intricate melodrama that has plot in abundance. Unfortunately, *Desperate Remedies* clearly illustrates Hardy's somewhat amateurish contention that 'a story, to be interesting, must be complicated and full of exciting events', a theory which undoubtedly originated in his youthful reading of gothic fiction. The novel itself contains a death-fall from a church tower, subsequent pitiable poverty for the children of the victim, a bizarre murder (the body is buried, exhumed, and reburied), a suicide, several ghosts and accompanying death rattles in the night, an intrigue centring on a bastard son, an involved chase scene, an attempted rape and the inevitable fight between hero and villain. Fortunately, a rigid time scheme guides the reader through this labyrinth, and consequently the strands of the story are seldom ravelled, as they sometimes are in Dickens, for example. From the events of Chapter 1, dated 12 October 1863, up to Chapter 21, at ten minutes past four on 30 March 1866, almost every hour is accounted for; the 'Sequel' is just as specifically set on 'Midsummer Night, 1867'.

Hardy warns the reader from the outset that his plot will be contrived. On the title page he quotes from Scott's introduction to *The Monastery*: 'Though an unconnected course of adventure is what most frequently occurs in nature, yet the province of the romance-writer being artificial, there is more required from him than a mere compliance with the simplicity of reality.'[1] In context

18

the quotation is a part of Scott's assertion that though many stories are made up of random incidents 'which are connected with each other by having happened to be witnessed by the same individual', and that though this method is probably more realistic, it is not the province of the romantic writer. Rather, we demand from him, just as we demand from the scientific gardener, 'that he shall arrange, in curious knots and artificial parterres, the flowers which "nature boon" distributes freely on hill and dale'; Fielding's *Tom Jones* is the ultimate example, but admittedly too high a goal for most novelists.

Hardy's choice of quotation indicates that he agreed with Scott, and that he was also prudent enough to know that Fielding could not be equalled by an inexperienced novelist. Consequently, he followed Scott's tenets, while patterning much of his novel after the convention exemplified by Wilkie Collins. In fact, *Desperate Remedies* somewhat resembles Collins's *Woman in White*, though it is not a copy. Both books contain three closely connected mysteries which are ultimately resolved; both involve illegitimate parentage and the identity of a mysterious woman; and in both one woman passes for another.[2] Along with these plot elements Hardy also owes some stylistic traits to Collins: it was probably from Collins that he learned his technique of gaining verisimilitude by accumulating minute realistic details, and though Hardy does not imitate Collins's unique method of telling a melodrama through characters, he does follow him in letting a character-narrator resolve the plot mysteries in the final chapter of the book.[3] However, though his first book does follow much of the sensation novel formula, complete even to the equation of white-knight hero plus virtuous heroine who combine triumphantly against evil, he none the less manages to transcend the bourgeois convention he is using by injecting into it his distinctive stylistic and philosophical elements.

When Hardy was to review *Desperate Remedies* from the vantage point of a successful, though embattled, novelist, he acknowledged in a prefatory note (dated January 1889) the immaturity of his early attempt:

The following novel, the first published by the author, was written nineteen years ago, at a time when he was feeling his way to a method. The principles observed in its composition are, no doubt, too exclusively those in which mystery, entanglement,

surprise, and moral obliquity are depended on for exciting
interest; but some of the scenes, and at least one or two of the
characters, have been deemed not unworthy of a little longer
preservation; and as they could hardly be reproduced in a frag-
mentary form the novel is reissued complete . . .

This accurate assessment of his book in the light of his maturer
critical standards indicates Hardy did not find the novel worthy of
extensive correction when he revised his canon for the definitive
Wessex Edition of 1912. A comparison of the 1871 first edition, the
earliest surviving form of the text, with the Wessex Edition
indicates that Hardy's main changes were to place-names: he
changed the early fictional names of Froominster, Palchurch,
Mundsbury and Traveller's Rest Inn to Casterbridge, Tolchurch,
Anglebury and the Rising Sun Inn respectively — all equally
fictitious, but by 1912 irrevocably established as parts of Hardy's
Wessex. Other revisions include combining short paragraphs into
better integrated wholes, and making identifications more
specific, as, for example, on p. 196 of the Wessex Edition, where
the rector, anonymous in the first edition, becomes Mr Raunham.
Hardy also takes pains to elevate Owen Graye and Edward Springrove in his revisions, making them both draftsmen, instead of
mere clerks; and Manston, too, is the object of descriptive revision
as he changes from 'deamon' to 'desperado'. The allusions remain
unchanged in both editions, except for Hardy's one attempt to
clarify the narrative by adding to it the identification of a passage
from Browning's 'The Statue and the Bust'.

Thus, Hardy let almost all of the novel remain exactly as it first
appeared. Even those places obviously in need of improvement he
left untouched; for example, the narrator's intrusive rumination
on Wisdom which concludes, 'Yet whether one's end be the usual
end — a wealthy position in life — or no, the name wisdom is
seldom applied but to the means to that usual end' (p. 52). His
decision not to undertake major improvements was a deliberate
and a wise one. To revise would have meant extensive rewriting, for
Hardy mastered the method he sought, and *Desperate Remedies*
contains obvious flaws when compared with his later masterpieces.
His efforts could be better spent elsewhere, especially since his taste
had returned to poetry; but students of his stylistic progress can be
grateful for this fairly pristine example of the birth-pangs of a
novelist.

In an analysis of Hardy's style in *Desperate Remedies*, and specifically his use of allusion, it should be remembered that here Hardy was striving for plot rather than character: hence his reference to Scott. Because of this emphasis on action in preference to character, the book contains comparatively few allusions: approximately twenty from the Bible, and some forty poetical ones, including three quotations from Virgil in the original. The majority of the references pertain to the principals, and are used to highlight or undermine some aspect of personality. However, Hardy also uses several allusions in conjunction with plot development. These allusions, when weighed in the light of their sources, enable the perceptive reader to foresee events. In consequence, both the device and the situation are basically Sophoclean irony.

The plot of *Desperate Remedies* is conventionally complicated, and its melodramatic events are difficult to remember in sequence, even for those readers familiar with Hardy's work. The book opens at a fast pace with 'The Events of Thirty Years' covered in Chapter 1; here is the life of Ambrose Graye, father of Owen and Cytherea, who has in his past a mysteriously unrequited love for a woman later identified as Cytherea Aldclyffe. Mr Graye dies as the result of a fall from a church tower; Cytherea Graye and Owen are left penniless, and they attempt to solve their financial problems by becoming a governess and a draftsman. Cytherea just happens to get a position with Miss Aldclyffe, who, as we ultimately discover, did not marry Cytherea's father because of her guilt over bearing a child after being attacked by a cousin. The major love interest concerns Cytherea's love for Edward Springrove, a colleague of Owen's. Miss Aldclyffe in turn loves Cytherea with a Sapphic passion unusual in Victorian literature, and hopes for vicarious enjoyment by arranging for Cytherea to marry Manston, her bastard son, whom Miss Aldclyffe brings to her farm as a steward. Manston refuses to court Cytherea because he is already married, but, just as his despised wife comes to live with him, she ostensibly dies in a fire. Manston now presses his suit on an unwilling Cytherea, who agrees to the marriage only to get the money needed to save her ailing brother, and only after she learns that Edward has been engaged to his cousin for years. Edward is jilted, much to his relief, but he arrives at Cytherea's wedding too late to stop the ceremony. Cytherea is saved from her marriage bed, however, by Edward's discovery that Manston's wife may still be living,

since new evidence proves that she did not die in the fire. At this
juncture the plot becomes unbelievably intricate, and affairs are
so entwined that Hardy found it necessary to untangle everything
in the last chapter by the rather artificial device of a six-page
suicide note from Manston. It seems that on the night of the fire
Manston had accidentally killed his wife and had hidden her body
in an old oven. After news of his wife's escape from the fire became
known, Manston had taken a mistress, Anne Seaway, to act as a
cover for the death of his real wife. The mistress begins to doubt his
motives; she and three other people watch in the night as Manston
tries to remove the body, and he is exposed — but not captured
before an attempt to get Cytherea. Edward rushes to the rescue,
Manston is caught and confesses all in his prison cell.

Hardy unfolds his plot methodically, but he is able to maintain
the suspense necessary for a mystery novel while giving the reader
helpful clues to the outcome by ingeniously concealing some of
them in his allusions. Since Manston is the prime motivator of much
of the mysterious action, he appropriately utters several of the
adumbrative allusions, and all are related to him. For example,
while Manston is refusing to court Cytherea, he sees his wife on an
arriving train. He quotes aloud a line from Jeremiah (which Hardy
identifies): 'A woman shall compass a man' (p. 177). In context
(Jeremiah 31 : 22) God sarcastically rebukes the children of Israel,
saying that this is a new thing: the woman, or Israel, shall 'surround'
(the Hebrew dictates this implication of 'compass') the man, or God
— and that the result will be Israel's downfall. This is precisely what
happens to Manston: the woman does surround him by her discoveries, cuts off his escape, and is killed for her efforts. Again,
when Miss Aldclyffe confronts Manston with her knowledge of his
marriage, he tries to unnerve her by candidly acknowledging his
status; he decides to 'burn his ships and hazard all on advance'
(p. 188). The reference warns us of his fate, for it alludes to Cortez's
tactics in Mexico when he attempted to prevent his men's panicky
return to Cuba. Cortez was unsuccessful in spite of his methods, and
so is Manston. In Chapter 12, still another foreshadowing is offered.
Manston, his wife dead, is now forcefully courting Cytherea, and his
system is pointedly compared to 'Dares at the Sicilian Games'.
Hardy quotes from Dryden's translation of the *Aeneid*, v, 587—91:

> He, like a captain who beleaguers round
> Some strong-built castle on a rising ground,

Views all the approaches with observing eyes,
This and that other part again he tries,
And more on industry than force relies. (p. 249)

The pronoun reference is to Dares, who is fighting Entellus. There is every indication that Dares will win because of his superior fighting ability, but he leaves the arena in shame after Entellus has summoned up a superior strength, attributed to his moral fortitude. Manston's situation is analogous: he accepts a favourable challenge, but shares Dares' failure.

Biblical references are also keys to future events. Manston is discussing his loss of Cytherea on account of the discovery of his earlier wife, and says with disarming casualness, 'Abigail is lost, but Michal is recovered' (p. 307) — a reference to David's early wife, and Michal, Saul's daughter, who was also given to David, lost and returned as a token of faith by Abner (1 Samuel 25—2 Samuel 7). Manston's comparison of Abigail to Cytherea is an obvious device to avoid revealing his true feelings. But it is his reference to Michal which forewarns the reader of Manston's fate; Anne Seaway comes to hate Manston just as Michal ultimately hates David. The final foreshadowing allusion continues this connection. Once Anne has begun to suspect Manston of chicanery, she adds fear to her hate. She feigns innocence as he nonchalantly looks for an opportunity to poison her. Here the narrator intervenes with another clue: 'but what is keener than the eye of a mistrustful woman? A man's cunning is to it as was the armour of Sisera to the thin tent-nail' (p. 378). The nuances of this situation are parallel to those of the source, Judges 4:21. Anne Seaway contributes to Manston's downfall, as Jael drove a nail into Sisera's temple after he fled to her following his defeat by Deborah's forces.

But Hardy does not limit his allusive technique to foreshadowing events; he also employs allusions ironically to intensify action, and to sharpen the reader's attention to the tone of the novel. Hardy blatantly informs the reader that he applies these allusions, in the light of their sources, by having one of his characters use the device and be discovered doing so. While Springrove is conversing with Cytherea about his poetic past, he admits, quoting Milton's '*Lycidas*', that he '"meditates the thankless muse" no longer'. The narrator then enters:

Cytherea's mind ran on to the succeeding lines of the poem, and their startling harmony with the present situation suggested

the fancy that he was *'sporting'* with her, and brought an awkward contemplativeness to her face.

Springrove guessed her thoughts, and in answer to them
simply said 'Yes'. (p. 79)

Many of the intensifying references are bi-functional, serving as
comments on character as well as on plot. For example, both
Cytherea's emotional state and the electric atmosphere of the
scene are accentuated by this allusive setting:

The congregation sang the first Psalm and came to the verse −

> Like some fair tree which, fed by streams
> With timely fruit doth bend.
> He still shall flourish and success
> All his designs attend.

Cytherea's lips did not move, nor did any sound escape her; but
could she help singing the words in the depths of her being,
although the man to whom she applied them sat at her rival's
side? (pp. 239−40)

However, Hardy's talent is rarely so well represented as in the way
in which he allusively frames one of the novel's central episodes −
the burning of Farmer Springrove's inn, which purportedly houses
Mrs Manston. In the chapter preceding the account of the fire, the
narrator examines Farmer Springrove's self-knowledge and foresight. Lest the reader miss important narrative comment, Hardy
emphasises through an allusion to Walt Whitman Mr Springrove's
opinion of himself: 'Like Walt Whitman he felt as his years
increased − "I foresee too much; it means more than I thought"'
(p. 154). The cause of the fire is Mr Springrove's failure to take
into account windshifts when he leaves a burning pile of rubbish
unattended; it is precisely his lack of foresight that destroys all his
life's work. And as the buildings burn, Hardy adds the crowning
ironic touch: the 'bewildered chimes' of the church play Psalm 113
('O Praise ye the Lord . . . /He raiseth up the poor out of the
dunghill' (p. 205).

While the various prophetic references and the handling of the
fire scene prove that Hardy can be allusively effective when merely
dealing with plot action, there is also ample indication in this first
novel that he is already partial to allusions which function

primarily as the author's comments on character, giving the reader an incisive view into Hardy's own attitude towards his subject. Once again Manston takes on the unusual significance tonally associated with melodrama, while the reader's approach to him is carefully guided by a chain of allusions. In keeping with Hardy's already budding philosophic tenet that men are not responsible for most of their actions, Manston is not depicted as a consistent villain. In fact in the first part of the novel he is made exceptionally attractive — so much so that Cytherea's feminine pride is pricked when he refuses to court her. This favourable impression makes him not only a believable suitor for the angelic Cytherea, but, later in the novel, also a credible victim of irrational forces. (Hardy describes Manston, in his introductory analysis, as a Theomachist.) The novelist sustains this necessary picture of a well-meaning Manston, while simultaneously making him into the villain he ultimately becomes by having him retain the respect of the other characters in the novel as the narrator undermines him through ironic allusive comments — a technique Hardy is to use with even greater success with Manston's successor in villainy, Sergeant Troy.

Hardy begins to erode Manston's façade two chapters after he enters the novel — sixty-six days after his arrival at Miss Aldclyffe's. The reader becomes retrospectively aware of the craft involved in the description of Manston: 'Like Curius at his Sabine farm, he had counted it his glory not to possess gold himself, but to have power over her who did' (p. 191). Here a base character is linked to a noble one; Manston, whose final aim is to possess everything, becomes ironic when identified with a man of legendary frugality and virtue who refused all spoils of war. When Manston hears of his wife's death, he is again the victim of an unflattering allusive connection with a noble character and a situation which inspires sympathy: David's receipt of the news from Cushi that his son Absalom has been killed (2 Samuel 19:32-3). But while the great man cries upon hearing the news, Manston shows no emotion, not even slight regret, and is an 'unmoved David' (p. 210). When he is once again required to show some response to his wife's death, he demonstrates his callousness by replacing emotion with cold intellect, quoting from Sterne's letters 'that neither reason nor Scripture asks us to speak nothing but good of the dead' (p. 217). And the allusions continue to inform us of his deliberate degradation: his religion is Laodicean, or lukewarm

(p. 243); he is Corinthian, the synonym for dissoluteness and love of luxury; and he 'preys on virginity like St George's dragon' (p. 356).

As the references accumulate, Manston is stylistically demeaned into the man who can perform the progressively baser deeds attributable to his initial accidental misfortune. But Manston is not unredeemed. In the story he confesses all to clear Cytherea's honour. When Manston loses Cytherea, he is given the stylistic balm of one dramatic restorative reference as Hardy allows him a moment of compensatory humanity: 'Yes, the artificial bearing which this extraordinary man had adopted before strangers ever since he had overheard the conversation at the inn, left him now, and he mourned for Cytherea aloud' (p. 308). He reveals his wound with a lament: 'A land of darkness as darkness itself; and of the shadow of death without any order, and where the light is as darkness.' The quotation is from Job 10:22, the Biblical voice for suffering man – the same voice Jude is to use twenty-five years later. The 'deamon' is only a 'desperado'.

While Manston is the object of gradual allusive erosion, his rival, the hero, is raised correspondingly. Manston must become the hard, fanatical villain, wicked enough to break into Cytherea's house and physically overpower her. Springrove, to complete the polarity that melodrama demands, must become better than the average man: more loyal and more sensitive. To establish his sensitivity early, and to elevate him above any ordinary suitor, Hardy introduces him as a poet, and continues throughout the novel to associate him with great poets. As early as the second chapter Springrove is described through references to Milton's 'Lycidas' ('that last infirmity of Noble mind') and Shelley's lyric 'One word is too often profaned' ('One hope is too like despair / For prudence to smother'). And, lest we forget, the allusive links continue to instruct the reader: Springrove's first meeting with Cytherea is described in the words of Duke Ferdinand in Browning's 'The Statue and the Bust':

> He looked at her as a lover can;
> She looked at him as one who awakes –
> The past was asleep, and her life began. (p. 79)

He attempts to coax Cytherea into pleading with him to write by quoting from 'Lycidas': 'meditate the thankless Muse' (l. 66, p. 79);

he draws on Virgil's *Eclogues* in his flattering description of
Cytherea as Amaryllis (p. 79); he is trodden by Keats's hungry
generations (p. 207); he calls on Shakespeare to express himself on
Cytherea's apparent fickleness ('Love is not love / Which alters
when it alteration finds' (p. 233); and even in church his meditations are 'Horatian rather than Psalmodic' (p. 240). Hardy never
changes his pose for Springrove; the allusions attached to him are
poetic, classical or historical. The usual Biblical allusions are con-
spicuously absent. Springrove is the poet—hero of the novel. But
Hardy's allusions also achieve another important effect here, for as
the poetic references accumulate, the reader becomes gradually
aware of the inveterate Hardian irony. The allusions help to exalt
Springrove to the position necessary for a supernal protagonist;
Springrove is Hardy's incipient active hero. But by drawing the
references overwhelmingly from the greatest poets, men whose
achievements are far beyond Springrove's capabilities, Hardy also
brings into obvious contrast his hero's limited talent. Springrove
himself is not without blemish: he deceives Cytherea by not telling
her of his engagement. Just as there are no double-dyed villains, so
are there no unadulterated heroes in this novel.

The prize of the Manston—Springrove conflict, and the heroine
of the story, is a young romantic girl who, in true melodramatic
fashion, regularly finds herself confronted with problems greater
than she can solve. But Cytherea is not weak; she is a Hardy
woman, even if an immature one. She does struggle against her
adversaries with some Eustacian strength. However, the picture
Hardy draws of her is often shadowy and uncertain. The allusions
attached to her are the most erudite and obscure in the novel, and
tend to intensify rather than solve the problem. Sometimes the
allusions elevate, and Cytherea becomes a fitting heroine for this
melodrama which requires more emotional depth of its characters
than most in the convention. On the other hand, an almost equal
number of references disparage Cytherea and ironically lacerate
the romantic love which is the traditional stimulus and sacrosanct
ingredient of such stories. Such a dichotomy suggests an ambival-
ence of temper, or tone, on Hardy's part, abetted by an amateur's
inability to identify the inconsistency fully, and to resolve it.

It is the darkly realistic Hardy who allusively considers
Cytherea's romanticism and her conviction that there has never
been a love equal to her own. First, her name itself is ironic, since
Cytherea, signifying Aphrodite, is a contentedly virginal girl who

is anything but a goddess of love. Next, when she is first alone with Springrove, the narrator approaches the pair with mock irony: 'Sweet, sweet Love must not be slain thus, was the fair maid's reasoning. She was equal to the occasion — ladies are — and delivered the god . . .' (p. 77). The ironic tone, though without the salve of comedy, continues: the hoped-for kiss comes five pages and several turns around the lake later. The scene is described as 'many a voice of one delight', ironically a line from Shelley's sad lyric, 'Stanzas Written in Dejection Near Naples'.

Cytherea's personality is also assessed as she is ironically compared to characters beyond her approximation: she unsuccessfully tries to scorn Edward like 'Beatrice accusing Dante from the Chariot' (p. 170); she is 'like another Blessed Damozel', but, unlike Rossetti's panting, passionate observer, Cytherea 'listlessly looked down . . . the vivacity of spirit which had hitherto enlivened her was fast ebbing under the pressure of prosaic realities . . .' (p. 98). And for an ironic comment on her handling of a love affair, Hardy again draws, with perhaps some empathetic bitterness at the way external circumstances, Springrove's ineptness and her own constitution have countered her happiness, from 'The Statue and the Bust', whose two lovers keep postponing action until they are too old to bother.

However, when Cytherea is confronted not with the trials of romantic courtship but with the seriousness of her brother's illness and the grotesque possibility of having to marry a man she does not love, the allusions, again revealing an aspect of tone, elucidate the narrator's reversal into sympathy. Her innocence and inability to cope with a woman of Miss Aldclyffe's strength and cunning are stressed through a comparison to *Head of a Girl*, a painting, until recently thought to be by Greuze, acquired by the National Gallery fifteen years before Hardy came to London, and one which illustrates the sweet and somewhat arch expression Greuze associated with childhood.[4] As Miss Aldclyffe's plan is beginning to work and Cytherea is caught in a vice between Manston and her brother's need of her, thus making her marriage to Manston inescapable, her plight is compared to De Quincey's bout with opium: 'Had a register of her pitiful oscillations been kept, it would have rivalled in pathos the diary wherein De Quincey tabulates his combat with Opium — perhaps as noticeable an instance as any in which a thrilling dramatic power has been given to mere numerals' (p. 249). Several lines later the depth of her sadness is sharply defined by a reference to Sunday sermons on Elijah and Elisha in famine and drought. Then her sorrow is immediately further compounded by still another allusion to tragedy, 'so like, so very like, was day to day', from Wordsworth's 'Elegiac Stanzas', motivated by the death of his brother. And when all seems hopeless, and she is married to Manston, she once again receives decisive allusive support from the narrator: Hardy again uses Wordsworth when Cytherea's eyes tell Owen of sensations 'too deep for tears' (p. 271).

Thus the dual picture of Cytherea: a romantic girl whose Arcadian innocence is ironically undermined, and a burdened soul with whom the narrator and audience commiserate as her trials increase. Unfortunately, Hardy never convincingly depicts the transitional maturing of Cytherea, and neither overt narrative comment nor the shifting allusions ever completely turns the young, flighty Cytherea into the young, sensitive Cytherea. The novel concludes with Cytherea, the 'young lithe woman in an airy fairy dress', who gives little indication that she has gained much emotional depth from events drawn as major formative experiences.[5] She is married to Springrove, but Hardy cannot resist a final ironic jab even at this supposed happiness. The lovers have returned full cycle and are again rowing on the lake — but now Cytherea is not lovingly co-operative, and we have a taste of things to come as she coyly contradicts every statement her husband makes.

The more minor characters receive sparse allusive treatment. Owen Graye is associated with two references, and both of these serve only to emphasise him as the moral itinerant he is: he mentions the Ancient Mariner in connection with a gate-man he met, and he compares his own obtuseness to that of Columbus: 'How unutterably mean must my intelligence have appeared to the eye of a foreseeing God . . . Columbus on the eve of his discovery of a world was not so contemptibly unaware' (p. 280). Miss Aldclyffe fares better, as is befitting her more important status in the novel. In keeping with Hardy's practice of sympathetically muting the evil of even his worst characters, and perhaps with a desire not to be too harsh on the Establishment, Miss Aldclyffe gains support in spite of her cruelty. Though initially the stereotyped virago, she gradually develops into a study of the sexually frustrated and inhibited woman — a woman who tries to arrange the marriage between Manston and Cytherea not out of jealousy or malevolence, but rather as vicarious gratification of her own sexual needs. Hardy was later to receive bitter criticism of Miss Aldclyffe's role in the novel: a propertied lady would not have an illegitimate child, especially not by a relative. Although this charge is of course ridiculous even for Victorian England, Hardy has created an unconventional character in Miss Aldclyffe. Not only is her sexual repression displayed with twentieth-century candour, but her affection for Cytherea, so graphically expressed in a scene where she comes to Cytherea's bed to embrace her both physically and verbally, is such an explicit treatment of Lesbianism that modern critics, such as Albert Guerard, are forced to surmise that Hardy himself — and, even more, his audience — would not have understood the meaning of the scene.[6] None the less, however neurotic Miss Aldclyffe's actions, and regardless of what some would consider a blot on her scutcheon, Hardy's portrait of her is ultimately favourable, and he allusively supports his bias. The references uttered by or attached to her all tend to compliment her, either by illustrating her knowledge or by commenting on her charm and sensitivity. She quotes the more obscure Shelley, and Hallam's criticism of Juliet; she has the charm of Mary Stuart, known for her ability to win over dissident Protestants.

But unfortunately all these allusive successes cannot be assayed without including the counter-weight of some stylistic shortcomings in this first book. In feeling his way to a method, Hardy stumbled many times, often simply because he lacked restraint. One consequence of this laxity is that his references occasionally intrude upon his story. His perfunctory discipline is clearly evident, for example, in one of the tense debates between Cytherea and Miss Aldclyffe. Cytherea is speaking 'in an agony of torture' and her opponent is in a jealous rage, when Miss Aldclyffe abruptly interrupts her railing to quote four lines from the last stanza of Shelley's 'Lines', 'When the lamp is shattered' (p. 117). The slight pleasure the reader derives from recognising the irony involved in having the perverse intellect of Miss Aldclyffe voice 'bright reason will mock thee' is heavily outweighed by the intrusion that such a long and ill-timed allusion injects. Similar stylistic faltering is also evident later in the novel. In an unusual instance where allusion is directly attached to action, the narrator deadens the excitement by interrupting the inevitable histrionic fight between the hero and the villain to quote 1 Kings 21:20:

Manston was on his legs again in an instant. A fiery glance on the one side, a glance of pitiless justice on the other, passed between them. It was again the meeting in the vineyard of Naboth the Jezreelite: 'Hast thou found me, O mine enemy? And he answered, I have found thee: because thou has sold thyself to work evil in the sight of the Lord'. (p. 398)

Another result of Hardy's early critical myopia was occasional lapses of taste. Although critics have justified it as a projection of his prejudice against the city, Hardy is none the less coarse in his description of the Dutch clock in a slum kitchen: 'its entrails hanging down beneath its white face and wiry hands, like the faeces of a Harpy' (p. 350). The line following, a distorted passage in Latin from the third book of the *Aeneid*, accentuates the gaucherie rather than redeems it.[7]

Hardy is also guilty of forcing his method beyond its strength. At times he is obviously straining for a reference. His second quotation from Dryden's translation of the *Aeneid* is a pertinent example. Hardy's allusion discussing Cytherea versus Manston reads

> One on her youth and pliant limbs relies,
> One on his sinews and his giant size. (p. 397)

To make the reference fit the context of his plot, Hardy has to feminise the pronoun – and even this is not enough, for the roles are reversed: in the source the 'youth' is the villain, the stronger man the hero.

At other times Hardy overworks his technique by being too erudite or obscure for all but a very limited part of his already select audience. He ostentatiously describes Cytherea's emotions by quoting Virgil, one of five Latin digressions in the novel. And only extensive research or chance knowledge of useless information would elucidate Manston's mention of 'the Flying Isle of San Borandan' as an allusion to the voyages of the sixth-century Saint Brendan to find the terrestrial paradise.

Such specimens of his early stylistic deficiencies in *Desperate Remedies* are only samples, and can be supported by a list of several other allusions which are not smoothly integrated or used. None the less, Hardy's allusive techniques of foreshadowing events in the plot, of elevating characters to a figurative rank beyond their immediate circumstances and of commenting ironically on his characters, undercutting their apparent positions in the story and thus revealing his own evaluations of them, all promise the genius that is to come in later novels. Admittedly there is some confusing entanglement, too little restraint. But even though the technique often fails, the inventive development of several scenes and more than one or two of the characters make it a book 'not unworthy of longer preservation'.

Under the Greenwood Tree (1872), because of its later date, would seem to promise a more mature manipulation of allusions. But this is an atypical novel, as demonstrated by the often recognised fact that it contains no sensational incidents, little suspense, no references to chance and only one coincidence. The story itself is a light one, its entire tone analogous to the title's reference to Shakespeare's *As You Like It*, II. v. 1.[8] This bucolic novelette, whose plot is reminiscent of some of the poems from William Barnes's *Poems of Rural Life*, deals with two coeval tales: the conventional courtship of Dick Dewy and Fancy Day, and the disbanding of the Mellstock Quire in favour of the more modern organ.[9]

Hardy subtitled his novel 'A Rural Painting in the Dutch School'. Barnes, in *Thoughts on Beauty and Art*, praises the Dutch School for its 'beauty and truth of colours and action'.[10] The Dutch painters are also known for their accuracy and finish, and for their 'warm fidelity to local truth in opposition to what are thought to be the cold idealisations of the "grand style" associated with Raphael'.[11] Hardy's novel is loyal to these same points: it gives a colourful, and though factual, somewhat idealistic portrait of English rural life. It is a sylvan idyl, and does not pretend to be otherwise; there is no tragedy in the main plot.[12] The preface states that this story of the Quire 'is intended to be a fairly true picture, at first hand, of the personages, ways, and customs which were common among such orchestral bodies in the villages of fifty or sixty years ago'.

Hardy set his story in an Arcadian world after the critical failure of his first novel, for reviewers of *Desperate Remedies* had praised the rustic figures in it while condemning nearly everything else. Though *Under the Greenwood Tree* is now frequently cited as one of Hardy's most flawless works, he discounted it as frivolous: 'penned so lightly, even so farcically and flippantly at times'. Because he felt this way about it, he did not devote a great deal of time to revision, and the Wessex Edition usually follows the original manuscript. There are some differences, however. The accidentals of the manuscript suffered considerably at the hands of compositors: commas, dashes and semicolons were added or altered at will to conform to varying concepts of house style. Hardy, in the course of revising for the 1896 and 1912 editions, emended some of these corruptions (deleting commas, for example), and made some changes in substantives as well.[13] The manuscript names have become Wessex names by 1912. There are also sporadic revisions in dialect − though these are inconsistent, for Hardy will change, for example, the manuscript 'martel' to 'mortal' (pp. 57, 161), thus taking out dialect spelling, and then reverse his procedure and revise 'keep' to 'kip', or add a whole paragraph of rustic speech which contributes nothing to the story except more rustic speech (p. 91). But perhaps the best illustration of Hardy's relative indifference here is in his excision of some of the choppy short paragraphs and intrusive chapter divisions, while leaving untouched rather trivial chapters such as Book I, Chapter 9 (2½ pages long and dealing only with the return of Fancy's handkerchief) or the one-page Book II, Chapter 1.

In that the novel hardly exemplifies the profundity implied in *Desperate Remedies*, Hardy was warranted in his apology for it. But modern taste has been kinder than Hardy and has since given it credit as a simple pastoral, a potential parable and a novel of rural manners. Unquestionably *Under the Greenwood Tree* does foreshadow his later skill in transmuting the natural world into an animate force acting on his characters, and also charts a marked advance in his ability to make his rural world real to a cosmopolitan audience. Much of Hardy's triumph stems from his precise description of scenery and customs, and from his inclusion of the dialect (though the *Athenaeum* of 15 June 1872 chastised him for occasionally making his rustics 'speak too much like educated people' − a criticism which perhaps precipitated some of Hardy's later revisions). But Hardy was also successful in making his particular countryside familiar to urban England through common references. These allusions serve as touchstones to the rural world, while fulfilling their internal function of heightening the comic tone of the novel. One excellent example of his desire to give an accurate picture of the 'personages, ways, and customs' of the villages, and of his best allusive talent, appears in Chapter 6, during a narrative digression on the gallery of Mellstock Church:

The gallery of Mellstock Church had a status and sentiment of its own. A stranger there was regarded with a feeling altogether differing from that of the congregation below toward him. Banished from the nave as an intruder whom no originality could make interesting, he was received above as a curiosity that no unfitness could render dull. The gallery, too, looked down upon and knew the habits of the nave to its remotest peculiarity, and had an extensive stock of exclusive information about it; whilst the nave knew nothing of the gallery folk, as gallery folk, beyond their loud-sounding minims and chest notes. Such topics as that the clerk was always chewing tobacco except at the moment of crying amen; that he had a dust-hole in his pew; that during the sermon certain young daughters of the village had left off caring to read anything so mild as the marriage service for some years, and now regularly studied the one which chronologically follows it; that a pair of lovers touched fingers through a knot-hole between their pews in the manner ordained by their great exemplars, Pyramus and Thisbe; that Mrs. Ledlow, the farmer's wife, counted her money and reckoned her week's marketing expenses during the first lesson − all new to those below − were stale subjects here. (p. 63)

Here is an adroit lightness of approach that is rare in Hardy, and one which proves that his talent is not limited to the sombre. The reference to Pyramus and Thisbe is a masterly touch, for immediately the situation becomes imaginatively familiar; and although the primary source is Ovid, it is difficult to suppress a picture of Bottom and his actors.

Other instances of this allusive maintenance of the comic tone are easily found in the novel. Biblical and political references, for example, produce a near farcical effect as they are reduced by the circumstances which elicit them. The country custom of smoking hams in the chimney is made comically vivid by the appearance of little Charlie, covered with soot after trying to play with the ham crook and chain − and his subsequent guilt is made an aspect of universal childhood as he looks 'back over his shoulder with an expression of great sin on his face, like Cain as the Outcast in the Bible pictures' (p. 70). (In order to make his meaning explicit here, Hardy has added 'as the Outcast', a post-manuscript revision.) Personalities gain an added vivacity through a reference to national politics: Mrs Penny plays Tory to her husband's Whiggism − but only at times of peaceful discussion (p. 90). And it is an analogy to Noah's pairing that heightens the comedy involved in

Mrs Day's custom of buying duplicate household items in anticipation of Fancy's marriage (p. 111).

Since much of Hardy's concentration here is on setting, there are surprisingly few allusions attached to the principal characters. Dick, the patient hero, is allowed only three important allusive references: to return Fancy's handkerchief he must 'screw himself up to enduring the cottage windows' (p. 84), recalling the chilling commands of Lady Macbeth (II. vii. 60); his hyper-sensitivity to Fancy's opinion of him makes him despair at the tranter's touch, 'coming down upon her shoulder the while like a Nasmyth hammer' (p. 81), alluding to the steam-hammer invented in 1839 to help forge large steamship paddle wheels; and his plan to ignore Fancy after she squanders his holiday is thwarted by a 'Venus' who planned other developments (p. 156). This series of allusions serves a dual purpose. Because none of the three is Biblical, they tend to isolate Dick from his scripturally oriented peers, contrasting his position as a main character with their choral function. More important, each of the allusions is amusingly incongruous, and thus mocks his emotions or his situation. With playful irony Hardy allusively exaggerates love's effect on Dick, while simultaneously depending on the seriousness of the references to check his twitting short of lampoonery. To link the fate of a handkerchief to that of Duncan, to compare a playful, flirtatious touch to a steam-hammer and to attribute Dick's failure to miss Fancy on the road to the machinations of Venus delightfully intensifies the comic atmosphere Hardy desired to establish for the mock heroics of his lovers.

While Dick gets his identity as an individual from his marriageability and the fact that his father is the unofficial leader of the parish, Fancy gains her superiority primarily because of her advanced schooling, her father's material circumstances and her own good looks. Her education, constantly emphasised by references to her position as schoolmistress, would make her the logical one to utter literary references. But just as this is an uncanonical novel, so is Fancy an atypical Hardy heroine. She is the only one who does not suffer – and the shallowness implied by her name and confirmed by her actions is not relieved by any stylistic elevation. Fancy is coy, selfish, flighty and vain. Horace Moule, commenting in the *Saturday Review* (28 September 1872) recognised this immediately: 'The portraiture of Fancy herself conveys a kind of satire on the average character of a girl with good looks, capable of sound and honest affection, but inordinately moved by admiration.' This picture is not allusively altered. Rather, her very allusive blandness is a comment on her personality. Only once is there any colouring, and this comes on the final page of the novel through a reference which primarily functions as an ironic comment on the plot rather than on her character.

Desperate Remedies proves artistically the ironic usefulness of allusions in plot development, and very early in *Under the Greenwood Tree* (Part I, Chapter 4) Hardy indicates that he has wisely retained this successful stratagem. Music naturally plays an important part in this book, and consequently, when Dick gets his first glimpse of his nemesis, Fancy, it is not surprising that the choir is intoning parts of an old hymn, 'Remember, O Thou Man' (p. 53). However, to induce the irony he desires, and to make the incongruity of comparing Dick to Adam work for the desired light tone of the book, Hardy deliberately omits the inapplicable first stanza of the hymn, and begins the singing with the admonitory lines, 'Remember Adam's fall, O thou man'. In the manuscript Hardy ends his reference with only two lines. But, perhaps fearing that his less ecclesiastical urban audience would not recognise his source and his ironic sample, he ensures identification by quoting five of the song's nine stanzas in the Wessex Edition. Here, then, by mere stanzaic selectively, a commonplace event is skilfully transformed into an ironic, and comic, comment on the plot.

Yet it is in the last two chapters that Hardy's allusive inventiveness equals that of his first novel. These chapters are the only ones with poetic titles. The first, 'The knot there's no untying', is ostensibly a forthright, impartial comment on the finality of marriage. But when placed in the context of its source, Thomas Campbell's song, 'How delicious is the winning', the irony materialises. The song warns, in the lines immediately following the chapter reference:

> Yet, remember, 'midst your wooing,
> Love has bliss, but Love has rueing;
> Other smiles may make you fickle,
> Tears for other charms may trickle
>
> . . . .
>
> Love he comes, and Love he tarries,
> Just as fate or fancy carries;

However, Fancy has already carried Dick too far for a retreat. In the final scene Dick and Fancy are returning from their wedding when he muses aloud, 'Fancy . . . why we are so happy is because there is such full confidence between us . . . We'll have no secrets from each other, darling, will we ever?' 'None from today', she replies, and then, 'Hark! what's that?' Here Hardy injects an inimitable double allusion which gives symmetry to the book and concurrently voices his undeviating cynicism on the subject of marriage. From a neighbouring copse comes 'Tippiwit! swe-e-et! ki-ki-ki! Come hither, come hither, come hither!' — a quotation from *As You Like It* (II. v. 5), the play which gave the book and the chapter their identical titles. The rhetorical 'Hark!' is then answered by Fancy herself: '"O, 'tis the nightingale", murmured she, and thought of a secret she would never tell' (p. 208). Dick remains ignorant of the coy irony of her reply, but the knowing reader is reminded of another pair of lovers, another deception: Juliet says to Romeo, 'Wilt thou be gone? it is not yet near day: / It was the nightingale, and not the lark, / That pierced the fearful hollow of thine ear' (III. v. 1–3). The allusion, then, in the book's last line nearly undermines the marriage with a playful irony in keeping with the fanciful tone of the novel — and Hardy leaves his characters in unusual happiness, but not flawless bliss.

After the mild success of *Under the Greenwood Tree* William Tinsley asked Hardy to write a serial for his magazine. Hardy responded with *A Pair of Blue Eyes*, first published in *Tinsley's Magazine* from September 1872 to July 1873. This was the first novel Hardy publicly acknowledged, and the first to be initially released as a serial — a practice he was to continue throughout his career. When *Desperate Remedies* was later designated a 'Novel of Ingenuity', and *Under the Greenwood Tree* a novel of 'Character and Environment', Hardy placed this novel among his 'Romances and Fantasies'.[14] The book proves to be accurately defined, and does not rise above its modest pretensions. However, even as an admitted 'Romance' it has enough depth to be a marked change from the frivolity of *Under the Greenwood Tree*.[15]

The reviewers of Hardy's serial judged by past attempts and were encouraged by the improvement. The *Saturday Review* (2 August 1873) chided him for minor errors of taste, but conceded that 'it is one of the most artistically constructed among recent novels'. The *Spectator* (28 June 1873), which had been so harsh towards *Desperate Remedies*, justified its earlier acrimony as constructive criticism, took some credit for Hardy's renunciation of 'inexcusable sensation writing' and finally allowed that under the sickly sentimental title 'we have a really powerful story . . .'. This praise, however, was somewhat tempered, and justifiably, by the critic's recognition that, although the talent was there, it still needed mellowing. The reviewer concluded, 'we heartily trust we may hear of Mr. Hardy soon, but not too soon again'.

Hardy himself was aware that *A Pair of Blue Eyes* was in some ways a weak novel, and that, as Coventry Patmore suggested, its theme was perhaps better suited to poetry than to prose.[16] None the less, he refused, in 1912, to correct his errors 'by the judgment of later years', contending that such a process would harm the freshness and spontaneity of the original. This decision was again a fortunate one, especially in view of the fact that Hardy did somewhat revise the manuscript before sending it to Tinsley. The book thus shows evidence of his developing critical taste, but without having undergone a mutation to become an example of the 'mature' Hardy.

The corrections Hardy made are more numerous than those in *Desperate Remedies* and *Under the Greenwood Tree*, perhaps indicating his higher regard for this novel; but they do not seriously alter the story. The major change is in the excision by 1895 of six pages at the beginning of the book which describe the heroine Elfride's method of novel-reading. Her personality is painstakingly analysed as she struggles to resist the temptation to read the ending first. Her curiosity engages her honesty as a reader, and the battle ends in compromise: she refuses to read the dénouement, but looks at the chapter titles, which tell her what she wants to know — her hero dies. The entire incident is minor enough, and the book does not suffer from its loss. On the contrary, the author's instruction to his public on how to read is presumptuous and harms the book, as does the prematurely sombre tone of one paragraph: 'it was the last time in her life that her emotions were ever won [unclear in manuscript] to any height by circumstances which never transpired; that the loves and woes, expectation and despair of imaginary beings were ever able so much to emulate her own experiences as to make a perceptible difference to her state of mind for a whole afternoon'.

Other revisions are less important, and are dispersed throughout the novel. For example, the original title of the romance

Elfride is reading, *The Court of King Arthur's Castle; a Romance of Lyonnesse*, was the *Court* [Count?] *of Kellyon Castle*; in the manuscript Elfride is 'nearly nineteen', while in the Wessex Edition she is 'nearly twenty'; in Chapter 15 Hardy tightens the prose of the introductory paragraph; the title of Chapter 4 is corrected ('swells' changed to 'heaves'); the titles of Chapters 18 and 22 are altered; the intrusive first manuscript paragraph of Chapter 7 is omitted; and some names are changed — for example, Port of Stranton becomes Castle Boterel. Such revisions are interesting for what they indicate about Hardy's meticulousness as he composed, but they have little literary effect. The novel remains a romance with a love triangle. Elfride first loves Stephen Smith, then shifts her affections to Henry Knight, his best friend and mentor. Knight emerges as the self-righteous moralist who cannot accept Elfride's previous love experience, details of which he has learned through a revengeful note from Mrs Jethway, who hates Elfride because of her mistaken notion that her son's pining for Elfride has caused his death. Knight's rejection of Elfride unwittingly perpetrates her marriage of convenience with the local aristocrat, Lord Luxellian. As the novel closes, Knight and Stephen, ignorant of her marriage, return to Elfride: Stephen hopeful that her love for him will be rekindled, Knight contrite for refusing her devotion. But the familiar Hardy irony of fate is unremitting; the train which carries the prospective suitors also carries Elfride's body. She is to be buried in the Luxellian vault.

Even a romance such as this ends with tragic irony, and other elements now recognised as Hardy conventions are apparent too. The plot is carefully worked out, with irony forming the bond; in every act of Elfride with Knight one easily sees a repetition of an earlier act with Stephen. Furthermore, the book differs from *Under the Greenwood Tree* in that coincidence now plays a major role: Elfride meets the only person she wishes to avoid when she returns from an abortive elopement with Stephen; her father secretly marries on the very day of her elopement, and so on. H. C. Webster contends that there are at least thirty-seven such incidents in the novel.[17] Still another convention, the natural world portrayed as an organic whole capable of enormous influence, is strikingly evident in the oft-discussed cliff scene. Here Knight, on the verge of crashing to certain death, finds himself staring compulsively at a fossil, and immediately mentally transforms his predicament into an epitome for all of evolution. He becomes painfully aware of the total human position: the insignificance of human beings in time, the ephemeral nature of the species. And — the final Hardian feature — Elfride becomes, like the Tess she foreshadows, the ironic victim whose punishment far exceeds her crime.

Supplying these particular plot characteristics are the familiar stylistic traits, which here show an advance, albeit an irregular one, over his previous novels. The awkward sentences are still here, as are the choppy paragraphs and the occasional useless chapter divisions. But these flaws are indemnified by a significant advance in his descriptive power, especially in the way he uses colour; by a deeper analysis of his principal figures; and by an increased confidence in his allusive method.

A Pair of Blue Eyes provides a marked contrast to the sparseness of *Under the Greenwood Tree*, though both occasionally suffer for their extremes. *Under the Greenwood Tree* has approximately twenty-six references, *A Pair of Blue Eyes* has five times that many. Though the latter novel is substantially longer and obviously more serious, one still cannot escape the suspicion that Hardy was trying to ballast the story with a plethora of references. Every chapter title is allusive — a fact that the *Spectator* noted as 'unusual' — though George Eliot had often used the device long before Hardy even started writing. And the text itself contains a welter of allusions, most of which follow his established practice of defining character. An inordinate number of the allusions are Shakespearean, though the balancing Biblical references, and the usual poetic, scientific and historical miscellany, appear too.

In the part of the manuscript excised from the Wessex Edition, Hardy justifies his allusive chapter titles by having the suspense of Elfride's novel-reading ruined by titles which blatantly reveal the conclusion. Hardy's system certainly protects the reader from this, but at the risk of being pedantic, for he over-extends the device.[18] Several of the allusions are pure ostentation, and are too obscure or imprecise to add anything of consequence to the story. 'After many days', 'A wandering voice', and 'Her father did fume' could wisely be replaced by more definitive titles, or at least ones which would flatter the reader by being only moderately difficult to identify.[19] 'Where heaves the turf in many a mouldering heap', from Gray's 'Elegy', 'Bosom'd high in tufted trees' (Milton's 'L'Allegro', l. 75), 'Fare thee weel awhile' (Burns's 'O my Luve's like a red, red, rose', l. 14), and 'A distant dearness in the hill'

(Tennyson, *In Memoriam*, lxiv) are titles of the latter type, but they, too, do little more than innocuously describe events in the chapter. Allusions such as these are simply decorative, supporting the judgment that Hardy had not yet completely decided to eschew quotation merely for its own sake.

On the other hand, several of Hardy's titular allusions do enhance the story and reward the reader's attention. The tone of the novel is projected immediately when on the title page Hardy quotes *Hamlet*, I. iii. 7–10:

> A violet in the youth of primy nature,
> Forward, not permanent, sweet, not lasting,
> The perfume and suppliance of a minute;
> No more.

In context, the allusion not only enlarges Elfride through a comparison with the tragic Ophelia, whose fate she will share, but also anticipates the shift of love that inaugurates the tragedy. Laertes is speaking to Ophelia just before he leaves. He tells her to take the attentions of Hamlet as being ephemeral – 'a violet in the youth of primy nature'. Elfride, too, could benefit from such a warning, for Knight's love, though sweet, does find alteration.[20] The reader is warned that even an apparent romance has overtones of tragedy.

The talent evident in the choice of motto is also observable in other chapter titles which variously complement, add humour to, summarise, intensify, and contribute irony to the story. Elfride first appears in a chapter entitled 'A fair vestal thron'd in the west' – a line from *A Midsummer Night's Dream* (II. i. 157), where Oberon is saying to Puck that he once saw Cupid aim at a fair vestal. The passage is commonly accepted as a compliment to Queen Elizabeth, and subtly enriches Elfride's position as heroine, thus preparing her for the queenly role she is to play. The comic spirit is injected when Stephen as lover is introduced under the heading 'Melodious birds sing madrigals', enabling Hardy to twit Stephen's inexperience with this reference from Marlowe's 'The Passionate Shepherd to his Love'. Further, a series of titles drawn from melancholy or tragic sources tonally operates to rehearse Stephen's predicament and accentuate the impending tragic renunciation by Knight. 'Adieu! She cries; and waved her lily hand', 'How should I greet thee', and 'Had I wist before I kist' referentially summarise past contingencies and predict events, all

with a slight touch of irony. 'Adieu . . .' is from John Gay's 'Sweet
William's Farewell to Blackeyed Susan', where Will's trip to India
and his admonition not to worry about his fidelity parallels
Stephen's situation. 'How should I greet thee' leads the reader to
Byron's 'When We Two Parted', a poem which, with startling
exactness, recounts Stephen's entire relationship with Elfride.
Elfride has decided in favour of Knight and against keeping her
long-awaited rendezvous with Stephen. The poem reads:

> When we two parted
>   In silence and tears,
> Half broken-hearted
>   To sever for years,
> Pale grew thy cheek and cold,
>   Colder thy kiss;
> Truly that hour foretold
>   Sorrow to this.
>
> The dew of the morning
>   Sunk chill on my brow —
> It felt like the warning
>   Of what I feel now.
> Thy vows are all broken,
>   And light is thy fame:
> I hear thy name spoken,
>   And share in its shame.
>
> They name thee before me,
>   A knell to mine ear;
> A shudder comes o'er me —
>   Why wert thou so dear?
> They know not I knew thee,
>   Who knew thee too well: —
> Long, long shall I rue thee,
>   Too deeply to tell.
>
> In secret we met —
>   In silence I grieve,
> That thy heart could forget,
>   Thy spirit deceive.
> If I should meet thee
>   After long years,

> How should I greet thee?
> With silence and tears.

And the third allusion, 'Had I wist before I kist', heading the
chapter containing the crucial fight between Knight and Elfride,
is equally pertinent for Knight. The line is from the ballad 'Waly
Waly', in a verse beginning:

> But had I wist, before I kisst,
> That love had been sae ill to win;
> I had lockt my heart in a case of gowd,
> And pinnd it with a siller pin.

Some artistically chosen titular allusions also serve to intensify
the tragedy of the ill-fated characters, and hammer home Hardy's
belief in a world not meant for human happiness. The pain
involved in Stephen's discovery that his teacher is also his replacement is reflected by Hardy's choice of 'Mine own familiar friend'
(Chapter 25), from Psalm 55 : 14.[21] This bitter song asks the Lord
to bring destruction on the wicked deceivers. It is the curse that
Stephen would feel only fleetingly in a moment of anguish; Mrs
Jethway would earnestly desire such vengeance because of the
imagined wrong done to her son — and she is covertly present
during the discovery scene.

Countering the artificiality and anticlimax of the actual
dénouement, the emotional climax of the book is also allusively
fortified in such a way as not only to exacerbate but also to unify
the crescendoing elements of tragedy, and inject the biting irony so
prevalent in Hardy's world. Certainly, Hardy's ironically-used
titles appear before this section of the novel: Chapter 11, which
describes the elopement, is announced by 'Journeys end in lovers
meeting', a line from *Twelfth Night* (II. iii. 44), which in the play is
part of a song on the instability of love; and the chapter dealing
with Elfride's deception is entitled 'A worm in the bud', another
allusion to *Twelfth Night* (II. iv. 115), where there is also the
Socratically ironic difference between appearance and reality in
the speech which the disguised Viola utters to Orsino about a
'sister' who concealed her love. And there are other instances. But
it is at the most crucial point in the novel that the developing skill
of Hardy is best shown. Chapter 33, describing Mrs Jethway's
death, is entitled 'O daughter of Babylon, wasted with misery';

Chapter 34, dealing with Mrs Jethway's Acherontic note to
Knight, is called 'Yea, happy shall be he that rewardeth thee as
thou has served us'. Initially it appears to be Mrs Jethway who is
'wasted with misery', for she is found dead; but when the two
chapter headings are recognised as the two parts of the same verse
of Psalm 137, the conjunctive titles become brilliantly devised
comments not only on Mrs Jethway, but on Elfride too.[22] It is
Elfride, the dual allusions reveal, who is wasted with misery — and
it is with virulent irony that Hardy includes 'happy shall be he that
rewardeth thee. . . .' Mrs Jethway gets her revenge — Elfride is
injured by her note — but Mrs Jethway earns death, not happiness. Chapter 35 draws the entire episode to a close: Knight has
left, Elfride follows him to London in one final attempt at
reconciliation. But the allusion in the chapter title echoes the
futility of her trip. Hardy uses Wyatt's bleak, plaintive 'The
Lover's Appeal' to provide the tone: 'And wilt thou leave me
thus? / Say nay — say nay!'

In addition to the allusive chapter titles, Hardy has freely dis-
tributed a large number of miscellaneous references, which
perform a variety of functions. As in *Desperate Remedies*, he
again uses allusive conversation by principals to familiarise his
readers with references which he has deliberately chosen for the
significance of the source as much as of the immediate context:
Stephen finishes a Latin quotation of Mr Swancourt's (p. 83);
Elfride and Stephen exchange verses from Keats's 'La Belle Dame
sans Merci' (p. 89) and question each other on the poem's rele-
vance; Elfride thinks of Coleridge's 'Three Graves' while she is in
church, mentally comparing herself to the poem as 'she wondered
if Mrs Jethway were cursing her . . .' (p. 209); and Knight quotes
Psalm 102 to Elfride, applies it to the death scene at hand, and
asks her to complete the verse. In each of these cases the reference
itself is important, but the reader is also explicitly reminded that
the source must be considered as well.

The disparate allusions also inject a note of humour into a plot
that is otherwise an unusually serious 'Romance and Fantasy'. No
comic relief is provided by the main characters, but fortunately for
the reader Mr and Mrs Swancourt can be laughed at. Mr Swancourt's Dickensian characteristic is his constant threat to tell a
story he remembers, then only to refuse on the grounds of
modesty. The only time he is specific about his tale is when he goes
into his 'I remember a story, but it's too . . .,' abruptly remembers

it is Sunday, and dexterously turns his subject from its secular beginning into the more professionally appropriate Biblical realm, letting the matter rest with an ostensibly pious reference to the 'story of the Levite who journeyed to Bethlehem-judah . . .' (p. 207). The reader joins Hardy in the joke on the parson, for his allusion is to one of the most sordid of Biblical accounts – Judges 19 – where a Levite's concubine is gang raped, dies, is cut into twelve pieces, and is sent to the tribes of Israel to incite a war. Mr Swancourt is too mild a man ever to tell an equally lurid secular tale. And this humorous tone continues to circumscribe the couple as Mr Swancourt describes his minor discomfort when boarding a boat with a quotation from Jeremiah (29:17), the prophet of doom, or when he compares his wife's people-watching with what 'Mr Puff saw in Lord Burleigh's nod' (p. 168), reminding the reader of the scene in Sheridan's *The Critic*. Burleigh enters, nods, and leaves. Puff describes the meaning to Sneer:

> Why, by that shake of the head, he gave you to understand that even though they had more justice in their cause, and wisdom in their measures – yet, if there was not a greater spirit shown on the part of the people, the country would at last fall a sacrifice to the hostile ambition of the Spanish monarchy. (III, i)

The more minor stylistic functions of the miscellaneous allusions can be quickly enumerated. Hardy's reading and his desire to impress is evident in the detailed scrutiny given to Mr Swancourt's theological library (p. 59); in the mention of Staunton and Morphy (p. 195), the English and American chess experts; and in the allusion to Smeaton's lighthouse (p. 186), an esoteric reference to John Smeaton's reconstruction of the Eddystone Light in 1756. The important influence of painting on Hardy at this time is exemplified by the numerous artists he cites: Holbein, Kneller, and Lely are used to intimate the wealth of the Luxellians; Rubens, Correggio, Greuze, and Guido Reni are also mentioned. And finally, to emphasise the special influence of Stephen's mother, Hardy stylistically segregates her from the other rustics by allusions to Coryphaeus and Dahl, though he is quick to maintain her earthy demeanour by choosing a painter who had no qualms about stressing the stodginess and plainness of his models.[23]

This galaxy of allusions employed in areas sparsely treated in earlier novels – that is to say, areas extraneous to the central issues

of the book — gives a clear indication of the massive use of allusion
in the novel as a whole; for Hardy applies all of these references
without subtracting in the least from those committed to his
principals. Stephen, Knight, and Elfride are the objects of multifarious allusions, all used to reflect tone, to manoeuvre the reader
in accordance with Hardy's narrative intention.

Stephen Smith is the first major male character presented and
he is thoroughly analysed allusively before his too convenient
departure for India.[24] When he is first introduced, Stephen is the
epitome of naiveté, and his inexperience is allusively annotated.
Keats's 'Ode to a Nightingale' is used to describe his innocence of
'the weariness, the fever, and the fret' (p. 47). His physical features
are delicate, and his mouth is compared to that of the perpetual
boy, Cupid (p. 47). Even his passion is diminutive, for the fire in
his heart is that of 'a small Troy' (p. 56). But once Stephen's
innocence is firmly established, the references take a more severe
turn. Even as the plot is progressing in his favour, the allusions are
gradually undermining his position in preparation for the ultimate
defeat which Hardy's view of the story required. Stephen receives a
series of references as he courts Elfride which superficially seem to
raise him to a position of social and educational equality with her.
But when the allusions are more carefully scrutinised, they become
stingingly ironic. Elfride compliments his manners, only to have
the narrator compare them to the feats of Euryalus (p. 115). This
gilding by the classics is sufficiently tarnished when one knowingly
recalls that Euryalus heroically followed Nisus through the enemy
camp only to get himself captured and cause both his own and his
friend's death. Again Elfride makes an attempt to defend him by
pointing out that he is the best member of his family, and again he
is demeaned by allusion, this time by Mr Swancourt's retort from
Hamlet, v. ii. 88: 'Let a beast be lord of beasts, and his crib shall
stand at the king's mess' (p. 116). As Stephen leaves the rectory
after planning the secret marriage with Elfride, the allusive irony
is even more intense: his path is compared to Jael's tent nail,
calling to mind a grim story of betrayal and alienated affection
similar to what Stephen will encounter. The fictional tension
mounts when Stephen meets Elfride for the elopement. He makes
a simple-minded mistake about the licence, forcing the couple to
travel to London for the ceremony. Elfride goes, but reverses her
decision and demands to return home. Stephen kindly, and
meekly, complies, but his acquiescence is assessed through an

ironic comparison to a figure beyond his reach; the waiting game was correct for the brilliant Fabius as he fought with Hannibal, 'but decision, however suicidal, has more charm for a woman. . . .' (p. 157). Stephen's passive chivalry is decisive: he loses Elfride forever, and is replaced by Knight. In the narrative he makes the contrived exit to India here, and, once learning of his fate, becomes the early prototype of the unaggressive, long-suffering Hardy hero. His role in the plot is merely secondary now, perhaps too abruptly so. But if his departure has been inadequately planned, his precipitous course as a lover has been allusively charted by a professional.

Henry Knight is the only purely intellectual figure among all Hardy's men, and critics have often commented that Hardy's treatment of him is consistent with his attitude towards such insularity. For Hardy avowedly admires the man of feeling more than the man of intellect. The *Spectator* (28 June 1873) accurately describes the portrait Hardy has drawn: 'For Knight is no carpet-knight, but quite the reverse, — a lonely, unloving man, an acute, uncompromising critic, of severe rectitude, unable to conceive of purity and faithfulness in combination with timidity and vacillation, and therefore harsh and unjust.' But Hardy does not make Knight a limited melodramatic villain. Quite to the contrary, he has a complex personality — nuances of which Hardy will later develop in the similarly intellectual Angel Clare and the infinitely more compassionate Phillotson. In Knight we see a man whose harshness and injustice are mixed with an honourable desire to be lenient and with the reasoned love his intellectualism permits. Unfortunately, however, he has never learned how to temper his exacting standards and his jealousy, and is thus incapable of tolerance. His perfectionism results in an obsession with feminine purity which in turn places demands on his lover which no human could meet. When Knight does find what he believes to be the 'pure woman', he approaches her reasonably, mathematically — and conditionally. Once he discovers a supposed flaw, he is unable, and unwilling, to compromise. Although he suffers for his rigidity, he never gains the nobility or compassion necessary to be an object of much of the reader's, or the narrator's, admiration. Granted, his course can be somewhat rationalised as guided by an innate lack of sensitivity, but his self-righteous cruelty, even while in love, cannot be exonerated. Having created such a character, Hardy gives him the allusive trouncing he deserves.

Knight first physically appears in the story when Stephen goes to him for advice. The transition from Stephen-hero to Knight is soon allusively transacted by another reference to Hamlet, the arch-procrastinator. Stephen has just unwittingly lost Elfride through indecision; now Knight is 'sicklied o'er by the unmistakable pale cast' (p. 159). But his connection with Stephen is quickly severed — in the plot by Stephen's departure, and stylistically by references to his Ciceronian library and the Roman poets, which firmly establish Knight as Stephen's intellectual superior. Knight visits Elfride as family friend and as a critic who has disparaged her novel. There is a brief allusive truce as Knight defends the task of reviewers with Pauline pomposity: 'To make you sorry after a proper manner, that ye may receive damage by us in nothing' (2 Corinthians 7:9). (Hardy must have had his tongue in his cheek here.) Then Knight's harsh absolutism gradually seeps in.

At first his standards, unusually Puritanical even for nineteenth-century England, appear to be rather harmless rules of the inexperienced — and the allusions tracing his position are neutral, though they tend to emphasise the depth of his convictions. In his first conversation with Elfride, he tells her that the best thing to hear about a woman is nothing: 'It is as Smeaton said of his lighthouse: her greatest real praise, when the novelty of her inauguration has worn off, is that nothing happens to keep the talk of her alive' (p. 186). And when Knight begins to suspect Elfride of a previous love, he is able to shake off his fears with a forced allusive laugh: 'it was as hard to be earliest in a woman's heart as it was to be first in the Pool of Bethesda' (p. 329), the miraculous healing waters described in John 5:2. But as Knight probes deeper, becomes more disillusioned, and consequently more unyielding, the reader's sympathy for him ebbs. Knight begins to use his intellect as a weapon, cutting at both Elfride and himself. In unbroken succession he utters three allusions which he believes serve him well: when he learns of the depth of Elfride's former attachment, he tries to salve his bruised ego with an exalted comparison and mutters Adam's reproach to Eve in *Paradise Lost*; when he pries further into her affairs, he responds to her plea to stop the cruel questioning with a vicious reference to Diogenes Laertius:

Diogenes Laertius says that philosophers used voluntarily to deprive themselves of sight to be uninterrupted in their meditations. Men, becoming lovers, ought to do the same thing . . . Why?

Because they would never then be distracted by discovering their idol was second-hand (pp. 344—5).

And during his most emotional confrontation with Elfride he is again the caustic pedant: 'Knight trifled in the very bitterness of his feeling. "In the time of the French Revolution, Pariseau, a ballet-master, was beheaded by mistake, for Parisot, a captain of the King's Guard. I wish there was another 'E. Swancourt' in the neighbourhood"' (p. 357). Knight's single-minded involvement, plus his egocentricity, do not allow him to see the devastating effect of his pervasive intellectualism — but the more objective reader is not so blinded, and the allusions become polyvalent. Fictionally they express Knight's feelings; technically they enforce an ironic tone as they expose Knight for the uncompassionate, coldly idealistic prig that he is. Once this has been established, Hardy plots an undeviating allusive course. Knight has cruelly rejected Elfride without a thought 'whether he did not owe her a little sacrifice for her unchary devotion in saving his life'. He looks wistfully at his books, and Hardy describes his scholarly regrets with a scathingly ironic reference to Antony's having 'kissed away kingdoms and provinces' (p. 365). Hardy gives Stephen the last allusive word on Knight's behaviour: 'You out-Hamlet Hamlet in morbidness of mood' (p. 374).

The heroine, Elfride, is clearly the central figure in the story. Apropos of this importance, she receives the most individual allusive attention; but like those applied to the women who have preceded her in Hardy's novels, the allusions have a more erratic success than those assigned to the male characters. Guerard has proposed that Elfride is a minor Eustacia Vye in that she is capable of great depth of feeling and passion, factors which also put her a step beyond Fancy Day.[25] But though Elfride is certainly evolutionary in Hardy's portrayal of heroines, she none the less makes it obvious that he is still learning about his women, and how to depict them allusively.

The unevenness of Hardy's allusive progress here is negatively illustrated when Elfride is first described, for she is almost obliterated by references. In three consecutive sentences of the novel's first pages she is linked with the Madonna della Sedia, Rubens, Correggio, Wordsworth, and Shakespeare's Miranda. All of these references are qualified — a Madonna without rapture, a Rubens without fleshiness — overtly beginning the allusive erosion that is

to come; but the plethora is somewhat heavy-handed, ostentatious. Thereafter Hardy does start to discipline his allusive style.

Throughout Elfride's relationship with Stephen she is almost
haughtily superior. She can best him at chess and riding, she has at
least equal intelligence, she wields a stronger will, and comes from
a socially superior family. Moreover, her provincialism has convinced her that her primacy is incontestable. Her allusions during
this interlude individually reflect this pre-eminence, but when
viewed collectively they reveal Hardy to be more devious. Like
Springrove in *Desperate Remedies*, she is consistently compared to
a figure much beyond her approximation, and though her façade
remains intact in Stephen's eyes, and nascently in Knight's, the
reader sees her status slowly deteriorate because of her mediocre
showing in the light of these comparisons. Her imperviousness to
gossip is made analogous to the wild-fowl's knowledge of Crusoe's
first shot (p. 144); her good name will be saved, she flippantly
asserts, by the orange tree, as it 'saved the virgins in St George's
time from the poisonous breath of the dragon' (p. 149); and her
assimilation of the London scene is compared to the admiration of
Aeneas at Carthage (p. 167).

Just as Elfride's personality is made more credible by these comparisons, so does the same device narrow the aperture of her
world. Elfride considers a chess game with Knight to be of para-
mount importance, but the hyperbolic seriousness of the allusions
used in the scene turns the tone into one of mock epic, and the
mode into that of satire. Elfride defends her vanity in the game
with the imperious 'Nelson's bravery lay in his vanity' (p. 190). She
continues in naive high seriousness to discuss the game in terms of
'the book of the prophet Shakespeare', quoting *Richard II*
(III. ii. 183); and her chess strategy is described in classical terms
through a reference to Rhadamanthus, one of the three judges of
the dead in the underworld, who had been known for his justice
while on earth (p. 198).

Concomitantly with this ironic commentary on her personality
and her provincialism, Hardy also works to destroy any sympathy
which the reader might feel for the coquettish game she plays.
Elfride realises the importance to Stephen of a planned reunion,
but since she no longer loves him, the liaison is onerous to her. She
initially decides, however, to take the noble course and go. Yet the
picture we get of her is not flattering: 'So during the day she looked
her duty steadfastly in the face; read Wordsworth's astringent yet

depressing ode to that Deity; committed herself to Her guidance; and still felt the weight of chance desires' (p. 229). And later, when Elfride's timidity, tinged with an element of precaution, makes her delay telling all of her past to Knight, she is again allusively censored (p. 281). The narrator ironically describes her by a reference to the *double-entendre* speech of the player-queen in *Hamlet* (III. ii. 181), citing the scene in which the queen asserts that to take a second husband quickly is to be unfaithful to the first.

This type of allusive erosion through exaggerated and contextual comparison continues to follow Elfride as long as the plot only skirts the impending tragedy. While she is emotionally self-supporting, and can receive such allusive barbs without eliciting the reader's defence of an underdog, she is stylistically trimmed to natural size and placed in measured perspective. But when her predicament becomes more painfully serious, and the romance turns towards tragedy, Hardy gives her the allusive shoring up she needs to enlarge her into a pitiable figure and ultimately to establish her as one of his characters whose suffering is harsher than her transgressions merit.

The emotional realisation of what she has done to Stephen crashes upon her when she and Knight meet her former lover in a tense, macabre scene staged in the Luxellian vault — the very place that will house Elfride in the final chapter. Hardy handles the encounter well, but once again he cannot resist stippling on allusions. Elfride has the 'conscience-stricken look of Guido's Magdalen'; she mentally quotes part of Claudius' prayer speech (*Hamlet*, III. iii. 56), and adds a verse of Psalm 102 to the conversation — all in three short paragraphs (pp. 287–8). Yet this effusiveness apart, these allusions are especially significant, for they initiate the change of course which will lead the novel into a new seriousness, and the reader into a new sympathy for Elfride. Each of these allusions, and every one appended to her hereafter, presents Elfride in a favourable light. We get Claudius at his only admirable moment; Psalm 102 predicts plaintively what is to happen to her:

> My days, just hastening to their end,
>   Are like an evening shade;
> My beauty doth, like a wither'd grass
>   With waning luster fade. (p. 288)

Subsequent allusions continue to support her: her devotion to Knight is discussed through a comparison to 'the susceptible daughter-in-law of Naomi', and Ruth 2:13 is quoted (p. 321); now there are 'no saucy remarks on "La Belle Dame sans Merci"' (p. 332); and her final allusion is a tender compliment from Psalms 61:3 (p. 336).

Hardy, then, proves that he can, even at this rather early stage, masterfully apply his allusions to shape his characters and control the reader's responses. Yet this last allusion of Elfride's is also a good example of how much Hardy has yet to learn. Elfride intones the verse to Knight: 'Thou hast been my hope, and a strong tower for me against the enemy.' She is completely subdued now, and the reader cannot help but regard such total disappearance of the daring Elfride who was once willing to risk everything for another lover as a lapse in character development. And the structural function Hardy imposes on the allusion is equally weak; for here he shows himself still the neophyte when he incorporates such an obvious device as having the church tower fall at just that moment — and, even more conveniently, on Mrs Jethway, thus giving her already important note a supernatural significance! This is all rather unconvincing characterisation, gratuitous coincidence, and elementary use of symbolism. Hardy is to do better in his next novel.

3 The Dimensions of Success and Failure

It is pleasing to meet with work that is so obviously the outcome of high aims: and one should not be grudging in
expressing one's conviction of the artist's thorough success.
'Far From the Madding Crowd' is not Mr. Hardy's first
novel, but it is so much more mature and powerful in every
way than his earlier efforts that in them he seems rather to
have been exercising himself with a view to obtaining a
command of his materials.

This part of W. Minto's review for the *Examiner* (5 December
1874) of Hardy's fourth novel reflects the general tenor of *Far
From the Madding Crowd's* critical reception. With its anonymous
appearance in *Cornhill Magazine* (January to December 1874),
during which several reviewers attributed it to George Eliot, and
its subsequent publication in two volumes in November 1874 by
Smith, Elder and Company, Hardy was established as an important novelist – and a popular one. *Far From the Madding Crowd*
was published seven times in 1874 alone: twice in London and five
times in America.[1]

Hardy's own estimation of his novel accords with the apprecia-
tion shown by his contemporaries: the usual Wessex Edition
apology is absent. Instead, in the only preface to the novel, Hardy
chooses to explain the whereabouts of his fictional region, Wessex,
specifically used for the first time here. Hardy did not have to
apologise or dismiss, since the novel proves that he had at last
struck the right vein.

The gestation of the novel was not painless, but its birth was not
as difficult as that of *The Return of the Native* was to be. Two
manuscript fragments now in the Dorset County Museum indicate
that he followed several false leads in the course of writing the
novel, and abandoned them when his concept of his characters

hardened: for example, when he discarded part of a section on
Sergeant Troy, or when Leslie Stephen advised him to reconstruct
weak parts, no doubt including the fragment headed 'Chapter
XXIII', which deals with the shearing supper. Very little –
approximately one page – of these 'first draft' fragments (as
Hardy designated them in red ink on the manuscript) found their
way into the published version. The manuscript for the complete
novel is currently in private hands. However, Robert C. Schweik,
who has examined the entire manuscript, has outlined several of
Hardy's revisions.[2] Fortunately, too, the crucial revision in the
manuscript has been summarised in print:[3] we now know that
from manuscript to serial Hardy did his important rewriting
primarily in the scene describing Fanny's wake. The text of the
two-volume edition is largely identical to that of the serial publication, except for some occasional word changes – for example, the
title of Chapter 48 in the serial reads 'Doubts arise – Doubts
vanish', instead of 'Doubts linger'.[4]

However, Hardy continued to make revisions in the novel
throughout his career, revising it for the Osgood, McIlvaine
edition, then reworking sections for Macmillan's first impression in
1902, and doing more revisions for the 1912 Wessex Edition. A
comparison of the 1874 first edition, for example, with the 1912
Wessex Edition reveals that he changes place names as he revises,
sometimes making the locations in the Wessex Edition less specific
and therefore more universal: for example, the 'Melchester gaol'
becomes the 'county gaol' (p. 121), and 'Melchester Moor' the
'aforesaid moor' (p. 118); but he often reverses this procedure
when he wants to pinpoint a scene: 'just out of Budmouth' (p. 288)
is added to the Wessex Edition.[5] Often these proper names are
changed for no apparent reason: Troy swims in Carrow Cove in the
first edition, Lulstead Cove in 1895, and Lulwind Cove in 1912
('Lulstead' is the Wessex name, 'Lulworth' the actual name);
Bathsheba faints in the 'Three Choughs Inn' in 1874, the 'King's
Arms Inn' in 1912 (the King's Arms Inn is still a hostelry in Dor-
chester, an unusual bit of realism for Hardy); and the surgeon in
the first edition, Mr Granthead, becomes Mr Aldritch in the Wessex Edition. His other types of revision are more understandable.[6]
By the time of the Wessex Edition the important reference to the
scandal in Troy's background, and Fanny's child, have been
restored. Stylistically, many of the long, rambling paragraphs still
prevalent in the first edition are later divided, and occasionally

Hardy condenses, excising the unnecessary detail, such as a paragraph on Bathsheba's father's second cousin in Chapter 8. There is more dialect speech in the Wessex Edition, indicating Hardy's well-established confidence in his rustics, though some long, intrusive passages of rustic conversation have been deleted for the sake of conciseness. And, especially important to this study, he drops one unnecessary allusion and continues to clarify hazy ones: the intrusive allusion to Gideon appended to Bathsheba at the corn market is omitted from the Wessex Edition entirely; in the serial edition he merely paraphrases Keats (Chapter 23), in the first edition he adds 'the poet', and in the Wessex Edition he states, 'Keats daintily calls . . .' (p. 190).

It is evident from the finished product that, because of the moderate public success of *Under the Greenwood Tree* and the even more promising showing of his third novel, Hardy was reluctant to abandon completely his fictional formula. Instead, he chose to embellish it — to take a middle course between the over complicated intricacy of *Desperate Remedies* and the unduly simple placidity of *Under the Greenwood Tree*. In constructing the fictional Wessex for *Far From the Madding Crowd*, he retained the rural setting but now involved his characters in one static, but important, area, and concentrated almost entirely on the mental struggles of his principals. Granted, the sensational elements are still here — but they are fewer in number and are not emphasised for their own sake. In fact, Elizabeth Drew points out that the novel has only three deaths and one life sentence — making it almost a comedy by comparison to other Hardy novels.[7] Coincidence, too, plays its familiar role: we need only recall that Fanny goes to the wrong church, Bathsheba's toss falls in favour of sending the valentine, Troy and Bathsheba meet Fanny on the road. But in this novel the reader is not overwhelmed with a plethora of star-crossing, and the coincidences which are here do have an aura of inevitability. (The bellicose critic of the *Athenaeum* — 5 December 1874 — differed: 'We are alternately attracted and repelled by admirable delineations of man and nature on the one hand, and gross improbabilities on the other, till we lay it down, unable to say whether the author is an ill-regulated genius or a charlatan with some touches of cleverness.')

Some Hardian conventions are also evident in the structure of the plot. In *A Pair of Blue Eyes* he has one story in the novel gradually encompass a chain of suitors, then he painstakingly discards them: Elfride is loved by Jethway, Smith, and Knight. Hardy uses this pattern time and again. Bathsheba is courted first by Oak, then by Boldwood, then by Troy, and ultimately returns to Oak. *The Hand of Ethelberta* is to have the same processional, though this time Hardy laughs at his formula through Christopher Julian: 'I have heard of one-sided love, and reciprocal love, and all sorts, but this is my first experience of a concatenated affection. You follow me, I follow Ethelberta, and she follows — Heaven knows who!'[8] *Far From the Madding Crowd*, however, marks a serious advance in his plotting, for here the love theme, a dominant motive in all of Hardy's stories, is raised above the stylised triangular relationship of *Desperate Remedies*, the coquettish teasing of *Under the Greenwood Tree*, and the wooden frustration of *A Pair of Blue Eyes*, into the passionate, scarring conquests of mature adults. These adults are easily recognised as over-balanced character types, and are candidly announced as such: Gabriel Oak is the paragon of angelic steadfastness; Bathsheba Everdene is initially an innocent temptress, like her namesake;[9] Troy represents decadent urbanity with a military air; and Boldwood is the reckless landowner. But even while he type-casts, Hardy manages to avoid oppressive authorial control by subtly studying in depth each of his major characters, revealing those contradictory nuances of personality which individualise and humanise, which protect realism from melodrama.

Along with this deeper probing of the human personality and its private and public conflicts, Hardy in this novel has also broadened his ironic approach. In *Desperate Remedies* the irony existed primarily in the relationship of individual events — events which were leaked to the reader while characters groped with their fate. In *A Pair of Blue Eyes*, a large part of the irony was again extrinsic, but this time more broadly structural: one half of the plot reflects the other with ironic symmetry. But what Henry Knight can only briefly contemplate on a cliff in *A Pair of Blue Eyes* becomes the object of a much more profound study in *Far From the Madding Crowd*, for here Hardy has his characters engage not only in the irony of temporary circumstance, but also in the irony of their entire relationship with their universe. Mere situation begins to play an increasingly important role, and attempts to change conditions become correspondingly futile. Bathsheba recognises it for all of us in the scene where she recoils from her discovery of Fanny's child: 'destiny . . . had thrown over herself a garish light of mockery, and had set upon all things about her an ironical smile' (p. 324).

As Hardy paints his Wessex and explores these new psychological levels he once again turns to allusion to reveal, enlarge, intensify, and solemnise. Happily his technique here keeps pace with his other developing skills, and much of the allusive artlessness is gone. But just as the novel has a depth new for Hardy, so is it heavy on allusions to support this seriousness — there are approximately 160 allusions in *Far From the Madding Crowd* — and in such a melange of references there are inevitably some weak ones. As in his previous novels, Hardy's allusive method is weakened most by what seems to be a compulsion to impress his audience by dropping obscure allusions which add little to the story save distraction. Thus, a queue of Bathsheba's workers is described by means of a reference to Chain Salpae, salt water fish which reproduce through a long chain of linked embryos (p. 111); Fanny's using a crutch becomes 'oddly exercising the faculty of invention upon the specialty of the clever Jacquet Droz, the designer of automatic substitutes for human limbs' (p. 293; here, at least, Hardy gives us the identity of the eighteenth-century Swiss mechanist); Gabriel's furniture is characterised by two lines from William Barnes's provincial 'Woak Hill' (Hardy again identifies his poet, but only in a footnote, and only as a revision — the footnote is not in the first edition); and Greenhill still remains obscure, even though it merits being called the 'Nijni Novgorod of South Wessex' (p. 361), for few would recognise its correspondence to the city in Russia, where a commercial fair is held annually.

Moreover, equally ostentatious is Hardy's use of Latin and Greek phrases. The Latin motto on Troy's watch strikes the reader as a piece of creditable traditionalism, and is consequently unobtrusive — especially since Hardy goes so far as to translate it; but to leave two chapter titles in Latin (Chapters 13 and 53), the latter of which is drawn from Horace's *Satires*, I, 7—8, and to cap the emotional peak of the book with an untranslated Greek phrase (p. 327), can only be judged snobbish pedantry. However, these relatively few weak spots are outnumbered by the overwhelming number of successful allusions, which fulfil not only intricate stylistic functions but also add a surface richness to the novel that the density of the story can at last comfortably support.

That Hardy has made major strides in his allusive technique is ensured from the outset by his brilliant choice of title, and by his judicious decision to abandon the clutter of allusive chapter titles. Since the novel is not a ratiocinative tale designed to test the reader's ingenuity, adumbrative allusive titles are unnecessary. And, because suspense is always rewarding to the reader, Hardy is equally careful not to spoil the story by announcing his plot through obvious titles. Consequently, a perusal of the contents page gives the reader some guide to the course of action, but never reveals actual events — in fact, the title of Chapter 55, 'The March Following — "Bathsheba Boldwood"', is deliberately misleading. The title of the novel, however, tells the reader a great deal with no harmful side-effects. By choosing it from Gray's 'Elegy', one of the most quoted poems in the English language, Hardy almost guarantees recognition. Further, by drawing on a pastoral poem, and in turn taking a line that refers to a serene location, Hardy both juxtaposes the superior natural world against the civilised, as does the 'Elegy', and also indicates his increased concentration on setting.[10] Finally, and most important, because Weatherbury people are far from placid, even in their isolation, the title epitomises the ironic universe that is to circumscribe the entire novel.

The new emphasis on setting intimated by the title and later summarised by Hardy's categorising the novel as one of 'Character and Environment' is supported by an unusual number of allusions. In *Under the Greenwood Tree*, also a novel of 'Character and Environment', this attention was turned on persons and places, but with an authorial casualness that resulted in a novel sometimes penned 'farcically and flippantly'. *A Pair of Blue Eyes*, though evolutionary in Hardy's development of character, is also hampered by its announced 'Romance and Fantasy' approach, and it is not until *Far From the Madding Crowd* that Hardy is able to unite his characters gracefully and inextricably with the natural world, which not only provides the stage for their playing, but also begins to perform a major role in their drama.[11]

Hardy's allusive treatment of this setting is uneven in almost direct relation to the importance of the subject to hand: when he attempts to embellish allusively the animals in his pastoral, he verges on the unintentionally comic. The seriousness of the occasion supports his forecasting the bankruptcy which is about to befall Gabriel when his sheep are all frightened into breaking a fence and then into falling over a precipice, by comparing the guilty dog to the unrepentant and self-justifying Napoleon at

St Helena (p. 72). In addition, the erotic implications of Bath-sheba's watching Gabriel shear a sheep are subtly and humorously complemented by the comparison of the sheep to Botticelli's *The Birth of Venus*: 'the clean, sleek creature arose from its fleece — how perfectly like Aphrodite rising from the foam . . .' (p. 176).[12] And to accentuate the fertility of the region by a reference to Lucina (p. 52), the Roman goddess who presides over the birth of people and animals, is also tonally appropriate simply because a touch of narrative levity indicates recognition of the hyper-seriousness of the allusion in this particular situation. But this same jocular tone is missing in the rest of the allusions connected to animals, with the result that the weightiness of the references is self-destructive. A comment on the indigo of Turner's pictures (p. 70) seems wasted when it is used in an effusive description of old George, Gabriel's dog, and even Bathsheba's 'sad, bursting heart' cannot colour the atmosphere enough to justify disturbing both the tension and the typography by quoting an entire line from Milton's '*Lycidas*' (l. 126) to describe the condition of her sheep (p. 170).

However, when Hardy uses this same allusive tool to build scenery, or to evoke the atmosphere of a particular location, he is now a master. The echoes of the Wessex valleys are given godly resonance by a comparison to the Theocritean story of the sailors' cry on the Mysian shore for Hylas, the lost favourite of Hercules (p. 72). The coming of spring takes on animated beauty 'when we may suppose the Dryads to be waking for the season' (p. 154); and man and nature are deftly integrated through metaphor when the sheep-washing pool is viewed 'as a glistening Cyclops' eye in a green face' (p. 157). The exciting vastness, the rugged boundaries, and the menacing power of the sea are adroitly established by a quick barrage of allusions (also connected to Troy): first to Balboa's gazing upon the Pacific (p. 348), then to the pillars of Hercules (p. 349), then to Gonzalo's prayer in *The Tempest* (i. i. 71) for a dry death (p. 349). And we see Hardy's descriptive skill at its ironic best when he catches the ambivalent atmosphere of Boldwood's holiday kitchen by having a pot, kettle, and saucepan appear as Shadrach, Meshach, and Abednego (p. 382). Nor is he to be equalled when he portrays the soft chiaroscuro of autumn evenings:

The interior was shadowy with a peculiar shade. The strange luminous semi-opacities of fine autumn afternoons and eves intensified into Rembrandt effects the few yellow sunbeams which came through holes and divisions in the canvas, and spirted like jets of gold-dust across the dusky blue atmosphere of haze pervading the tent, until they alighted on inner surfaces of cloth opposite, and shone like little lamps suspended there. (p. 367)

The majority of the allusions attached to setting etch particular scenes on the reader's mind through the medium of mutual familiarity. However, several of these setting references make an even more important stylistic contribution in that they are used not only to define a scene but also to accentuate its influence on the principals involved. Such is the case, for example, in the crucial storm chapter, where Bathsheba is threatened with financial ruin and even death. The hellishness of her predicament is made more acute when the narrator relates the blackness to 'a cave in Hinnon' (p. 280), the valley near Jerusalem where human sacrifices and filth were burnt during the time of Josiah. Further on, in the same vein but with an added touch of irony, a reference to Ruysdael and Hobbema, the seventeenth-century Dutch landscape painters famous for their almost-spiritual portrayals of the cool lavishness of nature, is used to sketch the backdrop for Troy's discovery that the flowers on Fanny's grave have been washed away (p. 342). Here the very beauty of the landscape, intensified by the allusion, ironically mocks both the situation and Troy's belated, maudlin sentimentally.

Songs, too, are employed to underscore the significance and the irony of the moment. The regiment leaves town singing 'The Girl I Left Behind Me', and the very gods seem to be laughing at Fanny Robbin — as well as 'the public-house people and the nameless women' (p. 116). Later, when the soldiers are gone, save one, it is Bathsheba who sings a song, and the narrator blatantly prompts the reader:

Subsequent events caused one of the verses to be remembered for many months, and even years, by more than one of those who were gathered there:

>   For his bride a soldier sought her,
>   And a winning tongue had he:
>   On the banks of Allan Water
>   None was as gay as she! (p. 188)

Once the soldier marries her, setting the tragic scene, the union is celebrated with the playing of 'The Soldier's Joy' (p. 270), and the ironic nails are driven in: Bathsheba is never to be 'gay' in the marriage, and the 'Soldier's Joy' means tears, nervous breakdown, and near-death. Finally, it is also a song which frames the scene where Bathsheba begins to escape her sorrow and her soldier-past. When Bathsheba meets Oak at Troy's and Fanny's graves, the choir is singing 'Lead, Kindly Light' (p. 412; Hardy illustrates the range of his musical knowledge in his choice here, for Newman's poem had been set to music by John Bacchus Dykes only five years before). The song unleashes Bathsheba's emotions, and she begins to cry as the stanzas contribute the words she is unable to speak:

> 'Are you going in?' said Bathsheba; and there came from within the church as from a prompter:
>
> > I loved the garish day, and spite of fears,
> > Pride ruled my will: remember not past years.
>
> 'I was', said Gabriel. 'I am one of the bass singers, you know. I have sung bass for several months.'
> 'Indeed: I wasn't aware of that. I'll leave you, then.'
>
> > Which I have loved long since, and lost awhile,
>
> sang the children.

However, even while Hardy is designing his environment, the reader is never allowed to forget that this is foremost a novel of character, and that the setting has only a supporting role. As in his previous novels, a woman has the major part. But, as was not the case in Hardy's early stories − *A Pair of Blue Eyes*, for example − the limelight is shared by a male character. Bathsheba Everdene and Gabriel Oak are equal protagonists − and they are protagonists whose destinies are inseparable, despite the Fannys, Boldwoods, and Troys who swerve in and out of their ken.

Although it is Gabriel who is first introduced, the centre of attention quickly shifts to Bathsheba. She is first observed by Gabriel, and by the reader, as she is gazing at herself in a mirror, reflecting both her presence and her vanity. Gabriel's, and the reader's, interest in her grows as she is captivatingly described in great detail, notwithstanding the narrator's protestation that he will not throw 'a Nymphean tissue over a milkmaid' (p. 55). However, together with details of her physical beauty, we also learn that Bathsheba is an independent, supercilious woman, who, while having little trouble attracting men, also has the callousness and impulsiveness of immaturity – qualities which make her magnetism hazardous. Her attractiveness stems initially from her looks, but also from the mystique which Hardy has skilfully instilled into her character. As William Dean Howells observed, we, and the men she encounters never come to know Bathsheba thoroughly. We feel her charm, we understand her mind – she is, her aunt points out, quite a scholar – but we never know 'that ultimate reason of her being'.[13] It is this mysteriousness, brought into the foreground by her reliance on emotion rather than on reason, that makes Bathsheba the intriguing woman who can completely ensnare three men of entirely different temperaments. All love her for her beauty – but Boldwood can also love her for what he sees as stately boldness, Troy for her sexuality, and Oak for her dependence.

But regardless of our fractional knowledge, we do know Bathsheba well enough to realise that at the outset of the novel she is a proud, capricious woman. At first she is another Fancy Day – a tease – though innocently so, the narrator assures us. In the course of the story, however, Bathsheba slowly loses her arrogance and becomes a sympathetic figure who can humble herself enough to ask Gabriel to marry her. This gradual erosion of Bathsheba's hauteur is brought about within the plot by a series of tragedies. It is stylistically accomplished in part by the now familiar ironic twist which Hardy adds to his allusions.

It is not until Chapter 4, well after the physical description of Bathsheba, that the reader, or Gabriel, learns her name: 'by making inquiries he found that the girl's name was Bathsheba Everdene, and that the cow would go dry in seven days' (p. 61). Even while the course of the plot favours her every move, the narrator, by his choice of references, continues his stylistic undermining. Her pride is continually punctured by the ironic linking of the supposedly noble Bathsheba to elements beyond her reach – and often this irony is reinforced by the fact that Bathsheba's allusion is inferior in its own sphere. The first allusion allotted to her after she attained her new material superiority places her in such a doubly ironic perspective: 'this Ashtoreth of strange report was only a modification of Venus the well-known and admired' (p. 85). Her next allusion has the same result:

> Gabriel was rather staggered by the remarkable coolness of her manner . . . But perhaps her air was the inevitable result of the social rise which has advanced her from a cottage to a large house and fields. The case is not unexampled in high places. When, in the writings of the later poets [here, Sophocles, Euripides and Aristophanes], Jove and his family are found to have moved from their cramped quarters on the peak of Olympus into the wide sky above it, their words show a proportionate increase of arrogance and reserve. (pp. 115–16)

Then, in quick succession, she is a 'small thesmothete' (p. 117), one of the six inferior Archons in ancient Athens, and 'a queen among these gods of the fallow, like a little sister of a little Jove . . .' (p. 125). The allusions continue to attack her, all save one being drawn from non-Biblical sources, thus stripping her of the protective anonymity of the Scriptural rustics who surround her:

> Bathsheba's was an impulsive nature under a deliberate aspect. An Elizabeth in brain and a Mary Stuart in spirit, she often performed actions of the greatest temerity with a manner of extreme discretion. Many of her thoughts were perfect syllogisms; unluckily they always remained thoughts. Only a few were irrational assumptions; but, unfortunately, they were the ones which most frequently grew into deeds. (p. 164)

Even her emotions are victims: when Troy kisses Bathsheba, she cries with guilt, but her tears are equated with the 'Liquid stream' resulting from Moses' striking the rock in Horeb (Exodus 17:5–6) – a most happy occasion; when she finds she loves him (p. 220), she receives Ophelia's admonition to Laertes'; 'she reck'd not her own rede' (*Hamlet* I. iii. 48). Her sexuality, too, is assaulted as she foreshadows Sue Bridehead: she marries her passionate soldier, but 'Diana was the goddess whom Bathsheba instinctively adored' (p. 303).

Hardy inexorably sustains his ironic pressure through the first forty-two chapters of the novel, deftly leading the reader into the emotional climax of the book, Fanny's coffin scene. Here Bathsheba's pride is at its height, her nobility at its lowest; but here she also begins to rise out of her own ashes. Before Bathsheba discovers the child, she is truly saddened by Fanny's fate, and she is allowed the narrator's sympathy: she does not feel victorious, though 'she was the Esther to this poor Vashti' (p. 320). But when she opens the coffin, and the child and the blond hair bring the truth inescapably upon her, her compassion for Fanny turns to self-pity — she is aware only of her own injured pride. Fanny's innocent white countenance becomes in Bathsheba's 'heated fancy' an expression of 'triumphant consciousness of the pain she was retaliating for her pain with all the merciless rigour of the Mosaic law: "Burning for burning; wound for wound; strife for strife"' (p. 324). Bathsheba indulges in contemplations of suicide, rants at Fanny for dying and thus depriving her of revenge, and just manages to prevent herself succumbing to a fit of malicious hysteria. In a dramatic finale that must have delighted Hardy's sentimental audience Bathsheba kneels, and then rises with a quietened spirit.

The scene itself, and especially the portrayal of Bathsheba, are excellent artistic achievements. Bathsheba convincingly reacts with all the pride that is in her. Her emotions, spurred by the macabre setting, are indefinably, almost indescribably complicated. This psychological state Hardy is able to depict without ever boring the reader with analysis or stifling his imagination by being clinically specific. Yet the artistry here was not easy or spontaneous. In the manuscript version Hardy's vision was not so precise. To achieve the scene's high finish, rough allusions (three lines of bad poetry and a reference to Giovanni Bellini) are removed, and a tension-dispelling description of Fanny is scrapped. The most important change, however, lies in Hardy's new attitude towards Bathsheba. In the manuscript Bathsheba's 'heated fancy' fails 'to endow that innocent white countenance with any triumphant consciousness', and there is no sense of, or reference to, Mosaic retribution. Consequently, in the manuscript the whole episode verges on pathos, for no rebellious heroine screams at what she imagines to be an unassailable, victorious opponent. By the time the novel was published Hardy realised the advantages of showing Bathsheba at her worst, thus making her transformation even more impressive — and impressive it is, as Hardy skilfully begins Bathsheba's climb to humility within moments after her frenzy. As she rises from kneeling, Troy enters. Once he comprehends the scene, his face reflecting an 'indefinable union of remorse and reverence', he kisses the dead Fanny. It is at this crucial point, and not until now, that Bathsheba's feelings of the preceding moments are defined: 'the revulsion from her indignant mood a little earlier when she had meditated upon compromised honour, forestalment, eclipse in maternity by another, was violent and entire' (p. 326). The narrator tells us she suffers greatly, and it is with 'childlike pain and simplicity' that she crawls to Troy. From this hour forwards Bathsheba is no longer the proud, over-confident girl of her youth. The narrator utters the benedictive last rites for Bathsheba's arrogance and innocence in Greek, somewhat pretentiously choosing the phrase which Christ uttered on the Cross (John 9:30).

Bathsheba rushes away from the house, out into the woods, and falls into an exhausted sleep. She awakes from her emotional descent into hell in artfully drawn Edenic surroundings:

> There was an opening towards the east, and the glow from the as yet unrisen sun attracted her eyes thither. From her feet, and between the beautiful yellowing ferns with their feathery arms, the ground sloped downwards to a hollow, in which was a species of swamp, dotted with fungi. A morning mist hung over it now − a fulsome yet magnificent silvery veil, full of light from the sun, yet semi-opaque − the hedge behind it being in some measure hidden by its hazy luminousness. (p. 329)

But all is never so well in the Hardy universe: 'the general aspect of the swamp was malignant'. Hardy's natural world tells us that Bathsheba is not to be relieved of her grief so easily. But his allusions also indicate that recovery is possible: when Bathsheba returns to the house, she first calls for Beaumont and Fletcher's *The Maid's Tragedy*, Congreve's *The Mourning Bride*, Edward Young's *Night Thoughts* and Johnson's *The Vanity of Human Wishes* (p. 333). With a fine sense of the dramatic Hardy then has Liddy, the maid, check the building maudlin sentiment by injecting some allusive humour. She suggests the addition of 'that story of the black man, who murdered his wife Desdemona . . . a nice dismal one'. Bathsheba immediately revises her requests: now Isaac Bickerstaff's *Love in a Village* and *Maid of the Mill*, William Combe's *Doctor Syntax*, and Addison's *Spectator* suit her tastes better.

This allusive transition from the dark to the lighter side is precursory to the new slant which the references attached to Bathsheba now take. Whereas Hardy has previously undermined Bathsheba's arrogance, once tragedy has mellowed her she begins to receive the referential boost her new struggle for maturity needs. First, borrowing from Wordsworth, Hardy allusively records the change:

> To the eyes of the middle-aged, Bathsheba was perhaps additionally charming just now. Her exuberance of spirit was pruned down; the original phantom of delight had shown herself to be not too bright for human nature's daily food, and she had been able to enter this second poetical phase without losing much of the first in the process. (p. 358)

Though Hardy stops short of continuing this Wordsworthian reference and calling Bathsheba 'a perfect woman nobly planned', he none the less soon has two of the men in her life compliment her. Boldwood goes to the Bible, so familiar to Hardy's country folk, and compares her to Rachel, asserting his willingness to play Jacob (p. 360); Troy appropriately draws from the pagan world to call her his 'dashing piece of womanhood, Juno-wife of mine' (p. 387).

Finally, when Bathsheba reaches her finest hour, the allusions ultimately record her triumph. Troy has been killed and Bathsheba has taken command of the situation. Hardy describes her metamorphosis:

> Deeds of endurance which seem ordinary in philosophy are rare in conduct, and Bathsheba was astonishing all around her now, for her philosophy was her conduct, and she seldom thought practicable what she did not practise. She was of the stuff of which great men's mothers are made. She was indispensable to high generation, hated at tea parties, feared in shops, loved at crises. (pp. 402–3)

Bathsheba has learned to face life squarely, the first Hardy heroine to do so, and though, typically, she has little control over her fate, she is able to avoid being crushed by it.[14] She is deservedly linked to the Muse of Tragedy as she regally suppresses her pain over the death of her husband in order to dress his corpse: 'her looks were calm and nearly rigid, like a slightly animated bust of Melpomene' (p. 404). And Hardy uses a hymn to make the final comment on her character: 'Pride ruled my will: remember not past years' (p. 413).

❚While drawing a person as complex as Bathsheba, Hardy is also careful to supply a counterpointing figure through whom he can give added perspective to his heroine and, not accidentally, infuse more adventure into his story. Fanny Robin plays this part as her humility is juxtaposed with Bathsheba's pride, her servitude with Bathsheba's authoritarianism, her ultimate failure with Bathsheba's success.❚Even Fanny's hair is significantly blond, while Bathsheba's is black. They share only one thing — a complete devotion to Troy. And even here Fanny's role is to illuminate, for by sharing this common ground of dedication Fanny proves that it is passion, not reason, basic instincts, not breeding or class, which draw Bathsheba to Troy. This introduction of Fanny into the novel was a good artistic decision by Hardy, especially since her actual appearances are few. It is her absence that is crucial, as Hardy makes it serve a twofold structural purpose.[15] Having established a favourable picture of Fanny in Oak's brief conversation with this 'slight and frail creature', Hardy subsequently pushes her into the background. With this sympathetic Fanny only talked about in the abstract, Hardy can then concentrate his action, and the reader's interest, on the principals, while Fanny's catalytic, mirroring presence is still felt. Secondly, since we do not initially see Fanny while she is pregnant her reputation is not destroyed before her plight has become too pathetic to arouse scorn. She consequently receives even the Grundys' reluctant sympathy, capturing a segment of the readers' emotion which would otherwise be untapped, since Bathsheba is too resourcefully independent to arouse such concern.

Hardy was particularly conscious of Fanny's reputation. In some pages of the first draft in the Dorset County Museum the devious Pennyways brings news that he has seen Fanny in Melchester and that she was dressed too well to be living as an honest woman. Hardy later discarded this aspersion, sensing the emotional and technical efficacy of keeping her merely strangely missing, for a prostitute would be so far below Bathsheba that she would not merit comparison with her. Hardy had to restrain himself in the opposite direction as well. In the original manuscript chapter dealing with the opening of Fanny's coffin he wrote an effusive passage on her childlike innocence:

She appear [sic] rounder in feature & much younger than she had looked during the latter months of her life. Her hands had acquired a preternatural refinement, & a painter in looking upon them might have fancied that at last he had found the fellows of those marvellous hands & fingers which have served as originals to Bellini.

The youth & fairness of both the silent ones withdrew from the scene all associations of a repulsive kind − even every unpleasant ray. The mother had been no further advanced in womanliness than had the infant in childhood; they both had stood upon the threshold of a new stage of existence, & had vanished before they could well be defined as examples of that stage. They struck upon the sense in the aspect of incipiency, not in that of decadence. They seemed failures in creation, by nature interesting, rather than instances of dissolution, by nature frightful.[16]

To represent her as completely degenerate might obliterate her value as a foil, but to overpraise an unwed mother in 1874 was more than stylistically unwise, as *Tess*'s subtitle was later to prove. The deliberate keeping secret of Fanny's condition illustrates with what skill Hardy walked this creative tightrope.

In the one chapter where Hardy does allow Fanny to take the centre of the stage, he comes dangerously close to heavy handed sentimentality, and might be justly accused of toadying to the Dickensian bathos for which many of his readers craved. (The *Saturday Review* of 9 January 1875, for example, praised this scene highly.) As Fanny becomes the epitome of unmerited suffering, the reader shares, inch by inch and pain by pain, the excruciating pilgrimage which the pregnant girl makes to the Union House. Dramatically, the incident is a qualified success, primarily because Fanny's lonely death strikes a note of universal sympathy. None the less, Hardy's possible discomfort with the overt pathos of his scene − only enhanced by the convenient dog who gets stoned for his life-saving efforts − is reflected in his compensatory over-intellectual allusions, the only ones allotted to Fanny, apart from those in the manuscript. Aided by a Droz device (see page 57) Fanny crawls along; the half-mile she must cover seems to her 'like a stolid Juggernaut . . . and impassive King of the World' (p. 295). Neither reference clarifies or intensifies Fanny's position. Allusively, too, she is better *in absentia*.

The three principal male characters in the novel all revolve round Bathsheba, and are all Hardian types. In ascending order of importance, Boldwood is the man who has disciplined himself too much — a Henry Knight without the intellectualism, a man who, once he gives his emotions rein, is rushed into insanity. Troy is Boldwood's opposite: completely undisciplined, often unprincipled, a man for whom 'the past was yesterday; the future, tomorrow; never, the day after' (p. 197). The golden mean, for Hardy at least, is Gabriel: stoic, stalwart, straightforward — and exhaustingly loyal.

Boldwood is primarily the catalytic protagonist. Bathsheba's whimsical valentine revives feelings which he has suppressed for decades, and his passive exterior suddenly gives way to the explosions within. Hardy affords him one of his best capsule descriptions:

> The phases of Boldwood's life were ordinary enough, but his was not an ordinary nature. That stillness which struck casual observers more than anything else in his character and habit, and seemed so precisely like the rest of inanition, may have been the perfect balance of enormous antagonistic forces — the positives and negatives in fine adjustment. His equilibrium disturbed, he was in extremity at once. If an emotion possessed him at all, it ruled him; a feeling not mastering him was entirely latent. Stagnant or rapid, it was never slow. He was always hit mortally, or he was missed. (p. 153)

It is Bathsheba who hits Boldwood mortally, and he spends the rest of the novel suffering through his decline, a victim of his grand obsession. He is now recognised as a fine example of Freud's melancholiac. But he does not 'go gentle'. Rather, by being a relentless agitator, Boldwood causes much of the discord. His nightmarish pressure on Bathsheba helps precipitate her hasty marriage to Troy; the intensity of his pursuit and the disclosure of his passion to Gabriel keeps the latter from pressing his own suit; and finally, killing Troy makes Boldwood a *deus ex machina*. While Boldwood is thus indirectly instigating most of the action, the allusions connected to him serve a complementary purpose, for almost all of them foreshadow the events of his tragic life. He is first allusively introduced as a Daniel in Bathsheba's kingdom — a nonconformist who is to disturb her complacency (p. 130). But he soon loses his advantage, with an allusion forecasting his inner upheaval. The first time Boldwood really looks at Bathsheba, the narrator ominously annotates, 'Adam had awakened from his deep sleep, and behold! there was Eve' (p. 149). We are adequately cautioned about Boldwood's fate. This warning is issued again only two pages later through another reference from *Paradise Lost* (v, 450): Boldwood feels 'the injured lover's hell', foreshadowing the jealousy which makes him shoot Troy. The futility of his love is announced with equal accuracy: during the farmer's most tender interview with Bathsheba (p. 190), the narrator warns of Keats's 'too happy happiness' ('Ode to a Nightingale', l. 6). His next allusion tells the living death of Boldwood's commuted capital sentence: 'Boldwood's dark form might have been seen walking about the hills and downs of Weatherbury like an unhappy Shade in the Mournful Fields of Acheron' (p. 264). Then Hardy makes Boldwood summarise the entire course of his courtship:

> 'I had some faint belief in the mercy of God till I lost that woman. Yes, He prepared a gourd to shade me, and like the prophet I thanked Him and was glad. But the next day He prepared a worm to smite the gourd and wither it; and I feel it is better to die than to live!'. (p. 286)

There is only one allusion left for Boldwood after this lament from Jonah (4 : 6—8), and it is a bitterly ironic one. He says he will gladly serve Jacob's seven years to win his Rachel (p. 360). He serves his time for Bathsheba, but in the gaol, incarcerated during Her Majesty's pleasure.

Boldwood's more masterful rival, Troy, shares Boldwood's passionate nature, but lacks his virtue. Obviously Troy plays the heavy, but, like most Hardy villains, he has redeeming qualities which invest his nature with a certain sophistication. Once again Hardy walks that fine, difficult line between an elevated anti-hero and an unregenerate villain — a distinction so important that he completely discarded an entire section of manuscript which describes a monster-Troy deliberately infecting sheep with disease so that they will fatten quicker and realise a higher price. The fact that he risks poisoning Londoners is of no consequence to him, as Gabriel learns when he confronts Troy with his guilt. The Troy of the finally published version is a much more even character, one who 'never passed the line which divides the spruce vices from the ugly; and hence, though his morals had hardly been applauded, disapproval of them had frequently been tempered with a smile' (p. 198). He is well-educated, aggressively masculine (to use

George Wing's phrase), and a wondrous flatterer — in short, a very plausible lover for the disdainful Bathsheba. But Troy is not an honourable man.

With a role such as Troy's, Hardy faced the difficulty of portraying an attractive man who is a realistic contender for Bathsheba yet clearly revealed as evil enough to drive one woman-with-child to her death, another woman to distraction, and a man to murder. All the while, the Troy who is shot must retain some of the sympathy he had originally aroused in order to satisfy the Hardian tenet that no man is completely responsible for his actions. The manipulation of Troy's image thus becomes quite complex, for there can be no simple unveiling of a born blackguard, with its inevitable just retribution, in Hardy's fictional formula. Hardy accomplishes this feat partially through allusions. At first, while the dashing Troy is entangling the enamoured Bathsheba in a Freudian net, the allusions are cutting away at his façade.[17] But, when Troy repents, the assaulting allusions give way to neutral ones. It is much the same scheme as the one which is so successfully used with Bathsheba, except that Troy, as the antagonist, never gains the allusive accolades finally earned by Bathsheba.[18]

Most of the abusive references attached to Troy occur in a quick barrage, designed to warn the reader that Troy's intentions and his actions represent two entirely different facets of his character. They thereby put in true perspective for the reader the romantic picture of him that Bathsheba has already obtained from their foreboding encounter in the darkness, 'black as the ninth plague of Egypt at midnight' (p. 192). We are told he is 'moderately' truthful ('perfectly' in the first edition — too much praise for a prospective villain), but to women he lies like a Cretan (p. 197; here Hardy relies on the Cretan poet Epimenides, who said, 'Cretans are always liars'). He is Corinthian in religion (p. 198); he is ironically compared to the saintly and dangerously truthful sixteenth-century Scottish divine, John Knox, who did anything but flatter his queen (p. 204); and he is premonitorily equated with the devil at the precise time that he finds the precious first chink in Bathsheba's armour: 'the careless sergeant smiled within himself, and probably too the devil smiled from a loop-hole in Tophet, for the moment was the turning point of a career' (p. 203). The allusions Troy utters in these introductory sections are equally damning: Cretanly he echoes a line from Thomas Campbell's 'How delicious is the winning', saying, 'I wish it had been the knot of knots, which there's no untying'; he refers to the Ten Commandments only because he has just broken one (p. 203); and even when he is protesting his honesty, his sentences are an allusion to the ironic *double-entendre* of Mark Antony's funeral address: Troy's 'plain blunt man, who has never been taught concealment, speaks out his mind . . .' (p. 202) echoes Anthony's 'I am no orator, as Brutus is; / But, as you know me all, a plain blunt man, / That love my friend' (*Julius Caesar*, III. ii. 222).

However, when the full magnitude of what he has done to Fanny is forced onto his conscience, Troy is shocked into repentance and a temporary conversion. Yet the allusions do not reverse for him; 'he that is accursed, let him be accursed still'; both the narrator and the situation itself tell us in the critically controversial gargoyle scene, where the destructive rain demonstrates what Richard Carpenter describes as the 'futility of belated good intentions when opposed by the ineluctable forces of nature'.[19] But while the allusions do not strongly support Troy even now, at least they remain neutral, or, if biased, mildly complimentary, and again serve to remind us of the complexity of his personality. Through a collage of references connected also to scene and plot we learn that he is sensitive enough to be moved like Balboa when he reaches the crest of a summit and the sea bursts upon him (p. 348); and that he is vulnerable to respectable fears, but views the prospect of drowning calmly, thinking of the comic lines of Gonzalo in *The Tempest* (I. i. 71) who 'would fain die a dry death'. (Troy, we remember, ironically enough gets his wish.) Moreover, in the travelling drama it is the adventurous hero, albeit a highwayman, he plays, enacting the role of Dick Turpin, a character from Harrison Ainsworth's *Rookwood* (p. 366). And his last allusive connection summarises both the tone and the intention of those which have preceded it. Troy describes himself as an Alonzo the Brave, then recounts the story of Monk Lewis's ballad 'Alonzo the Brave and the Fair Imogene' (p. 391). The allusion shows Troy to be disdainfully honest now about the perversity of his actions; it forecasts his death by comparing him with a ghost; it has the Hardian irony, for Troy is the opposite of the wronged suitor; and finally, it does all this while still letting the comparison be a complimentary one, for, as with our reaction to Alonzo, we have some sympathy for Fanny's lover, despite his deeds.

In contrast to his Boldwoods and his Troys, Hardy's most admirable characters are conventionally recognised as evidencing a deep-seated stoicism, coupled with intense reserve.[20] The noblest person is one who never shrinks from the indifferent but powerful forces he encounters, one who realises (albeit dimly) the seriousness of his conflict, yet, drawing his strength of character from the soil, continues to struggle against fate. Throughout this novel Gabriel Oak is Bathsheba's mainstay, the one whose opinion she always seeks, though often to be piqued at his answers. Gabriel is not saintly: he unjustifiably reveals to Boldwood Fanny's note, betraying her request for his silence; he does not warn Bathsheba by telling her the whole truth about Troy. Yet he always remains her staunch, selfless, tender-hearted protector. Gabriel's good qualities are woven into the fictional tapestry in several ways First, Hardy is careful to omit any black adjectival threads. In the first edition, the narrator disparages Gabriel's stolidness during a description of Boldwood: 'In all cases this state [a commonplace general condition] may be either the mediocrity of inadequacy, as was Oak's, or what we will venture to call the mediocrity of counterpoise, as was Boldwood's' (p. 201). By 1895 this passage has been deleted, and Gabriel is spared any such aspersion. Secondly, Hardy subtly builds Gabriel's personality by making it an overt contrast to Troy's. His Biblical and rustic name is obviously antithetical to Troy's urban, secular one, illustrating once again Hardy's preference for the country life;[21] Troy never disciplines his emotions, Gabriel is the arch stoic; Troy acts impulsively, Gabriel's passion is under constant control; Troy lies to women almost as a matter of principle, Gabriel tells the truth even 'at the fear of breeding aversion' (p. 220); and Troy has blue blood, though illegitimate, while Gabriel's lineage is honest rustic.

Unfortunately for Bathsheba, however, nearly all of Gabriel's attributes, buried under a poor man's exterior, are difficult to appreciate, and especially so when she is blinded by Troy's flashing flattery and physical magnetism. Nor does Boldwood's personality put Gabriel in a better light. His persistence and intensity, supported by his wealth and the rules of Victorian protocol, only help to push Gabriel further back in the line of suitors, until Gabriel blurs into Bathsheba's scenery, and is equally taken for granted.

Hardy's technical problem here, then, is to fortify the pious, poor, and slow-moving Gabriel in such a way as to keep him omnipresent before the reader as another believable, and interesting, suitor, while at the same time directing his most powerful floodlights onto his more active characters: Bathsheba, Troy, and

Boldwood. The *Examiner* of 5 December 1874 recognised the quandary:

> How Bathsheba, with her rare beauty, could be brought to rest her affections on this honest, uncouth fellow is the difficult problem that Mr. Hardy has applied himself to solve, and has solved satisfactorily, without investing the poor shepherd with any more heroic qualities than the constancy and business capability of Jacob.

The reviewer's allusion is perspicacious, as it hints at part of Hardy's solution: to maintain Gabriel's characterisation as a noble figure, who, though dressed in homespun and taking harsh orders, never loses the dignity required of his role as successful hero in a novel peopled by landowners, Hardy stylistically elevates him through a long list of ennobling references − primarily Biblical and thus apropos of Gabriel's rustic lineage − which constantly prick the reader into renewed admiration.

At the outset of the novel Hardy does not have to concentrate on lifting Gabriel above his immediate status, for he is a landed farmer whose position in society makes his proposal to Bathsheba an unpretentious request. The allusions in these two opening chapters reflect the narrative mid-course, but, even while doing so, by connecting Gabriel to people and events much larger than he, they create an aura around him which conclusively protects him from ever becoming just another rustic. In his religion, he occupies 'that vast middle space of Laodicean neutrality' (p. 41); his coat is as nondescript as Dr Johnson's (p. 41); physically, his 'features adhered throughout their form so exactly to the middle line between the beauty of St. John and the ugliness of Judas Iscariot . . . that not a single lineament could be selected and called worthy either of distinction or notoriety' (p. 45); and finally, echoing *Hamlet* (I. iv. 16), his approach to life is pictured as one of studied inertia:

> Yet, although if occasion demanded he could do or think a thing with as mercurial a dash as can the men of towns who are more to the manner born, his special power, morally, physically, and mentally, was static, owing little or nothing to momentum as a rule. (pp. 48−9)

Soon after this initial cluster of defining allusions, Gabriel gets to know Bathsheba. Hardy once again injects four consecutive allusions, to make a patterned comment on his now defined character, but this time also gives the reader an ominous, and Sophoclean, forecast of Gabriel's fate. The first dark note is struck by a somewhat incongruous reference to Gabriel peering at Bathsheba from 'a bird's-eye view, as Milton's Satan first saw Paradise' (p. 51). (Hardy indicates some concern for the reference by adding the 'Milton' between the serial and first edition, thereby clarifying the source.) Next there are two masterly allusions, only three pages apart, carefully drawn from tragedies in which the woman definitely causes her man to fall: Bathsheba saves Gabriel from suffocation, and as he clears his head he begins 'wiping his face and shaking himself like a Samson' (p. 58); *Macbeth* (v. v. 27–8) provides the reference which describes Gabriel's inability to compose love phrases for Bathsheba. Lastly, after Gabriel has proposed and been rejected, the narrator tells us that he has the bearing of one who has consigned his days and nights to Ecclesiastes: a world of gloom for Gabriel, and a reminder that Bathsheba is all vanity at this point (p. 69).

Predictably, soon after Bathsheba's refusal, fate, in the form of his inexperienced dog, enters to bankrupt Gabriel. Thematically and allusively he descends into his hell: 'he had sunk from his modest elevation as pastoral king into the very slime-pits of Siddim . . .' (p. 75). But while fortune is unkind to him, Hardy is not; the narrator continues his 'Siddim' sentence with

> but there was left to him a dignified calm he had never before known, and that indifference to fate which, though it often makes a villain of a man, is the basis of his sublimity when it does not. And thus the abasement had been exaltation, and the loss gain.

Hardy is quick to shore this exaltation with more allusions. We are immediately told that Gabriel plays the flute with 'Arcadian sweetness' (p. 77), but when he hears that such playing sometimes makes him resemble a scarecrow, he decides not to let Bathsheba ever see him play, 'in this resolve showing a discretion equal to that related of its sagacious inventress, the divine Minerva herself' (p. 102). The classical references continue to elevate him above his ostensible peers: he threatens the gossiping rustics with a fist that

falls like Thor's hammer (p. 140); he grinds the sheep shears like
Eros when he sharpens his arrows (p. 164).[22] Biblical citations also
contribute to his aura of grandeur, while reminding us of his ties to
the peasantry: his subordinate relationship with Bathsheba is that
of Moses to Pharaoh (p. 168), and Luke 18 : 11 is echoed to remind
us that the proud Gabriel has 'a pharisaical sense that he is not as
other shearers' when reckoning their knowledge of Bathsheba
(p. 182).

Moreover, the allusions emphasise not only Gabriel's superior
dignity and stature, but also his learning and his humanity. The
books in his library are carefully listed, with the narrator's
additional comment that Gabriel has acquired much sound information by diligent perusal of this admittedly limited collection
(p. 105). Nor has Gabriel himself forsaken the Biblical traditions
of his past. He can quote the Scriptures, and does so as he vents his
frustration with Bathsheba by reciting to himself Ecclesiastes 7 : 26
– again an appropriate book because of its castigation of vanity
(p. 183). His humanity, though constantly illuminated through his
acts, is also technically crystalised: his sympathy for Bathsheba's
sorrow, in spite of all she has done to him, is made painfully real by
a seemingly casual reference to 'the oft-quoted observation of
Hippocrates concerning physical pains' (p. 220): when two pains
occur together but not in the same place, the more violent
obscures the other (Aphorism II, 46).

Gabriel, thus enlarged, patiently waits his turn for Bathsheba.
He accepts his adversities, but is never overwhelmed by them, and
eventually wins his prolonged struggle against fate, gaining an
unusual victory for a Hardy character. The strands of the plot are
all either tied together or snipped off: Troy and Boldwood conveniently dispose of each other, and, in a *da capo* manoeuvre,
both Gabriel and Bathsheba return to their original positions,
even to the extent that Bathsheba is required to wear her hair as
she did when Gabriel first saw her.[23] As in *A Pair of Blue Eyes*,
Hardy's construction has again been criticised, this time by both
Henry C. Duffin and Elizabeth Drew. Duffin contends that Boldwood deserves a more artistic demise: Troy's murder is probable,
but to have Boldwood merely drop from view for ever behind
prison walls is to leave 'an exceedingly ragged end'. Drew maintains that the conclusion is unmotivated, that very improbable
crises remove the difficulties to the marriage.[24] Duffin's criticism
has some justification, for one's sympathy for Boldwood fosters a

wish that he could bow out with dignity rather than with ignominy. But Drew in her analysis fails to consider fully the universal irony which Hardy envisioned as perpetrating all of his 'improbables'; and in this novel, unlike *A Pair of Blue Eyes*, Hardy at least affords his Immanent Will some realistic covering. That Elfride's body inexplicably happens to be on Stephen's and Knight's train in *A Pair of Blue Eyes* certainly smacks of artistic gerrymandering; that the storm in *Far From the Madding Crowd* comes just when the men are drunk, that Fanny goes to the wrong church at a most crucial time, or that Joseph Poorgrass gets drunkenly delayed with Fanny's corpse and necessitates Bathsheba's harbouring it, are all also eerily coincidental. But in the latter novel fate is made to work through nature and personality, thus giving it a credibility that blind chance does not easily engender. If the universe is to be indifferent, at this stage of Hardy's career it can at least be indifferent to happiness as well as to tragedy.

Hardy of course concludes the novel with a marriage, ostensibly the conventional Victorian happy ending. However, as in *Desperate Remedies* and *Under the Greenwood Tree*, he seems to be unable to resist one final ironic touch. In the last chapter Bathsheba is preparing for the wedding, and the scene is apparently a jovial one (p. 422). She has just 'laughed with a flushed cheek', and Liddy, the maid, expresses her excitement at hearing of the imminent marriage with '. . . what news! It makes my heart go quite bumpity-bump!' Though the narrative gives no indication of a change of mood, Bathsheba incongruously replies, 'It makes mine rather furious, too . . . However, there's no getting out of it now!' The next line reads, 'It was a damp disagreeable morning', and then two allusions quickly follow: one to Keats's 'Eve of St Agnes', where Madeline is in a trance and has no idea of what is happening around her, and one to the bloody hands of Macbeth immediately after he has murdered Duncan (*Macbeth*, ii. ii. 62). As if these allusions did not fully establish the Hardian qualifications about the marriage, Joseph Poorgrass brings the story to a close with

> 'I wish him joy o' her; though I were once or twice upon saying to-day with holy Hosea, in my scripture manner, which is my second nature, "Ephraim is joined to idols: let him alone." But since 'tis as 'tis, why, it might have been worse, and I feel my thanks accordingly.' (p. 424)

Things do get philosophically worse, and artistically even better, in *The Return of the Native*, but not before Hardy was to reverse both trends on an unfortunate detour into social comedy.

Though some modern critics have come to revalue Hardy's next novel, most agree that it is one of his weakest.[25] The popular reception of *Far From the Madding Crowd* brought a request from the *Cornhill* for another story immediately, and Hardy hurried into production before learning what was of value in his previous work. Further, coinciding with the *Cornhill's* request, Hardy heard some gossip that critics were smirking about the 'house-decorator' author of *Far From the Madding Crowd*. Such criticism made him put aside what was eventually to become *The Woodlanders* and plunge into an untried area, social comedy. *The Hand of Ethelberta* was the result. Hardy was later to concede it to be a 'somewhat frivolous narrative', and it is relatively uninteresting if one is focusing on Hardy's stylistic progress. Consequently, the novel calls for only scant attention here.[26]

   That Hardy in a cosmopolitan milieu was out of touch with his talent is evident from almost any approach one might take, and the use of allusion is no exception. The sparseness of references is debilitating: there are about eighty-six, approximately half of them assigned to Ethelberta herself. In using these references, Hardy follows many of his now established practices. He analyses an allusion (Ruth—Naomi, p. 101) within the narrative to instruct the reader on the recondite importance of the device. The seemingly obligatory Latin allusions are here also, though only two; nor are we spared the teasingly obscure ones (Zamzummins, Kamtschatka, Pugin).[27] He also continues his practice of referentially bolstering the setting or sub-structure of the novel. As he unveils the society into which Ethelberta is fortuitously married and widowed, the dull and pedantic conversations are patiently drawn, with allusions used to create the name-dropping atmosphere and satirically to spice the jargon employed in analysing Ethelberta's poems.[28]

   Yet Hardy's most virulent assaults on the society he both despised and secretly admired come not so much in the events which take place in the stifling drawing rooms he describes but in the characters who people them. Two men in particular are studies in social decadence: Ladywell represents the new generation, Lord Mountclere the firm foundations of the past. Ladywell is first introduced by an allusive description which categorically defines him: 'a town young man, with a Tussaud complexion and well-pencilled brows half way up his forehead' (p. 56). Urbane, waxy, pseudo-artistic, effeminate Ladywell. Subsequent allusions (only two) continue to degrade or mock him in a relatively harmless way as he trails his bleeding heart after Ethelberta.[29] The few allusions associated with Lord Mountclere, on the other hand, give him the stylistic lashing his corruption deserves: both the man and his estate are in states of decay 'emulating in their surface-glitter the Escalier de Marbre at Versailles' (p. 304); and references to 'Walpolean scandal' (p. 306), Mephistopheles (p. 313), Rabelais, and 'cunning Friar Tuck' (p. 329) blacken him. Even when he is joined to an historically admirable figure, it is to King David in his old age, who could not be aroused by his Abishag (p. 379).

Allusively, most of the other peripheral figures are equally insignificant. Ethelberta's siblings are not developed as characters, and Christopher Julian, who does have a major role, gets less than half a dozen supporting allusions, all of which underline how short he falls of the saintly heroism his name promises. Faith, his sister, acts as a partial substitute for the largely absent rustic chorus, and through her the narrator inserts judgments on Ethelberta's ethics. Her position is allusively sustained by references to Tennyson (p. 60), the Bible (pp. 190–1), and even Hawthorne (p. 327).[30]

There remains the title character, an excellent contrast to almost everything that makes Hardy's other heroines successful. His tragic heroines are for the most part people whose emotions rule them, who undergo hours of moral agony for any moment of bliss. Ethelberta as a comic heroine is antithetical. She is cold, calculating, resolute, and self-controlled. Granted the polarities of comedy and tragedy, such a reversal should conceivably work for Hardy. But though Ethelberta is the heroine of a story billed as a comedy, and usually narrated as one, she is forced to deal with what she regards as deadly serious concerns. Moreover, she is made to carry out her charge humourlessly: she is determined, not nonchalant, grave rather than flippant, fully aware of consequences rather than naive. As a result of this tonal incongruity, the reader often finds himself pulled by divergent loyalties. Narration, atmosphere, and frequently situation all call upon us to take the heroine seriously – yet Hardy himself labelled the book as an intended satire on everything that motivates Ethelberta, everything that makes her fictionally what she is. Sometimes the satire is

effectively obvious, but more often it is buried in a pictorial pot-
pourri designed to show realistically 'that part of life they hide
which is behind the scenes', as the epigraph anticipates.

Considering the fact that Ethelberta is a character who some-
how got maimed by the contradictions of the author's intention
(the book veers between social criticism, comedy, seriousness, and
satire), her allusive treatment is surprisingly competent and
deserves some scrutiny. The allusions do not particularly enhance
her portrayal or her performance, nor do they harm them − a real
risk in a character so inconsistently developed. Initially the allusions elevate her. Her poetry resembles Sir Thomas Wyatt's
(p. 48), her prototype is Sappho (p. 50), and she is the great one
that the less prattle of (p. 84; *Twelfth Night*, I. ii. 33). Then her
developing resolve to marry well is meticulously traced. Fearing
that it might be said of her, as it was of Richard II by Henry IV (*1
Henry IV*, III. ii. 69−73), that she had 'Enfeoffed herself to
popularity . . .' (p. 184), and concerned that she could become
(p. 185) 'what Dryden called himself when he got old and poor − a
rent-charge on Providence' ('To My Dear Friend, Mr Congreve
. . .'), she decides to be more bold in her pursuit of a financial
alternative to poetry reading. She quotes *Macbeth* (III. i. 48−9) to
voice her objective: 'To be thus is nothing; / But to be safely thus'
(p. 257). Then Hardy momentarily allows her a sympathetic
wavering. With bitter sarcasm she surveys her position with a verse
from Hosea (2:7): 'She shall follow after her lovers, but she shall
not overtake them; then shall she say, I will go and return to my
first' (p. 282). But this emotion is quickly repressed: 'That's no
matter', she says, and Benthamism dominates only fifteen pages
later. In a scene tediously drawn, Ethelberta is supposedly swayed
by reading 'a well-known treatise on Utilitarianism' into viewing a
marriage with Mountclere as a justifiable sacrifice. As she is convincing herself, the narrator comments that she has made a 'sorry
but unconscious misapplication of sound and wide reasoning'. Yet
our established faith in Ethelberta's intellect makes her travesty of
logic doubtful, and we sense that much of the blame for the mis-
conception lies in Hardy; that the perversion is due to character
development rather than the heroine's reasoning powers. Her
regrets that fame has nearly departed, 'the last infirmity . . .'
gone, are convincing; but her metamorphosis from 'soft and playful Romanticism to distorted Benthamism' (p. 297), and her subsequent willingness to accept Mountclere, are not.

Ethelberta weighs four men in the balance, and chooses the one with the heaviest pockets. Having settled on the viscount, she predictably achieves her goal. Yet her victory is a sordid one, and the reader can never have the proper comic satisfaction in the result. Moreover, Hardy's temperament seems to preclude a bright dénouement, even for comedy. *Under the Greenwood Tree*, the rural counterpart of *The Hand of Ethelberta*, ends with a cynical comment on marriage, as do the bleaker early novels. *The Hand of Ethelberta* is no exception. Once Ethelberta is established in society, allusive garnishing is unnecessary, and she receives none. Yet the references to Shakespeare at one of Macbeth's most dastardly moments, and to Hosea when God is severely rebuking the children of Israel, infer the desired response from the reader. Then the last sentence delivers the fatal blow to a happy ending. Ethelberta has deliberately suppressed her love for Christopher to marry a decrepit roué. She gains power, money, security, but she also knows the excruciatingly high price she has paid. Picotee gets what Ethelberta has sacrificed. Hardy's mordantly ironic and stylistically redemptive last sentence is devastatingly successful. Picotee innocently answers Christopher's proposal with 'I think he [her father] will be very glad . . . Berta will, I know.'

4 The Rustic Chorus

Hardy's failure in *The Hand of Ethelberta* proves what is now critical dogma: his talent thrived best in rural England. This peculiarity of Hardy's talent is supported by the almost unanimous scholarly agreement on the success of Hardy's collective characters, his rustics — drawn from the Dorsetshire labourers he was later to praise in an essay for *Longman's Magazine* in July 1883. Every Hardy novel contains a group of these people, and they serve a growing function in the canon, earning separate consideration in a study of Hardy's stylistic development.

As early as *Desperate Remedies*, Hardy's rustics were singled out for special praise, or, occasionally, opprobrium. But even the *Spectator*'s reviewer of this first novel, after snobbishly calling Hardy's characters 'gaping village rustics', grudgingly recommends that his future efforts be expended in this rural direction, 'instead of being prostituted to the purposes of idle prying into the ways of wickedness' (22 April 1871). In subsequent novels Hardy does expand his rustics' role, until they become significant as a chorus, acting as spokesmen for comic relief, as indicators of the social norms of the countryside, and, most important, as the group which comments on the action, voices Hardy's world view, and eventually enters into the main line of the story as unwitting tools of an Immanent Will. And, as with the principal characters in the novels, allusions play a major part in the stylistic success of the figures involved; those spoken by the narrator tend primarily to elevate and enlarge, while those spoken by the rustics themselves branch out into the even more multifarious functions which their complex serio-comic position and outlook require.

Although each group of peasantry in Hardy's early novels is differentiated, they do share some common traits. He wrote about several rustic types: farm-labourers, tranters, shepherds, local shop people, domestic servants, furze cutters. Almost all are easily recognisable through their dialect; Hardy admitted:

> The rule of scrupulously preserving the local idiom, together
> with the words which have no synonym among those in general
> use, while printing in the ordinary way most of those local
> expressions which are but a modified articulation of words in
> use elsewhere, is the rule I usually follow . . .[1]

Robert Heilman and others have justly asserted that Hardy had a
good ear for dialect, and is consistent in his rustic speech
patterns,[2] though many critics have, with some justice, criticised
him for the too-intellectual banter that the rustics sometimes use.
However, much of the censure, and especially that of Hardy's contemporaries (the *Spectator* said, in 1874, that the rustics' speeches
'come most unnaturally' from their mouths) stems from unfamili-
arity with country ways, and a refusal to admit that any country
person could be intelligent. Time and communication have given
credence to Hardy's portraits as we have come to a better understanding of the linguistic and religious patterns of isolated regions.
Hardy's rustics speak in highly stylised tones, but they are
authentic tones inherited from their ancestors who gained them
from church and Bible and enlarged them to cover the serious
moments of their secular life.

Hardy's rustics, thus linguistically grouped, also share less
definite characteristics. In general they are usually self-deprecat-
ing, naturally cheerful, disarmingly frank, sometimes obstinate —
and are always treated with respect by their creator. The majority
of them are middle-aged men and women, though youth and old
folk do provide necessary elements of naiveté, wisdom, even
senility. Throughout the novels they are preoccupied with human
nature, though Hardy somewhat idealises them by sparing them
both ambition and remorse; and it is this preoccupation that
makes them credible in their recurring judgments on the story
which is being related.

The rustics also have a common ground in their profound knowledge of the Bible. This, coupled with their concern for human
nature and with the Scriptural intonation in much of their language, would seem to indicate a strong religious bent. Yet, quite to
the contrary: Hardy's rustics have a practical habitual attitude
towards the Church, occasionally going to services, but certainly
with no sense of piety.[3] The Mellstock Quire attends on Sunday
purely to supply the music, and takes turns sleeping during the rest
of the service. In *Far From the Madding Crowd*, the rustics often

add the Biblical quotations for the occasion, and voice the spiritual point of view, but their ties to organised religion are conveniently loose. Hardy records a malt-house conversation which summarises their stand:

> 'I won't say much for myself; I don't wish to', Coggan continued, with that tendency to talk on principles which is characteristic of the barley-corn. 'But I've never changed a single doctrine: I've stuck like a plaster to the old faith I was born in. Yes; there's this to be said for the Church, a man can belong to the Church and bide in his cheerful old inn, and never trouble or worry his mind about doctrines at all. But to be a meetinger, you must go to chapel in all winds and weathers, and make yerself as frantic as a skit. Not but that chapel-members be clever chaps enough in their way. They can lift up beautiful prayers out of their own heads, all about their families and shipwracks in the newspaper. . . .'
>
> 'Yes', said Coggan. 'We know very well that if anybody do go to heaven, they will. They've worked hard for it, and they deserve to have it, such as 'tis. I bain't such a fool as to pretend that we who stick to the Church have the same chance as they, because we know we have not. But I hate a feller who'll change his old ancient doctrines for the sake of getting to heaven'. (pp. 313–14)

Thus, willing 'to stick to [their] side; and if [they] be in the wrong', 'fall with the fallen', the rustics stand only in the nave of the Church of England. Hardy never allows them a religious experience, and such emotion would be out of their stoic, ironic character. Their interests are primarily of this world, even while they rely on Biblical wisdom and terminology to express them. The Church is certainly no anathema, and they superstitiously depend heavily on it, but this does not stifle a healthy celebration of the pagan life. The Maypole is as familiar as the communion tray, and by *The Return of the Native*, the mummer's play and the perverted personality of the symbolic Christian Cantle tip the balance decidedly in favour of the pagan world.

The rustics, then, are formed into a dialectal, traditional, humanistic group who gain strength and position through their very unity. Proximity, occupation, and sociability draw them together, and once they meet, they establish the common base of the novel, thinking collectively to voice the practical wisdom of their accumulated experience, thus rendering colloquial judgments which are tolerably shrewd approximations of objective truth.[4] Much like its Greek prototype (Hardy even introduces one speech by the rustics — an announcement of the arrival of a messenger — with '(All)', and in *Far From the Madding Crowd* calls them a 'chorus': p. 270), the rustic chorus at its most serious level performs according to tradition — that is to say, it gives significance to otherwise unimportant incidents, clarifies immediate events and fills in missing information on past ones, adumbrates the course the principals are to follow, lectures the hero when to do so is in order (with the same ineffectiveness which is so prevalent in Greek choral lectures), and voices the work's inherent philosophical position.

Hardy's method shows him to favour the classic pattern in other areas as well. Northrop Frye remarks that 'in comedy a society forms around the hero; in tragedy, the chorus, however faithful, usually represents the society from which the hero is gradually isolated. Hence what it expresses is a social norm against which the hero's hybris may be measured.'[5] This is especially true of the Hardian chorus, for, since all but one of the early novels are set in rural England, Hardy could not assume in his urban audience a common ground of moral and social standards. The rustics bridge this cultural gap by becoming the gauge for the rise and fall of the principals, and bridge the respectability gap by using allusions as they do so. Moreover, the peasants' corporate view is given added weight by Hardy's practice of drawing his main characters from their very stock. Since the rustics are intimately familiar with the hero's class and background, they are the evaluative 'neighbourhood' of both their peers and betters: Baily Pennyways is below them because he fails to meet their level of honesty; Bathsheba, Boldwood, Wildeve are above them because money and education make them better than the rustic mean. In addition, then, to their role as influential interpreters, the rustics establish what Hardy saw as the normalcy of the area, and, remaining for ever unencumbered by the artificial codes Hardy condemns in *The Hand of Ethelberta*, bring into the novels the undistorted and unrepressed behaviour that he so admired.[6] Secondly, and again like their dramatic predecessors, they contribute the conventional comic relief to the novels. Free of the high seriousness of English social position, they can laugh at themselves, and be laughed at, harmlessly. The rustic role, then, is quickly recognised as complex, diverse, and important. To help them accomplish their choral assignments as social norms, comic elements, and wise commentators, Hardy once again uses his allusive techniques to gain both credibility and comedy.

The rustics comment on the status of the principals often, but because the social strata are naturally familiar to the characters in the book, and because Hardy often tries to be seductively unobtrusive as he measures his people by the more humane standards of *his* Victorian England, there are few familiarising allusions used as liaisons in this particular type of description. In *Desperate Remedies*, the leading figures plot their intrigues oblivious to customs, and the complex machinations of plot make any set system for community judgment impossible. Furthermore, murder is condemned at any level, and the immoral pressures which drive Cytherea into marriage are kept from the populace. *Under the Greenwood Tree* is of course in direct contrast, but here every action and conversation reflect on the local standards, since the novel centres on the 'rustic' group. By the time Hardy wrote *A Pair of Blue Eyes*, however, his world was becoming more fixed, and he found it increasingly necessary to place his principals precisely in it. Stephen's relationship with Elfride revolves round his social status, and consequently we have a long discourse between Stephen and his mother on just what separates him from the vicar's daughter (pp. 123 ff.). No allusions are used in this conversation, and their absence is significant, indicating that Stephen is still a rustic. For any reference other than a Biblical one would separate him from his class, and Stephen is deliberately not a Bible-quoting man. But his father and his father's friends are — and when Elfride has risen even higher in position, they do comment on her lineage, and give their words the proper universal authority by using Biblical language and quoting Scripture (Ecclesiastes 12:6) to discuss the vagaries of titular descent (p. 277).

This same duty to inform the audience of relative social status also falls to the rustics in the succeeding novels. In *Far From the Madding Crowd*, the group first introduces Bathsheba as the mistress of the estate, assuring the reader at the same time that she is still 'as proud as Lucifer' (p. 78). It is again the rustics who supply Gabriel's background, and it is they who tell the story of Bathsheba's ancestry, revealing that her father, Levi Everdene, whose name ironically means 'adhesive', or 'joined', could only be faithful to his wife if he called her by her maiden name and pretended she was his mistress. Joseph Poorgrass speaks for the group, admitting that this is a most ungodly remedy; but Grundyism is not the mode in Wessex, as is illustrated by the rest of his sanctified comment, 'but we ought to feel deep cheerfulness that a happy Providence kept it from being any worse'. Billy Smallbury adds in benediction, 'the man's will was to do right, sure enough, but his heart didn't chime in' (p. 98). In *The Hand of Ethelberta* and *The Return of the Native* no allusions are used specifically to annotate local point of view, primarily because in his fifth novel Hardy drastically suppressed his rustic interest, and in his next his country folk are elevated in such a way as not to need additional support in their moments of social commentary. None the less, the rustics do reveal status in these two novels. In *The Hand of Ethelberta* the milkman and the ostler tell of Ethelberta's widowhood and present condition. In *The Return of the Native* it is the rustics who supply the details of Clym's regional social standing, give an account of Thomasin's rustic father, and tell Eustacia's past history. Here, as in each of the novels, the rustics reveal the standard by which they decide what is unusual; the extraordinary figures, in turn, become the central characters of the stories. Very often it is the allusions which substantiate their claims.

In addition to social standards, the rustics also provide the necessary element of comedy in Hardy's books. In the bleak novels it is much needed comic relief; *Under the Greenwood Tree* purports to be totally comic, thus the specifically facetious elements are merely complementary to the farcical plot itself. Allusions are important in building these comic scenes, not only because their universal familiarity allows them to be comfortably funny to an audience uninitiated in rural ways, but also because Hardy obtains much of his laughter by the technique Henri Bergson defined as 'transporting the natural expression of the idea into another key'.[7] The rustics often rely on God and the Bible to make their point, but their very personalities and philosophical outlook occasionally make these references humorously lack the serious tone or the sombre moment religious allusions usually elicit or require. And, as a second avenue into humour, Hardy, as narrator, often injects through allusion a surprise conjunction of ideas: references to highly serious persons or events are used incongruously to exaggerate the mundane into comedy.

Hardy uses both of these comic techniques as early as *Desperate Remedies*. In his first novel, the two gossips, Mrs Crickett, 'a fine-framed, scandal-loving woman', and Mrs Leat, 'an intimate friend of hers, and a female who sported several unique diseases and afflictions' (pp. 181, 183), use references comically when discussing the impending scandal surrounding Manston, and are in turn themselves objects of humorous narrative allusion. The two women cattily assure each other, in a rather trite reference which reflects the inexperience of its author, that 'Miss Somebody' is undoubtedly some poor street wench, an escapee from Sodom, 'only to find herself in Gomorrah'. The narrator, however, scoffs at the high seriousness of the two snoops by a hyperbolical comparison of Mrs Leat's hand, when she reaches for that major clue, a strange hair on Manston's pillow, as one which would have been 'an unmitigated delight to the pencil of Carlo Crivelli' (p. 183), the fifteenth-century Venetian religious painter known for the almost grotesque and repellent features and expressions seen in his work. And later in the novel it is a brief descriptive allusion attached to rustics that allows one of the intolerably few moments of comic relief in the melodrama. On the bleak day when Cytherea is to mismarry Manston, we are permitted a brief respite to smile at the clerk and gardener crossing an iced driveway 'bowed and stooping like Bel and Nebo' (p. 266), the Babylonian gods of heaven and earth mentioned in Isaiah 46 : 1.

In his next two novels, *Under the Greenwood Tree* and *A Pair of Blue Eyes*, Hardy again has comic scenes, but temporarily drifts away from using allusions to support his humorous technique. The chorus is not needed for comic relief in *Under the Greenwood Tree*, and the book has only two possibly humorous allusions, though it has been noted that all the conversations in the book are reminiscent of the speeches of Shakespeare's Justice Shallow.[8] Both references are voiced by the players themselves. One appears when Nat, a wedding guest, loudly proclaims, 'And the stores of victuals and drink that lad has laid in: why 'tis enough for Noah's ark!' (p. 197). Secondly, there is a reference to Ecclesiastes that might be expected to evoke a mood of doom but is here comically turned upon the vicar: 'the sermon might have been good; for 'tis true, the sermon of Old Eccl'iastes himself lay in Eccl'iastes ink-bottle afore he got it out' (p. 89). Hardy only slightly expands his method in *A Pair of Blue Eyes*, but does include an important addition in that one whole scene owes its structure to a secondary source. The first humorous allusion reveals a minor point about the natural Scripturality of the rustics' imagination as one of them explains a trick

box by saying that he could try to open it 'till the end of Revelations' (p. 258). More significantly, Hardy models an entire chapter
(26) on the grave-digging scene in *Hamlet*.[9] The nonchalance of
the clown as he throws up poor Yorick is echoed in the actions of
John Smith and his friends, giving a narrative breath of life to what
could otherwise be a ghoulish situation.

By the time he has come to write *Far From the Madding Crowd*,
however, Hardy has hit his comic stride, and the humour is not
only technically appropriate, but often, as Lascelles Abercrombie
has noted, 'searches life as deeply as tragedy itself'.[10] Often the
comedy here comes through conversational and narrative asides,
and is suitably brief: Liddy gives her marital position through a
reference from Psalms 102:6: 'what between the poor men I won't
have, and the rich men who won't have me, I stand as a pelican in
the wilderness' (p. 110); the narrator exaggerates into humour by
describing the hung-over farmers by an allusion to John Flaxman,
a sculptor whose work is known for its heaviness and infelicitous
arrangement (p. 285). But more notable than these asides are
those occasions when, at just the right moment, often when the
story is on the brink of pathos, the rustic chorus enters to stave off
impending gloom with a balancing facetious comment drawn
from their common sense world. So, immediately after Gabriel
meets Fanny in the woods and feels 'himself in the penumbra of a
very deep sadness' (p. 88), he goes to Warren's Malthouse to hear
Joseph Poorgrass's hilarious rendition of his encounter with the
devil and his subsequent rescue through repeating the Lord's
Prayer, 'the Belief right through', the Ten Commandments and
'Dearly Beloved Brethren' – all he knew of the 'book' (p. 95).
Later, the story of the unfortunate Cain Ball, so named because
his mother confused Cain with Abel, is told in a comic light, as we
learn that Ball has always been called 'Cainy' to soften his tragedy.
And before Joseph gets around to telling Bathsheba that her sheep
are dying, he rambles through a long Biblical list:

> 'Yes,' said Joseph, 'and I was sitting at home looking for
> Ephesians, and says to myself, "'Tis nothing but Corinthians
> and Thessalonians in this danged Testament", when who
> should come in but Henry there: "Joseph," he said, "the sheep
> have blasted theirselves—"'. (p. 167)

Then Cainy again enters for comic relief by interjecting, in the
middle of his tale of seeing Bathsheba in Bath, a discourse on the

new religious trends: the new style parsons wear long beards, and 'look like Moses and Aaron complete, and makes we fokes in the congregation feel all over like the children of Israel' (p. 252). Finally, in one of the most sombre scenes in the novel, as Joseph is bringing Fanny home for the last time, the sadness is momentarily relieved by Bergsonian humour when Poorgrass, drinking with his friends, talks of the 'horned man in the smokey house', and justifies his imbibing as a 'talent the Lord has mercifully bestowed upon us, and we ought not neglect it' (p. 313). Then he plaintively tells us of his sickness — that is to say, seeing double when he is drunk: 'Yes, I see two of every sort, as if I were some holy man living in the time of King Noah and entering into the ark' (p. 316). In each of these instances the comedy follows hard upon or stands in the midst of sorrow, and thus creates a contrast that brings both relief and perspective. Moreover, each time the vehicle for humour is the allusion; the irreverent, bantering approach to the religious is incongruous, unexpected, unusual, and thus funny — and perhaps a little unsettling for the orthodox in Hardy's audience.

Hardy repeats these techniques in *The Return of the Native*, with equal quality though less quantity, for his increasing sombreness of mind refused to let much humour blow across the wilds of Egdon Heath. Flaxman's group of suitors has sobered up in this novel, and now become a 'Tussaud collection of celebrities' who march to church on Christmas morning. The ultra-seriousness of Thomasin's aborted marriage is relieved by the rustics' account of her father's musical ability, a talent that maintains its reputation, as does 'Sheridan's renowned Begum Speech' (a six-hour speech against Warren Hastings made by Richard Brinsley Sheridan before Parliament in 1787), and 'Farinelli's singing before the princess', only because it is forever lost to the world and cannot be comparatively judged (p. 76). But, as is appropriate to Hardy's deepening cynicism, the comedy here can also be deceptive. The reader enjoys listening to Christian Cantle ward off his fears by chattering, 'Matthew, Mark, Luke and John, bless the bed that I lie on . . .' (p. 58), until he realises that the laughter is directed *at* Cantle, and the humour becomes as bleak as the story it inhabits.

As the rustic chorus provides the social norm and the comic relief for the novels, it is also engaged in its most important function: acting as a serious commentator on the plot, contributing both the standard of truth and the bleak world view. Eventually it gains such prominence that it surpasses its classic limitations and enters directly into the action. In order to succeed when sagacity is required of them, the rustics must overcome the imagery of buffoonery conventionally associated with such figures. Moreover, since they act as comic relief, their complementary profundity must always be firmly established. Remarks by and about them can be, and often are, funny; but for the most part the rustics' attitude is fatalistically serious, and even the comic scenes have a grave element of dark truth in them. In order to maintain his rustics in their high-serious position, and to surround their annotations with an atmosphere of veracity, Hardy again partially relies on allusions. When used by the narrator, they move the rustics to a separate, elevated vantage—point; when spoken by the rustics themselves — and in such cases they are almost always Biblical — the allusions give an historical and religious tone to their comments, thus assigning an air of importance to their common—sense judgments, helping them to gain the confidence of the sophisticated audience Hardy hoped to reach.

Hardy gives his rustics their serious choral part as early as *Desperate Remedies*, but since there the rustics have little to do, their exegetical role is not sharply defined, and much of his rustic allusive method in this book illustrates the immaturity of his early style. The coachman, as an individual, gives the definitive picture of Miss Aldclyffe (p. 70), but his clarifying references to Robinson Crusoe, Lucifer, and the Pharaoh's chief baker (Genesis 40:22) are rather commonplace. Mr Springrove, the hero's father, quotes Deuteronomy 28:67 to underline the gravity of his situation, but here the reference makes Mr Springrove sound pompously self-pitying, not pontifically intelligent (p. 225). And in the final chapter, where the rustics congregate for the all-important joining of the disparate strands of this intricate melodrama, though their commentary gains a minor note of authority by one reference to 'babylonish places' (p. 416), on the whole they are carelessly denied the support of elevating allusions. Moreover, Hardy further weakens this scene by introducing an unexplained, unnecessary, and disconcerting reporter as the catalyst of their conversation, rather than using the stronger device of letting the chorus reveal details by talking among themselves. But Hardy's failures with the rustics in this novel, and with the allusions attached to them, are correctable ones, as his later proficiency proves. And even here there are portents of the major role the rustics are to assume. It is the insignificant porter at the railway station who witholds the crucial information about Mrs Manston's being alive, while the Hardian bleakness so prominent in later novels is introduced as early as 1871 by the minor Mr Springrove: 'There's a back'ard current in the world, and we must do our utmost to advance in order just to bide where we be' (p. 401).

Hardy tries a new approach to his chorus in *Under the Greenwood Tree*, since the choral group is in reality the Melstock Quire, and thus one of the two central concerns of the story. The flirtatious affair between Fancy Day and Dick Dewy is the romantic, comic focus of the novel, but, as Hardy makes quite clear in his preface, the book is also about the more critical fact of the disappearance of the traditional choir. Just as the incongruity and exaggeration of the allusions attached to Fancy and Dick contribute an ironic levity to the novel's comedy, so do allusions bolster the antithetical plight of the Quire. In the midst of comedy, the chorus now adds what might be called 'serious relief', and allusions contributed both by the narrator and by the rustics themselves adroitly help to accomplish the shift in tone and elevate the Quire into an object of empathetic consideration.

This allusive device first appears in the chapter entitled 'A meeting of the Quire'. The men have gathered to discuss rumours of their fate, and to compare the hustling new ways of the present parson with the pleasant, nonchalant humanity of the previous one. Mr Penny, one of the chief members of the group, is quickly moved to the centre of the gallery by being described through an allusion to Moroni, the Italian portrait painter who influenced both Titian and Van Dyck (p. 88). As the rustics continue to talk, the sense of loss and disappointment they are experiencing is given symbolic extension as Old William Dewy, while expressing his sorrow, gains 'nobility of aspect' from the setting sun and projects a 'Titanic shadow at least thirty feet long' (p. 92). (The Titanic allusion is a post-manuscript addition, thus indicating that Hardy wanted to make quite clear the 'imposing magnitude' of his commentator.) And finally, when the Quire's Armageddon has arrived and they are forced out of the loft into the public pews, Grandfather William again voices their sadness, and the resigned fortitude with which they must face what is to them a tragic break with security-providing tradition, as he quotes Psalms 44:17–18: 'though this has come upon us let not our hearts be turned back or our steps go out of the way' (p. 179).

Since the Quire-chorus is a focal point in this novel, Hardy takes more than usual care to define sequentially each member, and to make their daily doings an integral part of the plot. Because they must be both individuals and chorus, only rarely do they have occasion to step outside their own immediate concerns and discourse objectively on events. However, when they do utter judgments, their tone is for the most part serious, as when, for example, they discuss Dick's infatuation with Fancy (p. 93). It is their most solemn pronouncement, however, that earns the added dignity of allusion, and the allusion in turn gives the tone of bleak truth to the conversation. The scene is their last one, and they are discussing Dick and Fancy's wedding. All is seemingly gay, until the rustics add the pessimistic Hardian view of marriage seen repeatedly in the novels. Grandfather James, with all the wisdom his experience has given him, asks the leading question: 'I wonder which she thinks most about, Dick or her wedding raiment!' (p. 202). Grandfather William answers with the cynicism of Jeremiah 2:32, and summarises much that will be wrong in the fastidious Fancy's marriage: 'Can a maid forget her ornaments, or a bride her attire?' The story has already answered 'no', for the couple's first quarrel was over a too-important dress. Hardy's allusive adjudication on the marriage, to come in the final scene with Fancy and Dick, tells us that Grandfather William is right; their first quarrel will be far from their last (see p. 37).

Though the peasant chorus only rarely elucidates in *A Pair of Blue Eyes*, it none the less has a significant part to play in this novel also, and gains increased developmental importance in that here it begins to act, within now clearly defined limits, as a cohesive unit which can reflect and refract the central concerns of the story. And once again allusions identify the country folk's credibly knowledgeable position. Mr Smith and his craftsmanship are given the praise of being despised by Adam Smith and respected by Macaulay (p. 120). Mrs Smith, as Stephen's mother and mentor, is spokesperson for the local group, and Hardy makes her authority (and, by extension, that of the other rustics) explicit with the remark: 'Mrs Smith threw in her sentiments between acts, as Coryphaeus of the tragedy, to make the description complete' (p. 120). Once she has definitively become the choral leader, Mrs Smith goes on to describe the hitherto unmentioned pragmatic side of Stephen's infatuation with Elfride. Later in the novel the rustics enter again to tell us of Stephen's advanced position in the world (p. 367), the group having defined his former standing in a previous conversation (p. 251); and it is the rustics who give the foreboding clue to the contents of the mysterious train carriage, again resorting to a Biblical source for their seriousness when they paraphrase Ecclesiastes. Finally, it is the almost too appropriately named Unity who draws the story to a close by filling in the details of Elfride's marriage and death that Stephen and Knight have missed. Fortunately, Hardy has now dispensed with the clumsy device of having a mysterious reporter enter, and the rustics in this novel deserve the praise the *Spectator* gave them.

In *Far From the Madding Crowd* Hardy's handling of the rustic chorus as serious commentators on the action keeps pace with the maturity of other aspects of his style. The group assumes a major role, for several whole sections of this novel are devoted solely to the peasants, and nearly all of the major elements in the plot are revealed during rustic conversations: the firing of Pennyways, Fanny's disappearance, the hiring of Gabriel, the revelation of Bathsheba's marriage to Troy, the fact of Fanny's death, the final return of Troy, the fate of Boldwood — all are announced by the rustics. In each of these instances the credibility of the group is given tonal support by allusion — and, contrary to Hardy's practice with his principals, the references are neither of the ironic nor of the *double-entendre* variety. The rustics seem to understand the irony of the universe, and have come to stoic terms with it. They therefore speak the truth straightforwardly, and, Hardy says allusively, we are to believe them.

The rustics here are given authority early in the story by receiving more introductory attention than Hardy has accorded such groups in his previous novels. Individual characteristics are recorded, and we see that the peasants' strength is going to lie in breadth of knowledge and temperament as well as in sheer numbers. Every age and type seems to have some representative in the crowd: Joseph Poorgrass, one of the top echelon in the rustic ranks, is extremely shy; Mark Clark, another leader, is young and merry; Henery Frey is vain; Jan Coggan is sensitive, a loyal friend, and a professional godfather in 'baptisms of the subtly-jovial kind' (p. 93); Susan Tall's husband typifies all such nonentities who do not even rate a private name; the maltster is the old man of all old men, and so proud of it that he can trace his age back 117 years (p. 100); his son, Joseph Smallbury, is given no individuality, and thus becomes sons everywhere; then there is the unfortunate

Cainy Ball, the babbling, giddy maid, Liddy Smallbury, and even two 'yielding women — as scarlet a pair as ever was', called Temperance and Soberness (p. 114). Given such a variety of experience, the group is a valuable storehouse of reliable comment, and the comment itself gains a trustworthy tool in allusions. At their most incisive moments, the rustics again turn to the Bible to voice their authority and give weight to their words. For example, after Cainy Ball's honesty has been confirmed by his frequent church attendance, his report of seeing Bathsheba and Troy arm—in—arm in Bath is put in its proper sepulchral perspective when he is asked to swear 'in the most awful form' to the truth of his statements. Joseph Poorgrass, in his most religious manner, reveals the gravity of the oath: "Tis a horrible testament mind ye, which you say and seal with your blood-stone, and prophet Matthew tells us that on whomsoever it shall fall it will grind him to powder' (p. 253). Cainy cannot stand such pressure, the 'spiritual magnitude of the position', and shrinks from revealing what all know to be the truth. Joseph rebukes him with Biblical curses, comparing him to Shimei, son of Gera, who denounced David when he thought Absalom's rebellion was gaining ground (2 Samuel 16:5—14). But Cainy has made his point painfully clear, and the allusions have made it profoundly grave. Gabriel is worried; the seriousness supplied by the Biblical oath tells us that he has reason to be.

Hardy continues to inject allusions into the rustic scenes and does it with admirable skill, especially when he lets the rustics do his referential talking. After Boldwood has killed Troy and is awaiting trial, it is Joseph Poorgrass, in his 'reflective way', who says, 'Justice is come to weigh him in the balances'; even though he sounds pompously pious here, he at least conveys to the reader the chorus's confidence that Boldwood will get a fair trial. However, Hardy compromises his success at this point by having the narrator intrude to describe Laban's return with the crucial news of Boldwood's fate, expressed with an untimely quotation from Scott's *Marmion* (p. 409). The reader, anxiously awaiting the results of the petition for a reprieve, may resent having to read these lines about a trampling horse. Fortunately, however, Hardy quickly redeems himself by having Joseph Poorgrass allusively undermine the marriage of Bathsheba and Oak (see p. 77), thus continuing the rustic, and Hardian, approach to marriage which, initiated in *Under the Greenwood Tree*, was to be used again in his next novel, *The Hand of Ethelberta*.

The Hand of Ethelberta, by now familiar as the most consistent failure of Hardy's early novels, does not break the pattern with a triumph in rustic commentary. The novel's urban setting, however, does excuse him, since his peasant chorus could hardly be feasibly imported and given great significance. The conversations between the milkman and the ostler, and the occasional asides by various servants, do sporadically enlighten us about the action, but for the most part they merely establish the social setting of the story. Moreover, because the speakers are city people and not country folk, they do not talk in Biblical tones, nor is their position enhanced by allusion. (To have provided them with allusions would, in fact, have placed them, stylistically, dangerously close to Ethelberta, for she is but a servant veneered with sophisticated intelligence and polish.) Because of their commonness, their lack of Biblical superiority, and their tenuous position in the delicate social balance, the 'rustics' of this novel, then, are unusually insignificant. They do reveal Ethelberta's Mayfair status, they do enter the plot for an important moment as the means by which Mountclere finds out Ethelberta's secret, and the coachman does bring Christopher up to date on Ethelberta's marriage; but with only these few entrances, as a chorus they play a transient part.

The rustics in *The Return of the Native* seem to have all the strength lacking in their counterparts in *The Hand of Ethelberta*, as here Hardy allots them even greater importance than he gives to the country folk in *Far From the Madding Crowd*. The group is familiar in type if not in name, and once again they act collectively while being defined individually. As a group they tell, conversationally, the scandalous tale of Mrs Yeobright's forbidding the banns; they sing a wedding song to Thomasin and Wildeve, thus forcing them to pretend that they really have married; they forecast Clym's arrival; they are all present at the moment of Mrs Yeobright's death; they inform the reader of Clym's condition after her death; and they even lead us out of the novel by preparing for the marriage of Thomasin and Diggory. However, through all of these actions they receive or utter only one direct serious allusion, and even this does not serve to elevate the group as a whole. Christian Cantle imagines the presence of the devil in all adders, and recalls 'the old serpent in God's garden', thereby adding a note of Biblical foreboding to the scene. But the ominous note itself is overshadowed by the tremendous irony Hardy achieves by having the half-wit Christian draw the inference of original sin from Mrs Yeobright's death scene.

The fact that Hardy does not follow his practice of using allusions to substantiate his rustics' choral position is in itself significant. For, much more than in previous novels, these country folk are irrevocably tied to the land on which they live. Egdon Heath houses these rustics, and it, rather than the locals on it, receives exalting allusions. As the heath becomes universal, it carries the chorus with it (see pp. 98–100). The group gains its air of truth from the land which nurtures it, and its rustic dignity is never in question. Secondly, Hardy expands his rustic chorus into unconventional areas, for, although they function as a group, as individuals they also make vital recurring entrances into the action: Christian carries and stupidly loses the money meant for Clym and Eustacia; the supposedly cursed Johnny Nunsuch is the liaison between Eustacia and Wildeve; Charlie saves Eustacia, his beloved, from killing herself. To have the group closely knit by a recurrence of serious Biblical allusions could diminish the importance of the rustics' individual acts. Finally, solemn Biblical references would almost be incongruous here, for the rustics of Egdon Heath are less religious than those of Weatherbury, and, although they know the Bible and often speak in Biblical tones, as a group they gain their imposing status by sharing the pagan and secular images connected with the heath. The rustic Biblical references in this novel have rightly been reserved for comic relief, where they were most needed, as the chorus itself steps into the spotlit position it deserves.

5 Stylistic Maturity in *The Return of the Native*

The worth of Hardy's early forays into melodrama, romance, social criticism, and tragi-comedy is proved in *The Return of the Native*. The publication history is now fairly well-known: the novel appeared first in serial (*Belgravia*, January–December 1878) and was simultaneously serialised in America by Harper's *New Monthly Magazine* (February 1878–January 1879) before it was published in book form (Smith-Elder, 1878). In the years between this 'first edition' and the 'last' authorised text (the 1912 Wessex Edition), and even between the manuscript, serial, and first edition, Hardy worked to polish and clarify the story, his revisions usually tending to economise his statements, to place his locations more specifically into his Wessex geography, and to correct contradictions in plot action. Occasional changes in character development bring individuals into sharper focus.[1]

That Hardy, in *The Return of the Native*, surpassed all his previous ventures into fiction is evident in both the broad and the particular avenues into the novel. Whereas his time scheme was carefully worked out in the past, here he goes a step beyond in a conscious attempt to observe the unity of time.[2] In a second use of the classical conventions, he gives tighter structure to this novel by dividing it into five parts, adding the last section later as an admitted bow to his audience's desire for at least one happy marriage. Once more Hardy follows his pattern of multiple lovers elliptically circling one woman, complicated here by marriage and implied adultery. And with the foreboding Rainbarrow as an axis of space circumscribed by the Heath, the Hardian topography is again detailed with great care and accuracy, but now with such adroitness that this novel is often recognised as a model of modern fiction's advances in the technique of spatialisation.

Hardy's more particular stylistic skills keep pace with his improved sense of structure. Since mental struggles are the major theme here, there are no allusions that deal solely with action. In the same vein a refined continuation of the use of allusion heightens or debases the characters, and thereby moulds them according to the author's philosophical vision. Moreover, an even greater advance in his use of allusion establishes the environment as a strong motivator of personality, for, to a degree found nowhere else in Hardy, the setting in *The Return of the Native* controls both physical and psychological action, imposing restrictions that force both character and author to meet its challenge.

Hardy opens his novel under the heading 'A Face on which Time makes but Little Impression', and follows immediately with a brilliant personification of a heath which is as timeless and as aloof as the tragic mode it projects.[3] In his 1895 Preface to the novel Hardy makes his original intention explicit by aligning his Egdon with 'the heath of that traditionary King of Wessex, Lear'. The personality of the Heath, well developed even in the manuscript, is defined through images of solemnity, vastness, inevitability, and an ironic silence that mocks the human cries it hears. Hardy was Wordsworthian in his religious feeling for nature, but reading both Burke and Darwin compromised his love for it.[4] Consequently we see a mixture of forms for Egdon Heath. It combines with the twilight to evolve 'a thing majestic without severity, impressive without showiness, emphatic in its admonitions, grand in its simplicity' (p. 34). Its demeanour is tragic; its mood dark, controlled by seasons and thus bound to the cycles of infinite time: 'the sea changed, the fields changed, the rustics, the village, the people changed, yet Egdon remained' (p. 36). Its features are those of 'man's nature — neither ghastly, hateful, nor ugly: neither commonplace, unmeaning, nor tame; but, like man, slighted and enduring; and withal singularly colossal and mysterious in its swarthy monotony' (p. 35).

While Egdon Heath is being shaped by these abstractions into a separate entity which simultaneously reflects, supports, and influences each character, Hardy uses at least twenty evocative allusions to embellish, solidify, and particularise the subtle dimensions of the Heath's personality. It is the intellectual, almost sonorous tone of the references which sustains the antagonistic, Olympian character of the land. The Heath becomes not only a familiar place for ordinary encounters among the populace, but also a symbol of the temper of the future — a time in which human souls will find themselves in harmony only among the sombre

things. As the race wearies it is Egdon which will soothe: 'the new
Vale of Tempe may be a gaunt waste in Thule' (p. 34). And as the
Heath projects the century's atmosphere, so does it provide a
forceful companion for the tragic players upon it. Recorded in
Domesday Book, described in the sixteenth century by Leland as
'overgrown with heth and mosse', this dark country is even now an
untameable 'Ishmaelitish thing' (p. 35), and thus a fitting foil to
the outcast Eustacia, and to the outcast that Clym is to become. Its
Titanic forms (p. 34), Atlantean brow (p. 41), and Limbonic
expanses (p. 44), join to implant in the setting the proper elevation
and dignity for the natives' 'Promethean rebelliousness' (p. 45).

Moreover, the brilliant abstract description, coupled with
accumulating allusions, infuse the personified Heath with a super-
natural atmosphere that acts as a tangible force — a force indifferent in its punishments and rewards, ambiguous in its loyalty.
Even while the Heath permits on its brow the bright festival fires,
which afford a momentary stay against black chaos, and which, as
unbroken lineal descendants from Druidical rites, supply the
heathmen with the comfort of historical continuity, it fetters its
charges for ever in a 'Tartarean situation', a classical hell. The
Heath is to be hated as much as worshipped, feared as much as
admired, respected as much as challenged. The Keatsian epigraph warns of impending sorrow. The description and allusions
defining the Heath tonally elevate this earthly setting for sorrow
into a universe and a fateful force for tragedy.

The triumvirate of the novel is, of course, Clym, Eustacia, and
Wildeve. The characters who circle round them, Mrs Yeobright,
Diggory, and Thomasin, are drawn in by the emotional ties of
affection and family relationship and by the physical restrictions
of the Heath, and are eventually caught in the vortex of emotion
and coincidence that destroys Eustacia and her lovers. Though
Thomasin has both the position and the personality to be given
second-billing, it is Mrs Yeobright and Diggory who supply the
major supporting roles. Mrs Yeobright acts as the emotional
catalyst of events; Diggory is the manipulator of most of the
physical changes of course. Both of these roles, so carefully integrated into the novel, are strengthened by an adroit use of allusions.

Mrs Yeobright's part in the novel is a ubiquituous one: she
variously foresees the tragic course of things, makes ineffectual
and often unexpectedly destructive attempts to divert the stream,

and ultimately dies voicing the bitterness Hardian characters are so often heir to. From the time of her introduction we are told that Mrs Yeobright, with her redoubtable gentility, is superior to her neighbours, and that her ties with the land are to the Heath of geological timelessness, not the heath of furze and furze—cutters. Allusions from antiquity link her to the more mythical Heath, and secure her exaltation: she looks at 'issues from a Nebo denied to others around' (pp. 59—60); she is unafraid even when surrounded by the 'Tartarean' aspects of Egdon (p. 63). But Hardy's choice of reference here also foretells the tragedy of her existence: Moses stood on Nebo only to look at the Promised Land, never to enter it (Deuteronomy 32:49); and her Heath is to become a searing hell and cause her death. Moreover, even as she enjoys her most complimentary description, we are bleakly reminded that her insight, though singularly profound, is inevitably limited. As Benjamin Sankey astutely observes, in Hardy's world every force obeys a logic of its own, and the limitations of human foresight maim even the most perceptive of characters. Being unable to take into account every variable, the characters are often at the mercy of the unforeseen, and are, moreover, further handicapped by the necessity to rely on an intuition based on the logic of experience when dealing with what is for Hardy an essentially illogical world.[5] Mrs Yeobright becomes emblematic of these aspects of the human condition in that her talents are tragically at odds with her situation, enabling her, Hardy tells us, to intuit the tendencies, but not the essences, of events. Both human blindness and paradoxical talents are doubly underscored by appropriately esoteric references to two blind men: Blacklock's accuracy in describing objects is mentioned, as are Professor Sanderson's lectures on colour.[6] Then, as if to compound this correlative for the compromised position of human intuition, he extends her description through two more fittingly abstruse allusions: one to the painter Sallaert, a friend and pupil of Rubens; the other to Van Alsloot, a sixteenth-century portrait and landscape painter. Hardy, with unusual explicitness, ascribes one specific meaning to these allusions:

Communities were seen by her as from a distance; she saw them as we see the throngs which cover the canvases of Sallaert, Van Alsloot, and others of that school — vast masses of beings, jostling, zigzagging, and processioning in definite directions, but

whose features are indistinguishable by the very comprehensiveness of the view. (p. 212)

Since Mrs Yeobright's world has become narrowed to the struggles
of her immediate family, 'comprehensiveness' seems a less appropriate word than 'definitiveness'. The allusions emphasise the
ironic contradiction between what is and what ought to be; stylistically, their very obscurity, even though pedantic, serves to
achieve a complementary shade of meaning by metaphorically
reinforcing the obliqueness, engendered by human nature and
circumstance, of Mrs Yeobright's insight.

Mrs Yeobright's insights rightly lead her to fear effects, but since
she can never fully contend with causes, she inadvertently makes
wrong decisions in almost all of her crucial actions. We remember
that she forbids Thomasin's and Wildeve's banns, only to have to
apologise later; she warns Clym about Eustacia, and drives him
into her arms; she presses Clym to return to Paris, only to increase
his desire to remain on the Heath; she questions Eustacia about the
guineas and Wildeve, turning her well-meaning gesture into a new
bitterness. (Hardy included Wildeve in the conversation when he
revised the serial for the first edition, thus deliberately compound-
ing Mrs Yeobright's mistakes.) But Hardy makes it clear that the
elder woman's misdeeds are not malicious, that her failures result
either from misdirected altruism, maternal jealousy, defensible
pride, or limited vision. It is the irony that pervades the universe,
working through human vulnerability, that determines Mrs Yeobright's life, and we are intended to sympathise with her situation.
Hardy allows her the consummate ironic comment on her condition when she quotes Ecclesiastes 3:4 as she hears the bells
announce the nuptials of Eustacia and her son:

'Then it is over', she murmured. 'Well, well! and life too will be
over soon. And why should I go on scalding my face like this?
Cry about one thing in life, cry about all; one thread runs
through the whole piece. And yet we say, "a time to laugh!"'.
(p. 239)

Mrs Yeobright, then, is developed as a character who can often
foresee tragedy, but is ineffectual in preventing it, partly because
her very closeness to the scene blinds her. Hardy supplies an alternative to Mrs Yeobright's proximity to events in Diggory Venn,

easily recognised as a descendant of Gabriel Oak. Unlike his predecessor, however, and in company with Mrs Yeobright, Diggory,
by his altruistic, patently correct manipulations, ironically pro-
duces disastrous consequences. Diggory first intervenes to try to get
Eustacia to give up Wildeve, and then asks to court Thomasin,
with the ironic result that he drives Eustacia back to Wildeve. He
wins the guineas from Wildeve but mistakenly gives them all to
Thomasin, thereby setting the stage for Mrs Yeobright's tragic
misunderstanding. He plays tricks on Wildeve, ultimately leading
him to Eustacia; and he contributes to the rupture between Clym
and Eustacia by telling Clym of Mrs Yeobright's visit. Critical
opinion on Diggory Venn's purpose in the novel is characteristically varied: Evelyn Hardy sees him as representative of a bygone
era; Chew, McDowell, Weber, and Holloway all seem to agree that
Venn, as a satisfied man, is a character foil to the more tem-
pestuous Clym, Eustacia, and Wildeve.[7] But while he can be
viewed as both or either of these, he is, most importantly, Hardy's
vivid personification of his belief in the futility of any attempt to
act wisely, in the disproportion between action and consequences.
It is with an ironic jab at this universe that Hardy paints his
Samaritan a devil's red.

Thematically, then, Diggory must be free to act independently,
but involved enough so that his actions have repercussions. It is
through both plot and allusions that Hardy establishes Diggory in
his dual position as concerned agent who is yet separated enough
from the emotional conflicts to make a futile attempt to divert the
slings and arrows. In broad terms Diggory is connected with his
environment and the lives lived in it through his name, his profession, and his relationship with Thomasin. 'Diggory' is a name of
Cornish origin, appearing as early as the medieval tales of *Sir
Degarre*, but by the nineteenth century it was used chiefly for
rustics and servants.[8] 'Venn' is the southern Middle English variant
of 'fen'. Both names bind Diggory to the land, as does his job as
reddleman. While nomenclature and profession rusticate
Diggory, his love for Thomasin provides the realistic circumstance
for remaining at least on the periphery of the main action.

But, even while securing Diggory's multiple appropriateness in
the novel, Hardy allows him a structural latitude that permits him
to act as a recurrent, and inadvertently malevolent, *deus ex
machina*. Though Diggory loves Thomasin, his love is unrequited
until the 'Aftercourses' chapter. Moreover, he is free of prejudicial

blood ties to any character.[9] Furthermore, Diggory's profession requires both that he travel constantly, and that he be cursed with an eerie red colour, thus segregating him by habit and skin from the other Heath people, and giving credence to the local superstition that regards the reddleman as bogyman.

Importantly, the allusions give specific technical support to these structural patterns. Diggory is first referentially introduced through Fairway's confession that he feared the reddleman to be 'the devil'; and, in order to emphasise mysteriousness, Hardy later added to the sentence 'or the red ghost'. The allusions attached to him continue in this vein until Diggory is definitely a preternatural figure separated by circumstance and aura from the normal functions of life on Egdon Heath. In rapid succession, in three short paragraphs (p. 104), he is first called a Mephistophelian Visitant – that is to say, an outsider who injects a disturbing force into the story[10] (this reference is also a post-manuscript shoring–up of Diggory's weirdness; the manuscript reads 'somewhat spectral visitant'); next we are advised that reddle has stamped him unmistakeably, 'as with the mark of Cain'; and in the third paragraph we are told that he shares bogyman status with England's archenemy, Bonaparte.

However, once Diggory has been allusively elevated from the mundane and thus freed to work unencumbered, and once he is firmly established as the mysterious stranger of the novel, Hardy tempers his allusive spirituality and concentrates on building up credibility for Diggory in his second role as an involved agent – namely, a possible suitor for Thomasin. He is compared to the classical hero Tantalus, and defined as a man capable of looking at 'disappointment as the natural preface to all realisations' (p. 108). Next, historical heroes are used by way of analogy: he is as coldly calculating against Eustacia as was Frederick towards the beautiful Archduchess, or Napoleon refusing the terms of the beautiful Queen of Prussia (p. 114). Hardy gets double value from his references here: both of Eustacia's counterparts are beautiful women, and Hardy adroitly joins the Mephistophelian-Bonaparte-bogyman-reddleman to the suitor by using a reference to a more heroic Napoleon. Then Hardy summarises by reconfirming Diggory's dual role, for in his very next allusion to him we are off-handedly reminded that Diggory is an Ishmaelitish creature (p. 173).

Diggory is maintained in this tensional state between supernal, archetypal ministrant and realistic, patient suitor throughout most of the novel. By being thus tangential to two worlds, Venn has license in both to work his own plan and, not inadvertently, illustrate Hardy's *Weltanschauung*, while never losing his credibility or verisimilitude. Diggory would have rattled out of the story in the following way had not popular opinion intervened:

> The writer may state here that the original conception of the story did not design a marriage between Thomasin and Venn. He was to have retained his isolated and weird character to the last, and to have disappeared mysteriously from the heath, nobody knowing whither − Thomasin remaining a widow. But certain circumstances of serial publication led to a change of intent.
> Readers can therefore choose between the endings, and those with an austere artistic code can assume the more consistent conclusion to be the true one. (p. 413, Hardy's footnote)

Hardy is prepared for either ending, since Diggory is free of incapacitating tragedy even after all the other houses have fallen (see p. 391). Yet, in all probability the novel would have been better as originally intended, though one can hardly begrudge the public a note of happiness after a plethora of tragedy. But whether the reddleman be finally veneered in red or in white, the last allusions associated with him embody the taste he is to leave − a taste of sweet ironically gone sour. Diggory is compared to Ithuriel, the angel with the spear-touch of truth, when he delivers what is Eustacia's farewell note to Wildeve − a farewell that ultimately turns on everyone. And when Diggory intervenes once more in an attempt to separate Wildeve and Eustacia − again, only to achieve the opposite of what he had intended − Hardy continues his allusive justification of Diggory's tactics:

> The doubtful legitimacy of such rough coercion did not disturb the mind of Venn. It troubles few such minds in such cases, and sometimes this is not to be regretted. From the impeachment of Strafford to Farmer Lynch's short way with the scamps of Virginia there have been many triumphs of justice which are mockeries of law. (p. 292)

Narrative bias, then, demands that the reader support Diggory regardless of his means or ends. That Diggory unwittingly contributes

to the very tragedy he works so hard to avert is Hardy's bleak comment on the irony of circumstance — an assertion that is graphically outlined through Hardy's manipulation of allusions.

If the novel can be said to have an antagonist, Damon Wildeve
must fill the role. But, even more than Hardy's earlier recreants,
Damon treads a narrow path between arousing the reader's
sympathy and deserving his scorn. Much like Manston, he is a
complex man caught in his passion. Experience has left him, as it
left Boldwood, sullen and melancholy, unable to accept reality.
Yet his inability to control his desires, or to alleviate the boredom
that fans them, are seen as universal human weaknesses, and
Wildeve ultimately emerges as a victim rather than a villain.

In a letter to Arthur Hopkins, his illustrator, Hardy places
Wildeve fifth in order of importance among his characters, below
Clym, Eustacia, and Diggory, and, strangely enough, even below
Thomasin. (Thomasin's stated importance is most likely due to her
position — in the second, alternative ending of the book — as
happy survivor and Diggory's wife.) But in spite of the fact that
Wildeve was not a favourite of Hardy's, he none the less plays an
unusually important and sympathetic role, for a supposed roué.
Admittedly, Wildeve flirts with adultery, and he is often less than
kind to his wife. But, as both a technical device and as an intrinsic
villain, he often skirts his original manuscript name, 'Toogood'.
He does, after all, act honourably by marrying Thomasin; he does
make peace with Mrs Yeobright, something Eustacia never accomplishes. And, even if his motives are ambiguous, he does agree to
help Eustacia when she is desperate to escape. Moreover, as a
device, he is important as a sensuous contrast to Clym's ethereal
nature; his inherited affluence is used to mirror clearly the sudden,
pervasive poverty of Clym and Eustacia; his sensitivity to Eustacia
and her physical attractiveness to him underscore Clym's indifference (one remembers the scene, for example, where Wildeve is
described as approaching Eustacia's house with the reverential
excitement accorded to 'the birthplace of Shakespeare, the prison
of Mary Stuart, or the Chateau of Hougomont', p. 299); and
finally his undeserved inheritance is an astute ironic comment on
poetic justice. Thus Hardy comes dangerously close to making his
antagonist too good.

Hardy only partially corrects this situation by casting narrative
slurs on Wildeve, both overtly and through ironic allusions. In
widely separated references (pp. 64, 176, 237) Wildeve is compared

to Amerigo Vespucci, who 'received the honours due to those who had gone before'; he is the Satan receiving Ithuriel's touch, and he is the Rousseau of Egdon — that is to say, a petulant, gloomy, masochistic man. But even when Hardy is stylistically demeaning Wildeve, he has already tempered his criticism: the manuscript version of the Rousseau of Egdon paragraph contains an even more pointed barb through a comparison of Wildeve's limited capacity for feeling with the Swiss painter Godefrois, 'the Raffaelle of Cats'. Hardy judiciously deletes this allusion by the first edition. Moreover, the Rousseau comparison, as it finally stands, is characteristically blunted. Wildeve's flaws become standard traits of what Hardy defines as a man of sentiment: 'to be yearning for the difficult, to be weary of that offered; to care for the remote, to dislike the near' (p. 237). Wildeve is designed as the knave of the story, but he is none the less allowed to remain in that nebulous Troyan limbo as a man in 'whom no man would have seen anything to admire, and in whom no woman would have seen anything to dislike' (p. 70). Hardy fashions for him a death mask which has less repose than Eustacia's; but the 'same luminous youthfulness overspread it [his face], and the least sympathetic observer would have felt at sight of him now that he was born for a higher destiny than this' (p. 393).

Surviving Wildeve is his wife, Thomasin, the fourth member (figuratively speaking) of the novel's triangle. Although Hardy admitted a partiality for Thomasin, she is one of his few failures in feminine character development. Much like Gabriel Oak, she is representative of the bleak Hardian tenet that contentment comes only through asking little of life and willingly accepting the inevitable. Yet, she crucially lacks Gabriel's depth and range of feeling and his humanising flaws. Everything that is wrong with her is unwittingly summarised in *Belgravia's* caption to her picture appended to Book II, Chapters 1—4: 'I wish all good women were as good as I.' It is appropriate, in a humorously ironic way, that Hardy's only allusion for her is to a martyred saint, St Sebastian (p. 380); but this time the joke turns on the narrator. Insipid, unrealistically complacent, melodramatically matronly, often tiresome in her condescension, naively loyal, she is no match for either her rival or her domineering aunt. On the contrary, her relationship with her aunt is often confusing in its sudden reversals, and her attempts to keep the peace with her are unrealistically successful even in their minor degree. Moreover, Thomasin is too good to be a

credible foil to Eustacia, and it is fortunate that the Heath forms
an effective counterweight by filling the gap that Hardy's inadequate development of Thomasin leaves. He tells us that
Thomasin 'seemed to belong rightly to a madrigal — to require
viewing through rhyme and harmony' (p. 66). There is little rhyme
on Egdon, and, in spite of Thomasin's professed affinity with the
Heath, she always seems out of place there. A story patterned after
the desolation of *King Lear* affords little room for a madrigal.

Critics have occasionally noted that Hardy presents the actions
of his characters neutrally, judging them with restraint. The
allusive pattern surrounding Eustacia Vye supports this notion of
restraint, but reveals that Hardy none the less desires his readers to
feel deep sympathy for this, his most conventionally romantic
heroine, even while he himself stops short of a total commitment to
her. A forerunner of the Lawrentian woman who appreciates,
though probably does not understand, the blood consciousness,
Eustacia is a dramatic and final departure from the conventional
Amelia Sedleys of the nineteenth century novel. She first appears
in the novel as a mere dot on the landscape in a scene that is an
exercise in composition and perspective, plus iconic communication:[11]

> There the form stood, motionless as the hill beneath. Above
> the plain rose the hill, above the hill rose the barrow, and above
> the barrow rose the figure. Above the figure was nothing that
> could be mapped elsewhere than on a celestial globe.
>
> Such a perfect, delicate, and necessary finish did the figure
> give to the dark pile of hills that it seemed to be the only obvious
> justification of their outline. Without it, there was the dome
> without the lantern; with it the architectural demands of the
> mass were satisfied. The scene was strangely homogenous, in
> that the vale, the upland, the barrow, and the figure above it
> amounted only to unity. Looking at this or that member of the
> group was not observing a complete thing, but a fraction of a
> thing. (p. 41)

But if Eustacia is an organic part of the Heath, so is she eternally
unreconciled to it — and herein lies the root of her tragedy, a
tragedy that Hardy builds through his fateful handling of plot and
personality, and one that he adroitly silhouettes with manipula-
tory allusions.

Not until some forty pages after Eustacia's appearance on the Heath does the reader learn her full name, but the process of allotting her an elevated and mysterious status has already begun. Susan Nunsuch, a rustic woman 'noisily constructed', tells us that Eustacia is a woman 'strange in her ways' (p. 57). Several hints of Eustacia's strangeness occur in this early part of the novel, until she is surrounded with an aura of near-witchcraft which both separates her from the Heath people and joins her to the mysterious superstition and demonism of the Heath itself: Eustacia offers Johnny Nunsuch a crooked sixpence for his wages; his mother tries to kill the witch-Eustacia by traditional black magic rites. But Hardy is careful to avoid combining these super-natural trappings to form a definitive portrayal, and they never overstep their function as a stylistic device intended to isolate Eustacia from, and elevate her above, the rustics around her.[12] His diligence in protecting his character from the concrete demonism which would compromise her realistic womanhood is illustrated by his having deleted from the manuscript a 'from fair to foul, from foul to fair' reference. Eustacia's allusions exalt her and keep her apart, as do the occasional hints at witchcraft, but they never cut her off from the reality of the heath; her elevated position is always firmly anchored.

Eustacia is, literally, a slightly exceptional Wessex girl of nine-teen − but she is also a Greek heroine (Hardy even makes her father a former Corfu bandmaster), and the partial perpetrator of a crescendoing adult tragedy. In order to elevate Eustacia above her environment and place her in the company of the tragic heroines he so admires, Hardy surrounds her with largely classical allusions. In so doing he also flirts with a theme which he was to explore more fully in his later novels − namely, the feasibility and practicability of following an Arnoldian Hellenism.[13] Initiating the sequence which will bridge the seemingly irreconcilable dicho-tomy between Wessex earthling and Greek goddess are contiguous references to Sappho and Mrs Siddons, one of Britain's great tragediennes − a mixture of timeless classic and still-familiar modern. (In the manuscript Hardy used Marie Antoinette and Lord Byron, but later altered his choice, thus strengthening his pattern.) Then, in his famous 'Queen of Night' chapter, Hardy builds her a solid allusive pedestal, for, in direct contrast to the paucity of references in Thomasin's case, Eustacia receives over thirty-three allusions in a scant twenty pages, and several of these,

when viewed in the context of their sources, acquire a double
importance as they foreshadow the events of the plot. The 'raw
material of a divinity', she would have done well on Olympus,
handling the 'distaff, spindle and shears' of Clotho, Lachesis, and
Atropos (the Fates). Her presence brings 'memories of such things
as Bourbon roses, rubies and tropical midnights'; her mood recalls
'lotus-eaters and the march in *Athalie*'. Racine is followed by
Artemis, Athena, and Hera, as Eustacia is linked with the moon
goddess and her supposed influence on erotic and organic life, the
goddess of wisdom and war (who, adumbratively here, is also the
virgin goddess, despising love and marriage), and the sister and
wife of Zeus, noted for her jealousy and factiousness (p. 94). (It is
worth noting that Aphrodite, a seemingly obvious comparison
here, is omitted,[14] thereby casting a shadow over Eustacia's reputed
sexuality, a shadow that only strengthens the deliberate ambiguity
of her moral limits when she is drowned in the weir.) Then, in the
next paragraph, we are informed of her 'true Tartarean dignity',
– ironically, the same dignity which was attributed earlier to the
Heath she so despises. In the manuscript this passage is preceded by
an awkward sentence which alludes to 'Demeter's daughter'; such a
reference to Persephone, who, though goddess of the underworld,
is also the goddess of fertility, could be misleading, and Hardy later
excised it. He was also careful to cut from the next paragraph some
other tonally incongruous, and probably facetious, allusions. He
struck out a sentence reading

> When she saw less sophisticated maidens with their decorations
> of lavender and boy's love she laughed and went on; unwittingly
> chiming in with Plautus, Martial, and Ben Jonson and others in
> holding that, though rather than smell sour a woman's robe
> should smell sweet better even than smelling sweet is that it
> should not smell at all. (ms. 75, Wessex 77)

Nor is Hardy content merely to affirm her dignity, but rhetorically
traces its source to both the classical and the natural world:

> Where did her dignity come from? By a latent vein from
> Alcinous' line, her father hailing from Phaeacia's isle? – or
> from Fitzalan and De Vere, her maternal grandfather having
> had a cousin in the peerage? Perhaps it was the gift of Heaven –
> a happy convergence of natural laws. (pp. 95–6)

Here Hardy verges desperately near farcical exaggeration (J. I. M. Stewart calls it 'uncomfortable falsity'[15]), but he saves his very deliberate allusive elevation — the note on Alcinous is an intensifying post-manuscript addition — by following it with a sustaining tone of narrative seriousness: 'Among other things opportunity had of late years been denied her of learning to be undignified, for she lived lonely. Isolation on a heath renders vulgarity well-nigh impossible' (p. 96). Then comes a conclusive, summarising comment: 'The only way to look queenly without realms or hearts to queen it over is to look as if you had lost them; and Eustacia did that to a triumph' (p. 96).

Such unornamented narrative support maintains the high tone necessary to carry the formidable allusive structure, and Eustacia's characterisation is sophisticated rather than overwhelmed when Hardy uses more historical, and — in this single series, on the borderline between narrative judgment and explanation of his character's predilections — Biblical references to define her personality further:

> Her high gods were William the Conqueror, Strafford, and Napoleon Bonaparte, as they had appeared in the Lady's History used at the establishment in which she was educated. Had she been a mother she would have christened her boys such names as Saul or Sisera in preference to Jacob or David, neither of whom she admired. At school she had used to side with the Philistines in several battles, and had wondered if Pontius Pilate were as handsome as he was frank and fair. (p. 97)

Once again adjustments in the text show Hardy reaffirming his determination to elevate Eustacia and emphasise her rebellious, anti-Hebraic spirit, for originally he merely stated that 'her chief priest was Byron, her antichrist a well-meaning polemical preacher at Crestmouth, of the name of Slatters' (ms. 78).

The classical, historical, and literary catalogue continues even until the end of the chapter ('In heaven she will probably sit between the Héloises and the Cleopatras') and beyond: when Diggory confronts her with her *femme fatale* position she suffers the mortification of Candaules' wife (p. 117); she is compared to Zenobia, the celebrated princess of Palmyra; even her dreams are described through a pastiche of allusions — Nebuchadnezzar, Cretan labyrinth, Queen Scheherazade, and that Immortal

Dreamer, 'the Swaffham tinker', John Bunyan (p. 142). And the list goes on, until, through sheer accumulation of ennobling allusions, Eustacia's rustic situation is transformed into a universal one — but not without the touch of Hardian irony, for even as the allusions elevate they only serve to emphasise, through the dichotomy between the rustic and the classic, through the disparity between Rainbarrow and Egypt, the futility of Eustacia's ambition.

As Eustacia is narratively separated from the heath and ennobled through classical, secular allusions, she is concurrently, through her own allusive taste for strictly Biblical images, made to reveal her rustic ties and symbolically exhibit her fatal flaw — namely, her unwillingness to follow what Arnold calls the 'uppermost idea of Hellenism', 'to see things as they really are'. She is a Cleopatra, who, like her prototype, is an expert at varying her moods to captivate the man she wants;[16] but Eustacia herself sarcastically resorts to Scripture to describe this role (p. 91): 'I merely lit that fire because I was dull, and thought I would get a little excitement by calling you up and triumphing over you as the Witch of Endor called up Samuel' (1 Samuel 28:7). Or she responds to Clym's optimism about being fairly well off, even though he cuts furze, with a scathing comparison to the happiness of 'slaves, and the Israelites in Egypt, and such people!' (p. 273). And we learn much of what we need to know about Eustacia's marital situation when she compares Clym to the Apostle Paul. Such asexual spirituality cannot satisfy the passionate Eustacia, and she bluntly confesses to Wildeve, 'Yes; but the worst of it is that though Paul was excellent as a man in the Bible he would hardly have done in real life' (p. 334).

This distinction between narrative secular images (which project Eustacia above the Heath and colour her with exoticism) and her own Biblical images (which underscore her strong ties to its rustic traditions) exists in the novel for as long as Eustacia is able to continue, with some hope, her struggle against her situation. Only when — in deep sorrow and, as Wildeve points out, circumstantial guilt — she finally gives in to the universal forces arrayed against her does the allusive suspension shift conclusively. The classical allusions, with their hint of freedom and superiority, give way as the narrator turns to the rigidity of the Bible to define and judge the extent of Eustacia's responsibility for Mrs Yeobright's death: Clym's suffering becomes 'as dreadful to her as the trial scene was to Judas Iscariot' (p. 329) — another sinner whose guilt is compromised by the role fate seems to have in store for him. And, on the night Eustacia makes her decision to flee — ironically, to her death — Hardy sets the scene for the sympathetic Aristotelian sort of pity he wants her to arouse by narratively calling up the great disasters of the Bible: the last plague of Egypt, the destruction of Senna-cherib's host, the agony in Gethsemane (p. 371).[17]

In this final scene with Eustacia Hardy is an accomplished master of symbolic and allusive structure. After allusively priming the reader for catastrophe, Hardy halts the time surge of his narrative long enough to pull together stylistically the various strands of the novel. Eustacia reaches Rainbarrow, the summit of her world, and stops to think. The combined chaos of her mind and the weather metaphorically unites her with her macrocosmic surroundings, while the unifying rain, symbolically dripping 'from her umbrella to her mantle, from her mantle to the heather, from the heather to the earth', makes the connection concrete. In this setting she surveys the dimensions of her dilemma: to stay on Egdon now would mean unbearable misery, yet she has no money for an escape; 'to ask Wildeve for pecuniary aid without allowing him to accompany her was impossible to a woman with a shadow of pride left in her: to fly as his mistress — and she knew that he loved her — was of the nature of humiliation' (p. 371).

Finding every alternative open to her despicable, Eustacia reaches the nadir of her despair, with the very 'wings of her soul . . . broken by the cruel obstructiveness of all about her'. All her dreams now piercing nightmares, Eustacia is no longer Queen of Night, Queen of Love, as she cries out, in the set speech of high tragedy, against a Heaven which tortures her, though she has done no harm to Heaven at all. Yet even in her wretchedness she is allowed — as few of Hardy's characters are — a final rebellion, and we are reminded, by previously used allusions to her heroes Saul and Napoleon, of the unbroken Queen.[18] Then Eustacia voices the Hardian view of human possibility: 'I was capable of much; but I have been injured and blighted and crushed by things beyond my control!' (p. 372). However, Eustacia is shaking her fist at an immovable force. She does not have the idealistic determination and almost unnatural patience of the Gabriel Oaks of Hardy's canon, but rather is controlled by a passion for extremes — a passion that Hardy seems to have both feared and admired, even while giving her a zest for existence that makes for the tragedy of her death. Elevated by the narrative and by her personal aspirations

into the Hellenic world of excitement and curiosity, but thematically and tonally fettered by circumstance and what De Laura has
defined as a rather clear discomfort on Hardy's part at her restless-
ness, Eustacia, as a character, is never clearly at home in either
world. Hardy stylistically underscores the duality by using secular
images to magnify her, Biblical images to keep the bleaker truth of
her position clearly before us and concomitantly to underline the
ambiguity of her responsibility. The two patterns merge in a scene
of futile revolt, and Eustacia goes on to die in transit, either by an
act of wilful defiance or, as J. I. M. Stewart postulates as a more
credible possibility, through the sheer accident of blind fate[19] − a
fate which indirectly supports a Hebraistic devotion to duty by
thwarting Eustacia's illicit escape. In this novel Hardy lets us write
our own ending to Eustacia's predicament; by the time he is
writing *Tess*, the President of the Immortals is in control.

One of Hardy's major accomplishments in *The Return of the
Native* is that here he has created two well-matched protagonists,
figures whose bizarre incongruities themselves provide a unifying
principle for the entire book, and whose differences allow Hardy to
analyse a broad range of human personality, while also generalis-
ing about man's chances in the universe. Clym Yeobright is an
amalgam of several of Hardy's earlier characters, having Henry
Knight's intelligence, Gabriel Oak's passivity, and Boldwood's
deterioration, while bringing to the mixture his own disillusioning
experiences and blind idealism. As such, Clym, in the role of
Eustacia's husband, is not only her animus in a relationship
emblematic of the potential disaster awaiting any two irresistibly
attracted people who are polar in mind and temperament, but
also represents Hardy's theory of the futility of trying to construct a
brave new world along the lines of Arnoldian Hellenism.
Moreover, whereas Hardy is calculatedly bi-polar in his allusive
depiction of Eustacia, in Clym's portrayal he heavily weights the
allusive scales to unbalance subtly what is otherwise, as Leonard
Deen and Robert Schweik have both agreed, a tonally ambiguous
stance on Clym's final role in the novel.[20]

That Clym is in important ways the antithesis of his future wife
is made immediately clear in direct narrative statement and the
continuation of the Biblical motif: 'Take all the varying hates felt
by Eustacia Vye toward the heath, and translate them into loves,
and you have the heart of Clym. He gazed upon the wide prospect
as he walked, and was glad' (p. 197). We have been prepared for

Clym's entrance by the rustic chorus, from whom we have already learned most of what we are ever to know of Clym's days in the French capital as a manager for a diamond merchant.[21] The rustics ensure an heroic entrance for Clym by speaking of his past reputation for potential greatness, a myth which his absence has kept alive. Retrospectively we are to realise that Clym has reached his zenith and has returned to the Heath to act out his decline. Yet, even at his entrance, what we already know of Eustacia's ambition and irresistible charm indicates that the inevitable mutual 'Fascination' can only be destructive. Within the structure of the plot the irony of circumstance is used to bring Clym to Eustacia, while the more inclusive irony of fate works to bring him down. Extrinsically, Hardy uses ironic allusions as a technical reflector of this fate. Undermining as they ostensibly elevate, they punctuate the unalterable, paradoxical course of his hero, while concomitantly enlarging Clym's position into universal significance.

Clym is first sighted by Eustacia, and physically described by the narrator, in a brilliantly sketched scene. He is spotlighted in an 'area of two feet in Rembrandt's intensest manner' (pp. 161–2); then the focus is immediately narrowed to his face. It is excellently shaped, but illustrates the age of 'Jared, Mahalaleel, and the rest of the antediluvians', for thought has become an eroding parasite which is eating away at him. Hardy cynically reminds us that Clym's thought is a disease — foreshadowing the destruction that is to come upon him and the women he loves partially because of his malady.

As in his initial pictorial treatment of Eustacia, Hardy follows his introductory canvas of Clym with a chapter–length mural. But in contrast to Eustacia, who must be elevated above her station on the Heath, Clym, the sophisticated wanderer, must be reduced and realistically placed in his. The allusive erosion begins with the chapter title itself, as Hardy chooses a line from Edward Dyer, 'My Mind to me a Kingdom is.' Ironically, Clym's mind, in a novel where thought is a disease, will be his only kingdom, one which is either to exclude or to destroy all others, and the allusion implies one of the novel's themes: Clym's academic hopes to instil 'culture' into the heathmen will always be at odds with the practical problems he will face when he attempts to educate them. The irony introduced by the title continues throughout the chapter as Clym and his scheme are allusively undermined at every turn. Ironically drawing his reference from the classics, Hardy says that some future Pheidias will be the proper sculptor for Clym's features, for his is the face of the 'dour modern type', where physically beautiful men are an anachronism – anachronistic, says Hardy through a negative echo of the aesthetic Hellenism of Pater, because thought and beauty are not complementary, but rather mutually destructive. 'Disillusive centuries [have] permanently replaced the Hellenic idea of life', the Greeks are immature, and a zest for existence is impossible to maintain – these are the contentions used to introduce a character who has come to the Heath to teach a vague culture-scheme which shows the influence of Hardy's reading of Arnold's *Culture and Anarchy*.[22] Moreover, as his features are placed in perspective, so are his talents assessed: in an allusion revealingly added above the line in the manuscript Hardy states, '"It is bad when your fame outruns your means", said the Spanish Jesuit Gracian'; and Clym's local fame is compared to Homer's – an 'accident of his situation'. His unwise choice of occupation – here as a diamond merchant but also, prophetically, as a teacher – is placed in the same stream of inverse fate that made Keats a surgeon, Clive a writing clerk, Gay a linen-draper.

Theoretically, Clym's intentions are good, his goal admirable. And Hardy allusively tempers his approach by soliciting a sympathetic understanding of Clym's ambitions, saying that Clym has at least escaped the well-proportioned mind that would condemn him, like the painter West, the preacher Tomline, and the poet Rodgers, to mediocrity. Clym, however, is sentenced to failure by personal, public, and universal flaws. He is doomed by his idealistic, egotistic temperament; by the fact that 'the rural world was not ripe for him', since his sceptical audience is like the ancient Chaldeans, the wise men and astrologers of Daniel's time who were unalterably convinced of the rightness of their ideas (p. 197); and finally by an Indifferent Fate. An anonymous rustic supplies the definitive judgment which the allusions mark as forebodingly correct: '"'Tis good-hearted of the young man", said another. "But, for my part, I think he had better mind his business"' (p. 195).

The ironic cruelty of circumstance counters Clym almost from the day he begins to prepare himself for his missionary activities: he meets Eustacia, who is both irresistible to him as a man and a cross for him as a preacher. Clym moves into the relationship with mild intellectual doubt, Eustacia with blind emotion. Yet the reader, unlike the characters, gets the Sophoclean hint that the partnership is calamitous. Clym meditates on Eustacia's fondness for Paris in a paragraph (p. 223) which also allusively recalls her emotional separation from the Heath; she is his 'Olympian girl'. We are then warned that his love is as chaste 'as that of Petrarch for his Laura', a foreshadowing of one of the conflicts of temperament that will destroy the relationship.

Clym, then, is circumstantially handicapped by a marriage to a woman whose passions and ambitions he does not understand, and also by his unawareness of his own lack of comprehension. His inability to relate to the less mental, more passionate Eustacia is, moreover, symptomatic of his intellectual blindness — a blindness Hardy makes symbolically explicit by having Clym lose his eyesight while studying. Robert Schweik notes that Hardy has introduced Clym as a potential Carlylean hero who does see through the social shams to the human condition beneath.[23] But Clym is also flawed in that he is a victim of the fantasies of his idealism, and is thus blind to the basic human passions which govern the intended objects of his teaching: the heathmen, Eustacia, his mother, and even the simple Thomasin. Individuals are blurred into a class in Clym's scheme to improve the peasants' lot, and one is forced to agree with D. H. Lawrence's observation of a deep but very subtle cowardice in Clym's altruism.[24] He wants to improve mankind rather than discover the very quick of his being, or of Eustacia's, and never grasps the practical reality that he must not only expand his academic knowledge, but also, as Lawrence contends, 'undertake his own soul', must explore the limits of his own insight and compassion, before he can teach others. Thus we see a man who, while preparing himself to elevate humanity and thereby relieve human ignorance and suffering, unwittingly heaps indignation upon those whom he is supposed to know and love best. Lured into insensitivity by his own dreams, he refuses to compromise with his mother's ambitions for him until driven to do so by the practical necessities involved in marrying Eustacia; he fails to comprehend the depth of Eustacia's disappointment and loneliness; he leads both Eustacia and his mother into even deeper disillusionment by taking up furze—cutting, a trade onerous to them, and compounds their despair by wearing furze—cutters' garb and sleeping on the floor.[25]

Consequently, in spite of his noble plans, his marriage, his position, and his temperament all work against Clym and his project. The allusions connected with him during his decline add dimension and acceleration to his fall, giving an emphasis first to the implication that Clym's Hellenic idealism is as doomed as Eustacia's romanticism, and secondly to Hardy's tenet, worked out in so many of his novels, that there is no correspondence between man's aspirations and his ability to fulfil them. The real always contradicts the ideal; the allusions hammer the point home. Clym asserts to Eustacia that he can rebel 'in high Promethean fashion, against the gods and fate as well as [she]' (p. 277). His past, present, and future give the lie to his brag, while the reader has already been allusively indoctrinated to associate the classical gods only with Eustacia. Clym has been compared to the too ascetic St Paul; but, with an air of self-pitying martyrdom, he sees himself akin to St Lazarus, though his tone and situation reduce him to Lazarus the crippled beggar, not Lazarus the saint (p. 279).

The erosion of Clym by the ironic twist of allusion continues, easing him into the desolation of the dénouement. Throughout the novel Clym has only perpetuated his limited state of enlightenment enhanced by his reformer's ego. Hardian fate mercilessly bows him down and he must steadily reduce his aims. His situation mocks the rhetorical allusive question proposed by the title of the chapter dealing with his death-in-life state after Mrs Yeobright's death. The title asks Job's question (3:20), 'Wherefore is Light given to him that is in Misery?' and the reader mentally finishes the verse: 'and life unto the bitter in soul'.[26] Only the universe can answer the plea, and the response is the same one that Eustacia received.

The novel draws to a close after Eustacia, Wildeve, and Mrs Yeobright have all died, Thomasin and Venn (in the second ending) have too conveniently married, and Clym is at last preaching on the Heath. Like *Far From the Madding Crowd*, the novel runs full circle, only this time it is Clym who is standing on the same hill where Eustacia was introduced, and, broken by the world's dark turns, a Clym ironically antithetical in every way to the strong, classic Eustacia of Chapter Seven. (Even the weather is now derisively fair.) Once again, but with greater intensity, the allusions are devastatingly ironic when juxtaposed with Clym's fate. Half-blind, searching out the riddle of his mother's death and then believing himself responsible, Clym enters the final scene as an overt parallel to the Oedipus of a reference neatly attached to him (p. 342). But Clym is a defective Oedipus, for his blindness remains spiritual as well as physical.[27] With the Oedipus analogy as background, the narrator establishes Clym as a Christ figure by calling his lectures 'Sermons on the Mount' and speaking of him as not quite thirty-three, but this is immediately after we have been reminded of Clym's ego as he wonders if he is missed at Thomasin's wedding, and inquires if the toasting is to him. (Here Hardy revised to emphasise the point: the manuscript reads 'less than thirty'.[28] Finally, Clym's closing sermon is based on 1 Kings 2:19–20, and clearly alludes to his own relationship with his mother. Hardy quotes the verse:

> And the king rose up to meet her, and bowed himself unto her, and sat down to his throne, and caused a seat to be set for the king's mother; and she sat on his right hand. Then she said, I desire one small petition of thee; I pray thee say me not nay. And the king said unto her, Ask on, my mother: for I will not say thee nay. (pp. 422–3)[29]

When put in context, the king, like Clym, does deny his mother's request. But the king is the wise Solomon, and Clym's self-aggrandisement is obvious. The narrator further underscores Clym's position by following the reference immediately with the admonition that Clym, once hoping to be a radical, idealistic force for change, is now an itinerant preacher of the eleventh commandment and other 'morally unimpeachable subjects' (p. 423). Overtly Clym's position here can be viewed as ambiguous (both Leonard Deen and David De Laura see it so). But Hardy is not so completely ambivalent, for as the action thus closes we have a final, allusively ironic vision of Clym as an Oedipus without insight, a Christ without humility, and a Solomon without wisdom. Even his name mocks him: 'Clym', short for 'Clement', meaning modest and merciful; 'Yeo', the archaic form of 'young'; and finally 'bright'. Divorced from the novel, Oedipus, Christ, and Solomon tell us what ought to be; placed in Hardy's world, they supply the tragically paradoxical touchstone for what is. The misplaced idealism of Clym, exaggerated by an Indifferent Fate, has made him cause rather than mitigate suffering. Hardy does not support Clym's devotion to a cultural aesthetic which is inattentive to the less intellectual human passions, but uses circumstance and allusion to shape and forecast Clym's defeat.

Thus, unalterable temperament, the laws of nature, restrictive social codes, and blind chance have worked their way with the natives. Every opportunity for escape is closed off; there is no

Lawrentian rainbow on Egdon Heath. None the less, says Hardy, the rebellion fostered by the human spirit compels men to continue their struggling search to answer the riddle of the labyrinth, and to grasp every moment of happiness they chance to encounter. But the fight is for ever a futile one on the microcosmic Heath, just as the ironic melancholy of the epigraph both forewarns and summarises:

> To sorrow
> I bade good morrow,
> And thought to leave her far away behind;
> But cheerly, cheerly,
> She loves me dearly;
> She is so constant to me and so kind.
> I would deceive her,
> And so leave her
> But ah! she is so constant and so kind,

Keats, *Endymion*, v, 173 ff.

6 Aftercourses: *Tess of the d'Urbervilles* and *Jude the Obscure*

Hardy came of artistic age with *The Return of the Native*, and by this sixth novel had thoroughly learned the technique of allusion. But a study of Hardy would seem incomplete without some investigation of the final results of the long process of stylistic honing, without a look at his two final great novels, *Tess of the d'Urbervilles* and *Jude the Obscure*.[1] By *The Return*, most key character traits were in place, and he continually intensified them: Eustacia's sexuality becomes Tess's passion; Thomasin's virginity, Sue's frigidity; Wildeve's propositions, Alec's rape; Clym's asexuality, Angel's devastating priggishness; and Jude's dual nature has remnants of both Wildeve and Clym. Technique still complements content, as Hardy allusively elevates his prose, dignifies his plots, and undermines his characters.

The publication history of *Tess* is familiar enough: it first appeared in serial form in the *Graphic* in twenty-four weekly instalments from 4 July to 26 December 1891. The manuscript had already been rejected by two publishers as unfit for family consumption, and, as Hardy tells us in Florence Hardy's *Life*, he therefore had to bowdlerise the novel before submitting it to the *Graphic*. He carried out this task with 'cynical amusement', 'the modified passages having been written in coloured ink, that the original might be easily restored'. Two excluded passages were then printed separately: 'The Midnight Baptism' in the *Fortnightly Review* of May 1891 and 'Saturday Night in Arcady' in the *National Observer* of 14 November 1891. The deleted passages were restored for the English first edition, published by Osgood, McIlvaine and Company in November 1891. The next distinctive versions are the first one-volume edition of 1892 and the Osgood Wessex edition in 1895. The last significant text is the Macmillan

Wessex Edition of 1912. However, even with bowlderisation, this seemingly direct line of transmission belies a complex history of revision, starting with the manuscript, which itself has five different layers. J. T. Laird, in his fine study, has thoroughly explored all of these changes and proves that, as with *The Return of the Native*, the evolution of *Tess* was gradual and painstaking.[2] In the course of his revising, Hardy progressively refined his concept of Tess as a pure woman, emphasising her innocence in the eyes of nature and transforming the seduction into near-rape. As he purified Tess, he correspondingly debased Alec and Angel. Alec grows from a figure of melodrama into an important symbolic character; Angel's asexuality and cruelty are intensified. Laird also notes in passing that the patterns of Biblical, and especially classical, allusion were well-developed in the *Ur*-version. My own comparison of the manuscript with the Wessex Edition confirms this fact, though it also reveals that as Hardy's concept of character evolved, he did indeed change his allusions with deliberate, even fastidious, care.[3]

Hardy's public problems with *Tess* have become a familiar metaphor for the Grundian pressures which Victorian novelists faced and feared. Hardy later called its publication the 'beginning of the end of his career as a novelist',[4] rhetorically asking himself why he should endure such ill-deserved abuse as, for example, the rages of Mowbray Morris (as editor of *Macmillan's Magazine* he had already rejected the manuscript) who, when writing for the *Quarterly Review* (April 1892) called the novel a 'clumsy sordid tale of boorish brutality and lust'. Many influential critics did praise the book, however. The *Athenaeum* of 9 January 1892 called it 'not only good, but great' and its judgment was supported by the fact that during the next three years *Tess* was translated into French, German, Russian, Italian, and Dutch.[5] None the less, those morally outraged by the book initially made a deafening noise, aiming their din first at the very title—page.

Hardy tells us that his last act before returning the proofs to the publisher was to redraft the title—page, and add the subtitle 'A Pure Woman', together with the quotation from *Two Gentlemen of Verona* (I. ii. 110—11; see below). Earlier, the novel had a working title of 'Too Late, Beloved' (or 'Too Late Beloved'), a line perhaps drawn from Shelley's 'Epipsychidion'. Hardy gave no reason for his change of mind, but if the allusion is to Shelley's great celebration of the perfection of spiritual love, a hymn to the seraph-like Emily, it can only be viewed as a bitterly ironic fore-shadowing of Angel's idealisation of Tess. One other possible source is Browning's 'Too Late', a poem Hardy knew well enough to quote at a dinner party. This poem is also relevant to the plot, especially if one identifies Angel with the narrator, who prophetic-ally muses, 'I ought to have done more: once my speech / And once your answer, and there, the end, / And Edith was henceforth out of reach.' Given either source, the title does adumbrate what Roy Morrell sees as a major theme: postponement. Angel's not dancing with Tess at their first meeting; Tess's delay in leaving Trantridge as soon as she suspects Alec; Angel's negligence in not seeing Tess before he leaves for Brazil; his tragically deferred return — all con-tribute to the dénouement.[6]

Thematic considerations apart, however, Hardy's change of title was fortunate, for both sources in context divert the emphasis — either from Tess to Angel or from Tess to theme. Moreover, Hardy's addition of the present Shakespearean epigraph, '. . . Poor wounded name! My bosom as a bed / Shall lodge thee', appropriately complements Tess's name, which precedes it, as well as comments on the root of much of her trouble — the d'Urberville name. And if the understood speaker is Angel, so, too, is the irony maintained, for Tess's bed is surely a hard one. Thus, with a deft stroke, Hardy's epigraph unites Tess, Alec, and Angel with ironic portent.

This initial quotation is Hardy's only non-contextual allusion. Departing from his earlier practice, he does not use adumbrative headnotes or chapter titles. He does, however, use allusions internally, as in previous novels, to foreshadow action, and, with scathing irony, to heighten a scene. Because of the emphasis on character rather than on action, the allusions used in this way are sparse. In contrast to the plethora in *Desperate Remedies*, only three references alert our expectations here. First Tess describes Alec as being 'dust and ashes' to her, echoing Job's repentence and anticipating Alec's. Later, when Tess is dressing for her wed-ding, lines from a ballad, 'The Boy and the Mantle' (Childe No. 29) spring to her mind: 'That never would become that wife / That had once done amiss.' In the ballad a boy brings a mantle to Arthur's court, saying that it will only fit a woman who had in no way misbehaved towards a husband or lover. Queen Guinevere fails the test. Directly referring to the text of the ballad, Tess wonders if her robe will 'betray her by changing colour as her robe had betrayed Queen Guinevere'. She passes the first test, but her robe is to change — into the pale cashmere one Angel finds her wearing when he returns. Third, where the narrator again reminds the reader of his technique, Tess, immediately after her marriage, fears her idolatry of Angel to be 'ill-omened. She was conscious of the notion expressed by Friar Laurence: "These violent delights have violent ends"' (p. 256). The reference to *Romeo and Juliet* (II. vi. 9) is of course prophetic.

Hardy is equally adroit, and much more direct, when he uses allusions to intensify the situation at hand. Three times he turns the knife. First come the two condemnatory messages of the sign-painter Tess encounters immediately after leaving Alec and Trantridge: 'THY, DAMNATION, SLUMBERETH NOT. 2 Pet. ii. 3.' (Hardy changed the original, too blatant line in the manuscript: 'THE WAGES, OF SIN, IS DEATH') and 'THOU, SHALT, NOT, COMMIT', which he follows with the ironic reminder that Mr Clare is going to preach a charity-day sermon on these texts (pp. 114–15). Later, after Angel has returned to bid his parents goodbye before leaving Tess for Brazil, Mr Clare reads a passage from the thirty-first chapter of Proverbs; Mrs Clare reminds the household that this is King Lemuel's praise of a virtuous wife, and applies the words to the absent Tess. She then compares Tess to the Virgin Mary, and assures Angel that Tess, 'since she is pure and chaste' (the manuscript reads 'good' for 'pure and chaste'), 'would have been refined enough for her' (pp. 307–8). The irony is not lost on Angel, and a page later Hardy reminds the reader:

> No prophet had told him, and he was not prophet enough to tell himself, that essentially this young wife of his was as deserving of the praise of King Lemuel as any other woman endowed with the same dislike of evil, her moral value having to be reckoned not by achievement but by tendency. (p. 309)

On the third occasion Tess is at her lowest: it is the last night she is to spend in her family cottage before she and her family are evicted. She asks the children to sing, and they respond with a hymn entitled 'Joyful', which promises life hereafter: 'Here we suffer grief and pain, / Here we meet to part again; / In Heaven we shall part no more' (p. 406). The song rings derisively in Tess's mind as the narrator hammers the scene into the reader's consciousness with another allusion that Hardy changed after the manuscript stage to ensure that his bitterness would be obvious. He tells us that for Tess 'there was ghastly satire in the poet's lines "Not in utter nakedness / But trailing clouds of glory do we come."' The original reference was also from Wordsworth's 'Ode', but read, 'Thou little Child, yet glorious in the night / Of heaven-born freedom on thy being's height.'

Particular scenes, then, are clearly fixed in the reader's consciousness by their allusive support. More generally, setting also is enhanced by allusions, though in a way quite different from Hardy's practice in *The Return of the Native*. In that novel the Heath has been elevated into a major character, and 'place' is a constant protagonist. In *Tess* place is also important, but primarily as a background for Tess's struggle. The allusions ornamenting setting perform the usual function of intensification, and of making Hardy's rural world more familiar to his urban audience. However, they also add a new dimension to Hardy's novel, for, especially in the first half, they comment ironically on Tess's position. That Flintcomb Ash is an earthly hell is obvious; we are told that a Land of Promise, when seen from a distance, becomes an Egypt at a close view, and the master of the hellish machine Tess must operate looks 'like a creature from Tophet' who serves a 'Plutonic master' (p. 373). (This last allusion was added after the manuscript stage to heighten the drama of the scene. The manuscript reads 'metallic master'.)

Other settings — the Vale and, particularly, Froom Valley — ostensibly offer contrasts to this barrenness. But a closer look at the allusions used with the settings warn of Tess's ultimate fate, no matter where she is. The Vale of Blackmore, for example, was known in former times 'as the Forest of the White Hart, from a curious legend of King Henry III's reign, in which the killing by a certain Thomas de la Lynd of a beautiful white hart which the king had run down and spared, was made the occasion of a heavy fine' (p. 40). Philip Griffith has written perceptively on this allusion, noting that the legend foreshadows Tess's fate. She is the White Hart of Blackmore Vale; Alec pays a heavy fine.[7] Immediately following, and describing the scene while preparing for Tess's entry into the novel, is another proleptic allusion. The occasion is the local 'Cerealia', a festival held in April (here T. S. Eliot's, not Chaucer's) to honour the Roman goddess of grain, Ceres, the Greek Demeter. The educated reader's sense of foreboding is

stimulated by knowing that her worship involved both fertility
rituals and rites for the dead. Prophetically, Tess is dressed in
white and is a member of her votive sisterhood on this very day,
when Angel first sees her yet does not pursue his interest. (In
Froom Valley, Angel will naively compare the deflowered Tess to
the virgin Demeter, allusively resurrecting the earlier scene — now
bitterly ironic, in view of the opportunity missed.) Later, in
another dance scene, the allusions serve an identical function. On
the night of Tess's seduction, she attends a bacchanalian market-
day dance where the dancers are described as 'a multiplicity of
Pans whirling a multiplicity of Syrinxes; Lotis attempting to elude
Priapus, always failing' (p. 96). The shift from plural to singular
evokes Tess's situation. The notable change of the allusion makes
it deliberately applicable: in the legend Lotis escapes priapic lust
by her metamorphosis into a tree.[8] Tess does not get away from
Alec, for the benign dust of the dance floor becomes the con-
spiratory fog of the Chase.

Almost three years later Tess leaves home for the second time,
determined to rally her spirits in the lush Froom Valley, so different both from the darkness of the Chase and from the sterility of
Flintcomb Ash which is to come. But again the allusions describing this setting cryptically warn the reader that, in spite of appearances, location makes no difference. When Tess first enters Froom
Valley, the narrator says the Froom water was 'clear as the pure
River of Life shown to the Evangelist' — a reference drawn from
Revelations 22:1, where John has been carried by an angel to a
high mountain to see the new Jerusalem. Tess, having yet to meet
her Angel, thinks she is seeing a new Jerusalem, a place where,
Revelations tells us, grows the tree of life, whose leaves heal — a
place where 'there shall be no more curse'. The cruel illusion in
this symbolically promised optimism is enforced by the next allusive setting, the garden in which Tess meets Angel, a place Hardy
portrays as Milton's world after the curse: 'damp', 'rank with juicy
grass', 'offensive smells', 'slug slime', 'sticky blights', 'madder
stains' (pp. 161–2). The only other allusion attached to Froom is
similarly weighted. What is supposed to be merely warm and
fertile is really a land of 'Ethiopic scorchings', of 'Thermodorean
heat' that 'seemed an effort on the part of Nature to match the
state of hearts at Talbothay's dairy' (p. 189). The reference evokes
the passions rampant in the eleventh month of the French Revolu-
tionary calendar, when the Reign of Terror ended with the fall of

Robespierre. Much later, when Tess and Angel have separated and Tess is about to arrive at Flintcomb Ash, Hardy uses still another allusion to underscore the hopelessness of her search for happiness. The narrator notes, 'she reached the irregular chalk table-land or plateau, bosomed with semi-globular tumuli — as if Cybele the Many-breasted were supinely extended there —' (p. 326). (The manuscript merely reads, 'pimpled with prehistoric tumuli'.) Hardy added this reference to the Phrygian goddess of the earth's fertility, who was worshipped with orgiastic rites, to fortify the irony of the rejected Tess's position. Even the world around her seems derisive — and she goes from here to Flintcomb Ash, where 'she was doomed to come' (p. 327). The goddess of the earth's fertility has not travelled to this place of 'myriads of loose white flints in bulbous, cusped, and phallic shapes. The upper half of each turnip had been eaten off by the live-stock' (p. 331), and Tess must grub for the rest.

Tess escapes from this hell, only to enter several others, while the allusions attached to the settings continue to suggest the erosion of her situation. Now with Alec, Tess is in Sandbourne, where Angel comes to find her. It is a fashionable, somewhat remote watering place, the narrator tells us, 'yet the exotic had grown there, suddenly as the prophet's gourd' (p. 426). The reference is to Jonah 4:6–7, and, when placed in context, it is ironic and foreboding: the gourd tree has sprung up to shelter Jonah and 'to deliver him from his grief' — but the next day a worm destroys the gourd. Tess's respite is equally temporary. When she has killed Alec and believes herself at last inseparable from Angel as they make their escape, she and Angel rest in Bramshurst Court, entering a room with 'an enormous four-posted bedstead, along the head of which were carved running figures, apparently Atalanta's race' (p. 440). They spend their 'honeymoon' in this bed, under the eye of a woman who had a premonition against marriage; failure for unsuccessful suitors meant death. And the final allusion attached to setting is an equally caustic gloss: Angel's name for Stonehenge is 'Temple of the Winds' (the deleted manuscript line reads 'hall of Pandemonium'), a reference to a building of the fourth century BC in Athens (also called 'Tower of the Winds'), which was well-known as a post-Grecian shrine to the whirling Dervishes, the Islamic fanatics convinced that they were favoured by God. In such a seemingly benign setting Tess is captured.

Thus the allusions integral to setting maintain the ironic tension so important to Hardy's style. When the world is seemingly docile, the allusions warn that the way of the world is never to be trusted; when the environment is obviously harsh, the allusions intensify the unremitting cruelty that fate has in store for Tess. Admittedly, Hardy is not unerringly successful with allusions attached to landscape. When he compares the cows in a field to the crowd scenes in Van Alsloot or Sallaert paintings (p. 139), or, several pages later, says the milchers' shadows are copied by the sun with as much diligence as it had copied Olympian shapes on ancient marbles, little is gained. Several other allusions in the novel are equally unhelpful. One may take, for example, a narrative mid-sentence interruption of two lines from Whitman (p. 194), describing Angel's purpose at the dairy. In the manuscript Hardy quoted Swinburne's lines from 'The Garden of Proserpine': 'Dead winds and spent waves riot / In doubtful dream of dreams.' The change to Whitman shifts the focus from place to people, but remains intrusive. In fact, the original allusion better fits the logic of the sentence. This is, however, one of the few occasions when he revised his allusions for the worse. Hardy also commits another familiar error by using arcane allusions that seem to be included primarily to give a veneer of culture: a note on Jeremy Taylor that adds little insight into Tess's attitude towards her own morality (pp. 134–5);[9] two obscure references – to the Wiertz Museum (p. 304) in Brussels and to Jan Van Beers, a minor nineteenth-century Belgian painter – are cited in one sentence in a weak attempt to delineate Angel's new post-confessional attitude towards Tess; and narrative references to the *Dictionaire Philosophique* and *Huxley's Essays* (p. 369) are introduced to describe Tess's explanation of her husband's views. In this novel, as in others, Hardy was chastised for his style, and when he used such terms as 'pellucid smokelessness' and 'autochthonous idlers' on the same page, he was legitimately vulnerable; but such minor lapses, both in vocabulary and allusions, are overshadowed by his skill in using allusions to provide, for example, much needed humour.

In the earlier novels the rustic chorus characteristically injects the levity. But *Tess* does not have this pronounced chorus, and, in fact, Irving Howe argues that no one, not even the secondary characters, has much interest in his own right, that all are dwarfed beside Tess.[10] 'Hodge' is, of course, present – but because Tess changes location often, there is no one group to comment consistently on her situation. Moreover, Hardy directly tells us through

Angel's musing about the dairy people that the group had ceased to exist as a unit, that it 'had been disintegrated into a number of varied fellow-creatures'; he uses a reference to Cromwell and Gray's 'Elegy' to make his point (p. 156). Minor characters are, however, often in the background. As in the past, Hardy uses these people for some levity, and to enlarge the plot. The referential humour comes from both exaggerated comparison and narrative tongue-in-cheek. The book of woe, Ecclesiastes 12:1, is quoted as the narrator apologises for dwelling on young beauty rather than wrinkled wisdom at the May-day dance (p. 41); Izz also calls on the Prophet, 'there is a time to embrace' (Ecclesiastes 3:5), when she is in long-awaited ecstasy as she is carried across the steam by Angel; the dairy people sing 'fourteen or fifteen verses of a cheerful ballad about a murder . . .' (p. 147). Pomposity is pricked when Tess's father traces his lineage back long before 'Oliver Grumble' (p. 48). The opposite end of the social scale is equally open to ridicule, as in this passage, which irremediably undermines Clare's brothers, who, Sankey notes, Hardy disliked so much that he failed to characterise them adequately:[11]

> When Wordsworth was enthroned they carried pocket copies; and when Shelley was belittled they allowed him to grow dusty on their shelves. When Correggio's Holy Families were admired, they admired Correggio's Holy Families; when he was decried in favour of Velasquez, they sedulously followed suit without any personal objection. (p. 200)

And there are several other moments of relief — the Queen of Spades elevated into a Praxitelean creation (p. 100); the country dancers transformed into satyrs and nymphs, Pans and Syrinxes, and, with a humour already noted as grimly foreboding for Tess, 'Lotis attempting to elude Priapus' (p. 96); the Durbyfield dresser compared to the Ark of the Covenant (p. 409). These light interventions are sparse, however, and the story unfortunately lacks the sardonic commentary of the rustics in *Far From the Madding Crowd*.

The few remaining allusions attached to minor characters are of a serious nature. When injected into the narrative, they establish and augment character; as parts of conversation, they lend credibility and dimension. For example, Mr Clare's religious position is

precisely delineated in a paragraph containing no less than fourteen allusions, a group which Hardy carefully revised, striking out,
most likely because of its obscurity, a reference to St Cyprian (the
bishop of Carthage, *c.* 248, who seriously disputed with Pope
Stephen I on the validity of baptisms performed by heretics —
shades of Sorrow, Tess's illegitimate son) and adding Philemon
(the slave master with whom Paul pleaded for an escaped slave,
who faced death by crucifixion if he returned) to a list of
Biblical writers whom Mr Clare 'regarded with mixed feelings'
(pp. 198–9). Mr Clare's ministerial role is further reinforced as he
describes, in the language of Luke 12:20 and 1 Corinthians 4:12
(p. 208), his attempts to convert Alec. His and Mrs Clare's
humanity is magnified by placing Tess's crucial failure to see them
in the context of Mark 2:16, when we are told that the Clares
might have loved her because she was a Publican and Sinner
rather than a Scribe or Pharisee. This same compassion is again
elevated by linking Mr Clare's love for Angel to Abraham's for
Isaac (p. 387). In a similar vein Izz is given a prophet's status when,
like Balaam or Peor, she praises Tess rather than condemning her,
thereby losing her chance to go with Angel to Brazil (p. 315). But
Izz's last prophecy, though gaining authority from the Bible,
proves to be tragically, perversely wrong. She says of Alec, 'he can
do her no harm', and uses Revelations 10:3 to explain her
judgment: '. . . nor the seven thunders themselves, can wean a
woman when 'twould be better for her that she should be weaned'
(p. 375).

The weaning of Tess, first from her parents, then from Alec,
then from Angel, then from Alec again, constitutes of course the
central action of the story. Certainly, too, these three central
characters are allotted Hardy's most extensive allusive concern.
Though the story clearly has a heroine, it has no unmitigated
villain, for both Alec and Angel call forth some sympathy together
with the opprobrium they deserve. Alec, at the opening of the
novel, is a direct descendent of Aeneas Manston — the stock villain
of melodrama, complete with the 'bold rolling eye', 'a barbarism
in his contours', and a 'well, my Beauty' line (p. 68). His confident
mastery of women also smacks of Francis Troy. He is, in short, a
cad. Critical opinion on Alec is, as one might expect, diverse.
Dorothy Van Ghent, for example, sees him as the 'smart Aleck in
the book of Job, the one who goes to and fro in the earth and walks
up and down in it, the perfectly deracinated one, with his flash

and new money and faked name and aggressive ego'.[12] There is little question that he is a satan-figure. F. B. Pinion notes that his entrance into the poultry garden is reminiscent of the entrance of Milton's Satan into Eden,[13] and later in the novel Alec himself draws the parallel when trying to get Tess to leave her life of harsh manual labour and return to him. This entire scene is a set-piece (p. 397). Alec is working, unknown to Tess, in the field beside her, when suddenly the fire is reflected in his devil-like fork and she recognises him. Alec laughs and identifies himself — 'You are Eve, and I am the old Other One come to tempt you in the disguise of an inferior animal' — and quotes from Milton's temptation scene (*Paradise Lost*, IX, 625–31), cutting out of the quotation the inappropriate section. (In the manuscript, Hardy includes the entire passage, then later revises for emphasis.) But most critics and readers alike seem to agree with William Rutland, who dismisses Alec as primarily a piece of plot machinery, introduced for the purpose of destroying Tess.[14] Allusively, Hardy gives him relatively short shrift — there are only fifteen allusions in the entire novel which bear directly on him. But the fifteen are interestingly handled. And would that Tess could have understood them. For Alec is consistently associated with Shakespeare's comedies, allusively preparing the reader for the game he is playing with her. The referential erosion of Alec's wooing begins even before he actually comes on the scene. His usurping of the d'Urberville name, and Tess's family's ignorance of such practices, are sardonically summarised with an echo of *Much Ado About Nothing* (III. iii. 14): 'to be well favoured might be the gift of fortunes . . .' (p. 68). Tess meets Alec immediately thereafter, and in the ensuing conversation (p. 70) he uses the 'my pretty Coz' line that Rosalind and Celia repeat to pass the time in *As You Like It*, and, Hardy tells us, 'Thus the thing began.' When Tess moves to The Slopes and Alec begins his flirting in earnest, his conversation again draws on the comedies. In the scene in the chicken yard, when the tempter Alec comes out of the ivy, he twists a line from *Twelfth Night* (II. iv. 113–14) to tell Tess that she is like 'Impatience on a monument' (p. 91). The lines from the play continue: 'We men say more, swear more: but in deed / Our shows are more than will: for still we prove / Much in our vows, but little in our love.' Moments later he whistles a song from *Measure for Measure* (IV. i. 1): 'Take, O Take those lips away.' Hardy warns, 'the allusion was lost on Tess', ensuring that it does not escape the reader's attention.

After Tess's unfortunate fall, Alec does not allusively reappear until he has been converted by Mr Clare. Varley Lang advances the hypothesis that Alec's becoming a zealot is itself possibly a borrowing from George Crabbe's poem 'The Maid's Story', where the central character becomes a fiery preacher and offers to wed the heroine.[15] Even given the loan, Alec as divine rather than devil strains credibility, especially since there has been no real trauma in his life to motivate such a change in personality. Here Hardy requires of the reader a suspension of disbelief — a suspension he facilitates by having Alec, with ostensible legitimacy, now quote Scripture rather than Shakespeare to suit his purpose. In this role Alec begins a new process of seduction. First he uses Matthew 3 : 7 to help him woo Tess back to religion (p. 355); then he expresses his pious and arrogant disappointment at Tess's marriage in the words of Paul (1 Corinthians 7 : 14): 'The unbelieving husband is sanctified by the wife, and the unbelieving wife is sanctified by the husband' (pp. 364–5). But a pious Alec is too much for reader, Hardy, and Tess alike. In a last bow to his new role, Alec describes (pp. 369–70) his backsliding with ironically appropriate references from James 2 : 19 (the verse is in a chapter dedicated to condemning rich men) and 2 Peter 2 : 19–20, where the context of Alec's admission that he is 'one of those servants of corruption . . .' reads 'For when they speak great swelling *words* of vanity, they allure through the lusts of the flesh, *through much* wantonness, those that were escaped from them who live in error.' Immediately, at the end of the same paragraph, Alec's return to his proper party is complete, and he reveals his old colours; he taunts Tess: 'surely there never was such a maddening mouth since Eve's,' and a 'hot archness shot from his own black eyes'. With a demonic shift of guilt he then accuses her of being the temptress, and calls her the 'Witch of Babylon', perhaps toning down his language from the 'Whore' which his source (Revelations 17) supplies because such exaggeration would expose to him the cruel absurdity of his attack.

Tess fights back, and Alec recants his accusation, but his pursuit is unremitting. Hardy never lets the reader forget Alec's politics. He reinforces the Satan imagery, and even has Alec recall his old role as philanderer when he echoes both the Bible (1 Timothy 1 : 20) and Shakespeare in another attempt to convince Tess:

How could I go with the thing [his preaching] when I had lost my faith in it? — it would have been hypocrisy of the basest kind!

Among them I should have stood like Hymenaeus and Alexander, who were delivered over to Satan that they might learn not to blaspheme. What a grand revenge you have taken! I saw you innocent, and I deceived you. Four years after, you find me a Christian enthusiast; you then work upon me; perhaps to my complete perdition! But Tess, my coz, as I used to call you, this is only my way of talking, and you must not look so horribly concerned. Of course you have done nothing except retain your pretty face and shapely figure. (pp. 376–7)

Relentlessly he uses more references from Scripture. The paragraph continues, drawing on Luke 9:62: 'He regarded her silently for a few moments, and with a short cynical laugh resumed: "I believe that if the bachelor-apostle, whose deputy I thought I was, had been tempted by such a pretty face, he would have let go the plough for her sake as I do!"' In the manuscript Hardy wrote, 'and gone to the devil for her', then struck it out in blue, the colour he used for expurgating. Two pages later Alec twists the meaning of Hosea to suit his own arguments, and fires what is ultimately to be his most convincing and mortal shot:

The works of the stern prophet Hosea that I used to read come back to me. Don't you know them, Tess? – 'And she shall follow after her lover, but she shall not overtake him; and she shall seek him, but shall not find him; then shall she say, I will go and return to my first husband; for then was it better with me than now!' (p. 378)

Tess responds by hitting him with her glove – drawing the symbolic blood which is to flow more freely later, after she, having been persuaded by his 'real wife' arguments, her desperate financial condition, and his kindness to her family, has returned to him.

It is this last kindness that saves Alec from total villainy, for in the final chapters of the novel he does gain some sympathy by offering to help Tess when Angel fails to return. Hardy embellishes this mark of virtue on Alec's scutcheon by letting him remind Tess, in the words of Tennyson, 'that the old order changeth' (p. 413). But it has not changed much. Alec still expects Tess to pay for his favours, and never really understands that anything he gives her family now is in payment of old debts, not the creation of new

ones. He is momentarily allowed goodness to make him human, in
accordance with Hardy's notion that no one is totally bad. But
Tess must remain a 'pure woman'. So that we retain our moral
sympathy for her, Alec must constantly remind us of the spoiler
that he is: the allusions attached to him overwhelmingly reverber-
ate with the image.

Having explored hell, Hardy does not allusively neglect heaven.
Angel Clare is one of the most complex and indefinable characters
in Hardy, perhaps because his own attitudes towards Angel, both
philosophical and personal, were divided. On the one hand Angel
is to be admired for his courage – he has broken away from rigid
creeds and puritan parents (one has only to recall Mrs Clare's
pursed reaction to Mrs Crick's mead, which is banished to the
medicine cabinet). He has also ostensibly thrown off his class-con-
sciousness enough to aspire to be a farmer, and does not have
Alec's sensuality. On the other hand Angel's shedding of these
restrictions has few positive results. Irving Howe posits that Angel
'is a timid convert to modernist thought who possesses neither the
firmness of the old nor the boldness of the new'.[16] David De Laura
extends the same point, arguing convincingly that, philosophically, Angel's new Hellenism is dangerously defective. 'In
Angel,' writes De Laura, 'the "sample product" of a quarter–
century of English intellectual life, Hardy conveys his judgment of
the consequences of the residue of irrational idealism still infecting
even advanced thought in the ethical sphere.'[17] In practice,
Angel's idealism leads to his dangerous sentimentalisation of Tess,
and to his subsequent double-standard rejection of her. With a
history of philosophical vacillation he discards the old, assumes
what he believes to be the new, and in the process loses his
humanity. He does not find it again until he meets a philosophical
deus ex machina in Brazil, who forces him, in Arnoldian terms, to
'see things as they really are'. He returns to England and Tess, but
too late.

Angel's sexuality, too, is obviously integral to his treatment of
Tess. Robert Gittings, in his recent biography of Hardy, tells of
Hardy's own 'perpetual adolescence' with regard to love affairs,
and the unhappiness of his marriage has long been documented.
Peter Casagrande argues even more convincingly that Hardy was
troubled by his own physical fastidiousness, and that he had
residual problems with his relationship with his mother which possibly influenced his continual search for the ideal woman.[18] Such

biographical connections are of course difficult to prove con- clusively. It is clear, however, that Hardy's attitude towards Angel's spirituality is deeply divided. After she has deliberately rejected the physical, Tess sees Angel as her spiritual elective affinity, and Hardy says that his 'coldness is the source of much of his appeal to her'. But, as Eustacia found out, admiration is a poor bedfellow — and Hardy admits as much by saying that Angel was 'rather bright than hot — less Byronic than Shelleyan'. Hardy's personal response to Shelley was also ambivalent. He was a great admirer of his poetry,[19] but thought that Shelley's poetic sexual reserve was less than admirable. This comparison with the well- known potency of Byron leaves Angel as ethereal as his name. Ulti- mately, Angel's reticence is worse than Alec's rape — just as Sue's frigidity is later to be worse than Arabella's lustfulness.

Angel, then, is a paradoxical character, both in his own per- sonality and in Hardy's treatment of him. Though his new doctrine is 'modern' rather than Church-inspired, he is never totally free of his temperamental rigidity, of Arnold's strictness of conscience. Hellenism has replaced Hebraism in mind but not in ego, and even the Hellenic replacement is incomplete and untrust- worthy. Half-liberated, half-captive, enigmatic, William Buckler has called him, and it is this division of self that is so destructive to Tess.[20]

The dichotomy that is Angel both within and without, and the consequences of this fateful schism, resonate in his allusive context. When he is first seen in the novel (p. 43), his appearance 'would hardly have been sufficient to characterise him' — but what des- cription he is given, in the continuation of this sentence, is borrowed from *Macbeth*, III. iv. 24: 'There was an uncribbed, uncabined aspect in his eyes and attire . . .' It is a foreboding echo. For, just as all the early Shakespearean allusions associated with Alec are from the 'play' of the comedies, so are those attached to Angel, save two, from the tragedies and one sonnet.[21] They provide the ironic discord which directly contrasts with the harmony that Angel's personality ostensibly promises. For example, Angel expresses his interest in old families in the first of a series of refer- ences to *Hamlet*: 'Some of the wise even among themselves "exclaim against their own succession", as Hamlet puts it; but lyric- ally, dramatically, and even historically, I am tenderly attached to them' (*Hamlet*, II. ii. 368; p. 207). The narrative discussion of Tess's reluctance to marry is from *Hamlet* (II. ii. 338; p. 215), and, after Angel has heard Tess's confession and is still stunned, *Hamlet* serves again. Angel returns to the wedding house, sees Tess sleeping, and spies the d'Urberville portrait that ironically now changes his irresolution into determination. He turns away from Tess's door, his face wearing a 'terribly sterile expression . . . It was the face of a man who was no longer passion's slave' (III. ii. 77; p. 277). The sleep-walking scene in which Angel subconsciously buries Tess is reminiscent of *Macbeth*, but we are returned to *Hamlet* once more when Angel is confronting his philosophical inconsistencies in Brazil: 'But the reasoning is somewhat musty; lovers and husbands have gone over the ground before today' (III. ii. 359; p. 390). The line Hamlet speaks reads, '"While the grass grows", the proverb is something musty.' A fourth allusion in the *Hamlet* series then follows, when Tess and Angel are discussing their course of action and he refers to the familiar 'To be or not to be' soliloquy: 'Don't you think we had better endure the ills we have than fly to others?' (III. i. 81–2; p. 286). The final Shakespearean allusion draws similar parallels with the Dane's vacillation, for Angel is now trying to win Tess back, having realised that his has been a love 'which alters when it alteration finds' (Sonnet 116; p. 419). The cumulative Shakespearean evidence, then, points the tragedy that Angel's relationship with Tess causes. Alec plays; Angel, though seemingly offering deliverance, deals destruction, and leads her down the road to dusty death.

The clusters of Biblical references are equally ominous, and work in several ways to erode Angel's character, even when other narrative descriptions are neutral or even positive. When placed in context, the references are often ironic — but their mere presence offers a clue to his disposition. Angel meets Tess thinking himself a Hellene, a free-thinker dedicated to 'spontaneity of consciousness', and she comes to agree with his beliefs. But while Angel's exterior is classical, the allusions constantly emphasise that the Hebraic is dominant in his soul. Of the non-Shakespearean allusions attached to him the majority are Biblical. Only two major references and four brief ones (a list of names) are drawn from the classics. And in each classical notation the reference is immediately juxtaposed with a Scriptural allusion, the juxtaposition serving as a touchstone of the deep faults in Angel's character. Thus, in their original context, or when viewed as a part of the novel's own form, the Biblical allusions are often Sophoclean in nature, resounding both with Hardy's condemnation of Angel and with his dislike of Hebraic morality in general. For example, Angel explains his apostacy to his father by quoting Mr Clare's favourite verse from Hebrews (12:27): 'My whole instinct in matters of religion is towards reconstruction; to quote your favourite Epistle to the Hebrews, "*the removing of those things that are shaken, and of things that are made, that those things which cannot be shaken may remain*"' (p. 154). Already we recognise how little Angel knows himself. Offering still more evidence that he has not purged his ecclesiastical past, he woos Tess with whispers from Genesis 29: 'Three Leahs to get one Rachel' (p. 185). This allusion in particular is multi-layered, for it also reminds the reader of one of the most terrible aspects of Old Testament judgment – generational guilt. Angel speaks truer than he knows, for the Biblical Rachel, before dying in childbirth, called her son 'Benomi', Hebrew for 'son of my sorrow'. Hardy explicitly notes in a post-manuscript addendum that Genesis is Tess's source for her baby's name.

Angel at his worst is also cloaked in Scripture, though Hardy, with great technical virtuosity, directly turns form on content by allusively illustrating the paradox of Angel's nature and his blindness to it:

Whatever one may think of plenary inspiration, one must heartily subscribe to these words of Paul: 'Be thou an example – in word, in conversation, in charity, in spirit, in faith, in purity.' It is the only safeguard for us poor human beings. 'Integer vitae,' says a Roman poet, who is strange company for St. Paul—

The man of upright life, from frailties free.
Stands not in need of Moorish spear or bow.

Well, a certain place is paved with good intentions, and having felt all that so strongly, you will see what a terrible remorse it bred in me when, in the midst of my fine aims for other people, I myself fell. (p. 267)

Horace (*Odes*, Book I, xxii) is indeed strange company for St. Paul (1 Timothy 4:12). The ode, with its first line frequently used out of context to support the moral life, is in its entirety an ironic comment on just such cloistered virtue, the poet ultimately affirming his greater reliance on a woman's love. Moreover, that Hardy chooses this particular apostle is equally ironic, for, as we have seen with Clym Yeobright, he often uses Pauline references pejoratively.[22] Alec at his slimiest has also preached a sermon on the justification of faith as expounded by St Paul, and compared himself to the Bachelor Apostle. Certainly this failure of Angel to recognise Horace's irony, coupled with his unconscious reliance on Pauline morality, are symptomatic of the very weaknesses that destroy Tess. He neither understands his Hellenism nor has rejected his Hebraism. The Biblical erosion continues. Angel wakes from his sleep-walking, like 'Samson shaking himself', (Judges 16:20; p. 294), a revealing allusion, for Samson is now shorn and, like Angel, awakes only to be blinded. Yet the presence of the classical element which Angel wants to predominate is illustrated in the next sustained description of his contradictory state. He is going to tell his parents about his impending departure for Brazil when he draws on Marcus Aurelius and Jesus to channel his thoughts: '"This is the chief thing: be not perturbed", said the Pagan moralist. That was Clare's own opinion. But he was perturbed. "Let not your heart be troubled, neither let it be afraid", said the Nazarene. Clare chimed in cordially; but his heart was troubled all the same' (John 14:27; p. 304).[23]

Angel stays in this allusive limbo, seeing through all glasses darkly, until in the jungle in Brazil the stranger inadvertently makes him realise he must modify his ineffective modernism and reject his misguided traditionalism. In a paragraph added during revision, Hardy summarises:

> His own parochialism made him ashamed by its contrast. His inconsistencies rushed upon him in a flood. He had persistently elevated Hellenic Paganism at the expense of Christianity; yet in that civilization an illegal surrender was not certain dis-esteem. Surely then he might have regarded that abhorrence of the un-intact state, which he had inherited with the creed of mysticism, as at least open to correction when the result was due to treachery. (p. 389)

Angel has begun at long last to reason himself into right action. He thinks on Tess's d'Urberville history and realises that it was only useful 'to the dreamer, to the moraliser on declines and falls'. Rather than demand the prize of a Rachel, he tries to accept that 'the gleaning of the grapes of Ephraim [is] better than the vintage of Abi-ezer' (Judges 8:2; p. 390). The debate and the jungle take their toll of Angel, and when he returns, he looks like a drab Christ – 'Crivelli's dead *Christus*' (p. 417). But the reality of Tess has at last begun to overcome his inherited rigidity and force him to examine his perverted idealism. The allusions record his new awareness of his previous distortions by contrasting appearance with actuality. Faustina was the wife of Marcus Aurelius and famous for her debauchery; Cornelia was the Roman ideal of motherhood; Lucretia was famous for her chastity; Phryne was an Athenian prostitute; Bathsheba was the wife of Uriah and the mistress of David:

> He had undergone some strange experiences in his absence; he had seen the virtual Faustina in the literal Cornelia, a spiritual Lucretia in a corporeal Phryne; he had thought of the woman taken and set in the midst as one deserving to be stoned, and of the wife of Uriah being made a queen; and he had asked himself why he had not judged Tess constructively rather than bio-graphically, by the will rather than by the deed? (p. 419)

The tragic remorse of this question is not to be resolved, nor is the one last Biblical question to be answered. Here Angel's very silence shows that his conversion to humane flexibility, though too late, is at least sincere. His last Biblical allusion, another link with Christ, is pyrrhically positive. Tess, just before her last night at liberty, asks Angel if they will meet after death. 'Like a greater than him-self, to the critical question at the critical time he did not answer; and they were again silent' (p. 446). No longer the Pauline moraliser or the Hellenic idealiser, Angel stands mute, with only his new awareness and the 'ache of modernism' as rewards.

W. P. Trent, one of the founders of the *Sewanee Review*, said of Hardy in November 1892 that 'his gallery of women is unique, even if he has seldom drawn one whom his average male reader would care to marry'.[24] Tess, given Hardy's own taste in his heroines, is one of the exceptions. That Hardy liked Tess, and that he meant her to be viewed as pure even to the end of the novel (though he frankly owned that she lost a certain outward purity when she returned to Alec) we know from his autobiography and his letters. These are probably the only two real areas of critical agreement on her character. Reception of the world's most famous dairy maid has ranged from vituperation to sanctification. Most contemporary Grundies, of course, hated her, and were glad to see

her hang. Others, a little more compassionate, wanted her to live,
but refused to believe that − even if faced with dire poverty,
loneliness, and a conviction that she had been abandoned by both
Angel and heaven − she would return to the vile clutches of Alec.
Mrs Oliphant, liking Tess and feeling betrayed, wrote in *Blackwood's* (March 1892) that Tess would have flung that cashmere
robe out the window first. Academic criticism has been more
understanding, but, similarly, offers no consensus. D. H. Lawrence gives her the full Lawrencian treatment:

> And Tess, despising herself in the flesh, despising the deep
> Female she was, because Alec d'Urberville had betrayed her
> very source, loved Angel Clare, who also despised and hated the
> flesh. She did not hate d'Urberville. What a man did, he did,
> and if he did it to her, it was her look-out. She did not conceive
> of him as having any human duty towards her.[25]

Douglas Brown, using a traditionalist's argument, sees Tess as a
victim of the social disintegration caused by the coming of indus-
trialisation; Arnold Kettle arrives at much the same position, using
a Marxist approach. She has also been variously labelled a scape-
goat and a Christ-figure. Her journey has been compared to Pilgrim's, with a progress not towards a Celestial City but towards
murder and death. And her personality and fate have been
identified with Antigone's.[26] The manuscript shows that Hardy's
early plans for Tess were not so complex, for in this *Ur*-version the
emphasis was on the common enough situation of a country girl's
being seduced by her first employer.[27] Moreover, due to editorial
demands for publication, the serial Tess is anything but morally
pure, for she kills without creditable provocation. As noted, however, Hardy's revisions do show a gradual ennobling of her
character, and Tess, as we now know her, is a worthy heroine. She
calls forth our sympathy, partially, as Bernard Paris for one has
recognised, because 'she is loved by the author, because her feelings have for him and are made to have for the reader, an intense
reality'.[28] He builds up this intensity through sheer technical skill,
fading at crucial moments (the Chase, the confession, the murder
scene) to maintain the ambiguity, zeroing in at other times
(Sorrow's baptism, Tess's response to her mother, and to her
motherhood) to give us a full view of her developing complexity.
Supporting this chiaroscuro effect is Hardy's manipulation of

allusions, where he both enlarges Tess through allusive juxtaposition and projects her fate by ironic comparisons.

In creating a Tess to be loved, Hardy faced an obvious challenge: a country girl must be made appealing to his less-than-
socially-tolerant London readers, and a fallen woman must be
purified. To make her live in a realm familiar to those who knew
books better than country lasses, Hardy embellished Tess's matur-
ation with sometimes incongruously pedantic allusions, but ones
which none the less suggest the dimensions of her personality, her
situation, and her appeal. The Durbeyfield family is discussed
with a sceptical questioning of 'nature's holy plan' (p. 51; Wordsworth, 'Lines Written in Early Spring', 1. 22) that allows improvi-
dent parents to have seven living children; Tess's attitude towards
her mother's nine (to date) pregnancies is described as Malthusian;
and the generation gap between Tess and her mother is expanded
into a metaphor for the differences between the Jacobean and Victorian ages (pp. 50–1). Then her position is further elevated by the
way Hardy allusively emphasises that Tess is more victim than
vixen. The whole question of what actually happened to Tess is
weighted in Tess's favour as the narrator tells us that she had
learned 'that the serpent hisses where the sweet birds sing' (p. 110),
a line from Shakespeare's *The Rape of Lucrece*. And the similarity
between the two situations is striking: both Tess and Lucrece trust
men who betray them; both are victims of the immediate moment;
both are attacked at night; both are aristocratic; both are moral;
and both take a different view of life after they are attacked.[29]
After the night in the Chase, Tess's views on life totally change –
we are yet to learn how – but she slowly matures, and continues to
be enhanced by the references bestowed on her. After the searing
loss of her child, Hardy enlarges what she has learned and stresses
her sensibility with a reference to Ascham's *The Schoolmaster*:
'"By experience", says Roger Ascham, "we find out a short way by
a long wandering." Not seldom that long wandering unfits us for
further travel, and of what use is our experience to us then?'
(p. 134). In context Ascham is saying that wise parents teach their
children rather than trusting them to life's hazards – an injunc-
tion Tess also levels at her mother when she asks why Joan did not
warn her that there was danger in men.[30] And on the same page,
the narrator further supports Tess's transformation from simple
girl to complex woman by quoting St Augustine's justification of
the Christian Church, *The City of God*: 'Thou hast counselled a

better course than Thou hast permitted.' Even when she errs, that, too, is excused by an allusion that raises her above her own private motives. She accepts Angel's proposal, against all she feels to be moral, because she is swayed by an '"appetite for joy" which pervades all creation' (p. 232) – a line which places her in the company of another misguided searcher, Browning's Paracelsus (I, 92). Or, when her actual virtue is called into question, Hardy draws on King Lear to argue that she is 'more sinned against than sinning' (p. 274).

The allusions surrounding Tess, then, expand her personality, intensify her intellectual development, minimise her mistakes. They also do a great deal to increase and explain her appeal by impressing her physical beauty upon the reader. Her lips and teeth look like 'roses filled with snow' (p. 191; Thomas Campion). When Angel places the gems on her, her face and neck reflect the warmth of the fire, 'which each gem turned into an Aldebaran [brightest star in the constellation Taurus] or a Sirius [brightest star in the sky] – a constellation of white, red, and green flashes, that interchanged their hues with her every pulsation' (p. 266). Tess is at her most beautiful in this scene, just moments before her fateful confession. Later, the results of her honesty are recorded in an allusion which elevates her, and, when remembered in its original context, comments bitterly on her circumstances. She is deserted, walking to Flintcomb Ash, having 'just mercilessly nipped her eyebrows off', 'no sign of young passion in her now'. Hardy quotes Swinburne's graphically sensuous 'Fragoletta' (ll. 41–5; p. 326): 'The maiden's mouth is cold / . . . / Fold over simple fold / Binding her head.' These last two lines are not in the manuscript; Hardy also revised his text by deleting from the manuscript a line referring to hair, thereby highlighting Tess's deliberate ugliness. His awareness of the taste of his readers probably made him omit the remaining line of the stanza: 'her breast-blossoms are simply red.' But those familiar with Swinburne cannot help but mourn the loss of sensuality that Tess's association with this poem recalls.

By serving to keep Tess's superiority before us, the allusions stylistically support our conviction that it is a noble person who goes to the gallows. Though we are emotionally devastated by Tess's end, technically we have been subtly warned of it. For, while the secular images attached to Tess are heightening her worth by placing her with lasting figures of art, the Biblical images have been concurrently cautioning us that she rises only to fall.

Benjamin Sankey has pointed out that Tess herself integrates three very strong forces: animal vitality, alertness to moral scruple, and personal devotion.[31] None of these qualities need be contradictory, were she operating in a moral universe or among men who would not prey on all three of them. But the world makes no allowances for Tess's values, nor for her post-lapsarian sensitivity and intelligence. Tess is destroyed, Hardy implies, by forces she has neither the will nor the way to resist. The philosophical determinant of Tess's situation he never totally defines. As Dorothy Van Ghent has argued, the great crises of the book are indeed psychologically motivated: Alec's seduction of Tess, Angel's rejection of her, her murder of Alec.[32] But fate also works through coincidence – Clare did not meet the 'pure' Tess at the May festival; the mail cart kills the horse; the letter slips under the carpet; Angel's parents happen not to be at home. But whatever the source, human or divine, Hardy makes clear that it is Hebraic morality, with its emphasis on obedience to God and on an awareness of sin, that acts as the catalyst which allows all of these events to be destructive. It is the rigidity of church-oriented convention that ultimately crushes Tess, not her actions, nor her innate morality, nor the morality of the natural world around her. Despite the shock of her seduction, Tess cares for her baby and is prepared to live in her world – but Hardy continually banishes any hope for her happiness by shadowing it with Biblical allusions. Symbolically, just as is done with Angel, the allusions, when their irony is exposed, indict the Hebraic tradition and preach that Biblical morality is harsh and unjust.

The narrator begins this indictment overtly, and at a crucial juncture. At the moment of Tess's violation in the Chase (p. 108) he speaks of Tess's guardian angel (a foreshadowing pun?), saying that he, like the pagan gods of Elijah's time, has turned his back on his charge (1 Kings 18:17–27). In the next paragraph he questions the justice of Tess's ruin, this time sardonically criticising what may be viewed by some as progressive retributive morality; Tess's aristocratic ancestors had undoubtedly been even harsher with peasant girls. But that hardly signifies. Ecclesiastes 20:5 is used to reveal the injustice of both history and religion: 'But though to visit the sins of the fathers upon the children may be morality good enough for divinities, it is scorned by average human nature; and

therefore does not mend the matter' (p. 108). That nothing will
mend the matter continues to be echoed Scripturally. Tess knows,
and Hardy expects his readers to know, the history of Aholah and
Aholibah (p. 128), prostitutes described in Ezekiel 23, whose lewd-
ness called down the wrath of God. They are stoned, dispatched
with swords, and their sons and daughters slain. (Hardy added
these two allusions in revision to argue the desired connections.)
Tess can accept her own fate, not with equanimity, but passively.
Burn she must; she cannot fight a system that equates seduction-
rape with whoredom, though the reader, through the allusion, is
again reminded of the gross injustice and the enormity of the
forces working against her. But she has enough fight left to refuse
to accept such arbitrary judgment for her child, Sorrow — whose
very Biblical name shames the forces which have killed it. Tess
baptises her son, and as she does so is transformed by an 'ecstacy of
faith' into a divine beauty: 'it set upon her face a glowing irradia-
tion, and brought a red spot into the middle of each cheek; while
the miniature candle-flame inverted in her eye-pupils shone like a
diamond' (p. 131). In the eyes of her brothers and sisters Tess is
divine, but her veneration is bitterly ironic. They beg her to have
another child, hoping for another baptism; the Vicar refuses the
baby a Christian burial. Her eyes, shining like diamonds, are a
grim imagistic link with the next occasion on which we see her in a
jewelled glow — the night of her confession and Angel's betrayal.

After Tess has buried her baby, she starts out again, determined
to lead a new life, but she cannot avoid, either within or without,
the condemnatory strictures of the ecclesiastical tradition. She
struggles to comprehend, to place her situation in perspective, to
return to the faith she had before 'she had eaten of the tree of knowledge', but, as for Eve, so for Tess that is not possible (pp. 140–1).
She quotes a psalm, 'Bless ye the Lord . . .'; the irony is obvious to
her and the reader, and she accedes: 'But perhaps I don't quite
know the Lord as yet.' To get to know Him better is little help.
Hardy tells us Tess really 'wants to walk uprightly', but she cannot
shed her past, neither in fact nor in fancy. In a cluster of allusive
images (pp. 163–4) she sees herself as an 'unhappy pilgrim', for
whom it is a mishap to be alive; she aligns herself with Job; and she
compares herself to the poor Queen of Sheba (1 Kings 10:5). Angel
delights in all of this, Hellenically transforming it into the 'ache of
modernism'. To the perspicacious reader it gives a different order
of perception. Tess sees herself in the condemnatory terms of

systematised religion. Angel unknowingly loves her in those very
terms, seeing her as a paragon of self-discipline, a concept central
to Arnoldian Hebraism. Tess uses the Bible's own words to question divine and earthly justice: 'I shouldn't mind learning why —
why the sun do shine on the just and unjust alike' (Matthew 5 : 45;
p. 165). The question remains unanswered, as Hardy soon tantalises us with allusions that alert the reader, while the principals
remain tragically oblivious: Angel little thinks that 'the Magdalen
might be at his side'; he calls Tess Artemis and Demeter, which
'she did not like because she did not understand them' (p. 170).
Had Angel recognised and accepted his Magdalen, he could have
grounded his love on truth; had Tess known that Artemis and
Demeter are goddesses of purity, she would have recognised in
time Angel's perverted veneration of chastity.

But such salvation is not to be. The Biblical allusions continue
to emphasise the ironic contradiction between what is and what
ought to be. Angel's father, paraphrasing Psalm 121 : 8, tells Angel
to marry a 'truly Christian woman, who will be a help and comfort
to you in your goings-out and your comings-in' (p. 203). The
source has promised that 'the Lord is thy keeper . . . The Lord
shall preserve thee from all evil: he shall preserve thy soul.' Later,
Tess is ecstatic at her wedding, and her feelings are compared to St
John's when seeing the angel (p. 255). But the story in Revelations (19 : 17—21) is one of destruction, of death by the sword.
And at a crucial juncture in the confession scene, 'Christian'
charity again turns ironically upon her. Instead of challenging
Angel's cruelty, Tess accepts it in Christian humility and self-
sacrifice: 'she sought not her own; was not provoked; thought no
evil of his treatment of her' (p. 284). She seals her fate. After she
has been abandoned, and she is on the road to Chalk-Newton, she
makes a nest for the night, and then questions her wretched life,
finding the words of Solomon, 'all is vanity' (Ecclesiastes 2), hope-
lessly inadequate. One could live if it were only vanity, but it is all
'injustice, punishment, exaction, death' (p. 323) — Tess's future.
She rallies enough to believe in 'the spirit of the Sermon on the
Mount' (p. 368), but the practice is never there until it is too late.
Whatever hope there is to be must come from 'Liza-Lu, and that is
Pyrrhic at best, qualified at least. 'Liza-Lu and Angel watch for
Tess's black flag in a pose reminiscent both of Adam and Eve leav-
ing Paradise and Giotto's 'Two Apostles', a fragment from *The
Burial of St John the Baptist*.[33] Neither image promises the happy

ending readers and critics alike have wished, even discovered, for
Tess. Because of an 1835 law that made it illegal for a man to
marry his sister-in-law, Angel and 'Liza-Lu cannot marry — and
perhaps Angel's knowledge of it is the reason for his charitable
silence at Tess's suggestion.[34] But this tangential technicality
apart, artistically, Hardy has prepared us for such bleakness from
the beginning. The President of the Immortals has sported with
Tess. And if the result was not too bitter even to contemplate, one
would also say that Hardy suspected that Tess's unjust torture
would continue eternally. Her response to Angel's return, just
moments before she killed Alec, had been a low moaning, 'as if it
came from a soul bound to some Ixionian wheel' (p. 431). Angel's
modern thought does not suffice; Hebraism, with its uncharitable,
fixed moral laws, is not only inadequate, but purposefully paves
the way with its good intentions.

Michael Millgate and J. I. M. Stewart call *Tess* Hardy's greatest
work of art; Irving Howe sees the novel as the centre of his achievement, and Tess as an archetype of feminine strength — quite an
increase in status for a woman described by Mowbray Morris (see
p. 122) as rising 'through seduction to adultery, murder and the
gallows'. The final view we have of Tess is as victim sacrificed on
the altar of social and moral order unsuited to human nature. Her
unremitting tragedy is supported by an elaborate allusive structure, that repeatedly alerts the reader to remind him of the tragic
incongruity between the ideals of Hardy's heroine and the world in
which she exists. The allusions also afford momentary humour,
and enhance the settings — but the world remains tragic, not
comic; the setting, even when promising rebirth, is always a cruel
place. The appetite for joy is whetted, but never even remotely
satisfied. The allusions supply the seasoning to highlight the in-
herently bitter taste.

Jude the Obscure, Hardy's last novel, affords even bleaker philosophic fare than does *Tess*, but with an equally rich aesthetic
design. The book is his most autobiographical, though he dis-
claimed much similarity between the story and his life. He also
denied that the book was intended as a manifesto on the 'marriage
question', asserting instead that there are two themes: 'the labours
of a poor student to get a University degree', and the failure of two
marriages because of a curse of 'hereditary temperament peculiar
to the families of the parties'.[35] Hardy's obfuscation here of both

source and purpose is a token of the problems that confronted him from its conception and have faced the book's critics since.

The experience of his publishing problems with *Tess* did little to affect the content of *Jude*, but they did resign him to the solutions he had adopted for the former novel: again he bowdlerised for the magazine public, producing a serial version even more absurd than that of *Tess*. In the serial of *Jude* Arabella traps Jude with threats of another lover; Sue's elopement with Jude is twisted beyond recognition; Jude and Sue do not live together in Aldbrick-ham; they shake hands when they meet for breakfast each morning; they adopt a child; Arabella puts the drunk Jude in a spare bedroom; the Sue–Jude church scene is omitted, as is Sue's penance – the list could go on.[36]

The birth of the manuscript was not easy either. The revisions are not as complex as those of *Tess* – no five layers here – but the evolution of *Jude* was not linear. John Paterson argues convincingly that Hardy had not got far into the novel before he lost control of it, and, rather than the 'safe' book he promised *Harper's*, conceived quite another. Manuscript revisions (those not in bowdler blue) indicate that the original situation of the story called for Jude's initial presence in Marygreen for a month, no early relationship with Phillotson, and dreams of Christminster inspired by an orphaned Sue who had been raised by the provost of a college there. Once the novel was under way, Paterson says, the 'dynamics of the author's imagination' forced him to abandon his blander scheme in favour of the present virulent attack on marriage laws, narrow Christianity, Victorian perversity, and human relationships – both secular and divine.[37]

Fortunately, the final unbowdlerised manuscript contains much of the story as we now know it. Hardy did continue to work on the novel after it was first published (Robert Slack records some eighty-seven changes between the 1903 and 1912 editions), but these changes are more stylistic than conceptual.[38] Hardy admitted that 'on account of the labour of altering *Jude the Obscure* to suit the magazine, and then having to alter it back, I have lost energy for revising and improving the original as I mean to do.'[39] When he did direct his attention to the story, however, he was again particularly aware of the allusive superstructure, going so far, for example, as to add all of the epigraphs after he had finished the manuscript. And he revised his allusions as his original concept of the novel and his subsequent concern for it required.

The public reception of *Jude* is notorious; it was a terrible experience for Hardy. The Bishop of Wakefield said he burned his copy (though Hardy was highly sceptical, since it was summer and the book was almost too large to burn in a grate). Margaret Oliphant, previously dismayed by *Tess*, was now outraged: 'There may be books more disgusting, more impious as regards human nature, more foul in detail, in those dark corners where the amateurs of filth find garbage to their taste; but not, we repeat, from any Master's hand' (*Blackwood's*, January 1896). The general vituperation was of course enough to end Hardy's career in fiction, though he could laugh with Swinburne over 'having been the two most abused of living writers; he for *Poems and Ballads*, I for *Jude the Obscure*'.[40] As with *Tess*, however, the novel also received a share of contemporary praise. The critics of the *Westminster Review*, *Cosmopolis*, and *Savoy Magazine*, among others, lauded the book, though the support was often qualified by a distaste for Hardy's unrelenting bleakness. More recently William Rutland also dislikes the novel for its negativism, finding it a 'terribly wearisome book', a treatise on the misery of human existence which is ultimately false to life because it allows for nothing positive.[41] There is little question that it contains some of the imperfections Hardy himself worried about; as J. I. M. Stewart admits, 'those who amuse themselves with the oddities of Hardy's prose style have a happy hunting ground' here.[42] However, the flaws result from an excessively ambitious design rather than from a failure in skill. The book is, as Swinburne said, a great tragedy, 'beautiful and terrible in its pathos'.

The grimness of *Jude* is inevitable, given Hardy's aim in the book and his own darkling vision. F. R. Southerington contends that the power of the novel lies deep in the soul of Hardy, and if there is a death wish in the story, it perhaps comes from a longing for death in Hardy himself.[43] Certainly there is little to live for, either when the book opens, or at its close. Society is indifferent, the university impregnable, morality vicious; human relationships are doomed, and the best we can hope for from the universe is to be ignored. Because of its assumptions about inevitable loneliness, sterile intellectualisation, permanent doubt, and wasted sensitivity, Irving Howe has labelled *Jude* Hardy's most distinctly modern work.[44] Clearly it is his most allusive one. For, as Hardy incorporated a series of contrasts that he himself had outlined — 'Sue and her heathen gods set against Jude's reading the Greek testament; Christminster academical, Christminster in the slums; Jude the saint, Jude the sinner; Sue the Pagan, Sue the saint; marriage, no marriage; etc.'[45] — he integrated a plethora of references to support the multiplicity of themes that he explored.

In *Jude* Hardy returned to a device he had abandoned in *Tess*: the standard Victorian epigraph for each section of the book. Each serves the traditional function in that it directly points to events to come, but it is also explicit enough to highlight particular aspects of individual character. The first, for example, is from the Apocrypha (1 Esdras 4:26,27,32). The verses quoted warn of Arabella's power over Jude, but, placed in context, also tell of Jude's other weakness: strong drink. Part II is introduced by quotations from Ovid in the original Latin and from Swinburne. The Ovid obviously predicts Jude's growing love for Sue; but — more elaborately, since it is from the Pyramus and Thisbe story in the *Metamorphoses* (IV, 59–60) — also foreshadows Jude's suicide and Sue's happiness only after death. Swinburne's 'Prelude to Songs Before Sunrise' (l. 158) provides the second epigraph here, and, in context, again enlarges upon Jude's fate. The first four stanzas could serve as an outline of his early history with Arabella. The lines Hardy includes are equally indicative of Jude's isolation and his future: 'Save his own soul he hath no star.' In Swinburne the sentence continues, 'And sinks, except his own soul guide, / Helmless in middle turn of tide.' Jude's soul loses control to Sue's psychosis and Arabella's liquor. Part III, 'At Melchester', opens with 'For there was no other girl, O Bridegroom, like her!' It is a benign enough tribute, but bitter in the light of Sue's abhorrence of marriage and erotic love. Moreover, the line from Sappho is preceded by 'Aphrodite has honoured you above all others', an ironic taunt to Jude and a reminder of Sue's reticence. The line is followed by the bride's lament for her lost childhood, again prophetic of Sue's desire to stay physically inviolate.

Milton's *The Doctrine and Discipline of Divorce* heads Part IV: 'Whoso prefers either Matrimony or other Ordinance before the Good of Man and the plain Exigence of Charity, let him profess Papist, or Protestant, or what he will, he is no better than a Pharisee.' The quotation offers, first, direct approval of Phillotson's decision and a corresponding condemnation of the society — so well exemplified by Shaston, the town where he lives — which opposes such charity; secondly, it serves as a gloss for Phillotson's reversal — he does become a Pharisee. The epigraph to Part V is from Marcus Aurelius, and reminds the reader of the inevitable power of the flesh over the spirit. The epigraph is also revealing for its suggestion that humanity is doomed to unrealised potential. The final epigraph, by its source, returns the novel full circle. Once again the Apocrypha, rather than the Old and New Testaments, provides the emblem. The verse is from Esther, where the queen is humbling herself before God in order to save the Jews. 'She abased her body, and every part that she had delightfully adorned she covered with her dishevelled hair,' reads one translation. Hardy quotes a more explicit version: 'And she humbled her body greatly, and all the places of her joy she filled with her torn hair.' Esther's petition, and her subsequent God-guided manipulation of the king, are successful; the Jews are saved. But Sue's attempt to save her soul and Jude's is only a sick distortion of all that is just. She puts on her 'sackcloth' nightgown − but it is a curse, not catharsis. The second epigraph underscores the futility of her action and prepares for Arabella's final words. It is from Browning's 'Too Late': 'There are two who decline, a woman and I, / And enjoy our death in darkness here.' Arabella concludes that Sue 'never found peace since she left his arms, and never will again till she's as he is now' (p. 428).

Thus the epigraphs are avenues into the novel, illuminating both character and action. These epigraphs are in turn all accompanied by place-names that serve as division titles, recording Jude's pilgrimage and his pathos, while reminding us that environment, too, is extremely important. However, following the example of *Tess*, and perhaps because the scenes of Jude's life are set primarily in a town rather than in the country, Hardy again does not transform place into character; few elevating allusions are attached to settings. A minor one is used to embellish Aldbrickham, whose clammy fog is described with Milton's 'At a Vacation Exercise in the College': the fog is blowing in 'from "Royal-tower'd Thame"' (p. 302). There are also four allusions associated with Shaston. In a two-page description of the town which Hardy inserted after he had finished the manuscript, he intensifies the 'pensive melancholy' induced by the place through a quotation from Michael Drayton's *Polyolbion* and with a reference to the bones of King Edward the Martyr, Shaston's principal claim to fame (p. 220). Thirty pages later Hardy again draws on *Polyolbion*, and also on William Barnes, to describe Phillotson's view of Shaston as he walks over to Gillingham's house for his discussion of Sue's future. Hardy identified these two allusions in footnotes, so he must have been troubled by their obscurity. That he chose one of the dullest poems in the language to quote twice with reference to this most stultifying of towns is appropriate, though it is doubtful whether it was deliberate. The allusions do universalise the scene and do emphasise the town's atmosphere. But, in the third instance especially, they are intrusive. Our attention here is concentrated on Phillotson's mood, not on the view before him; six lines of poetry at this point impede both his progress and our understanding. In summary, then, the allusions connected with place here are relatively weak. But this is a quibble when weighed against Hardy's adroit choice of place-names, and his ingenious use of references to intensify the impact of particular scenes.

More than in any previous novel Hardy creates referential place-names that are ironic touchstones of the events they witness. For example, Jude sees Christminster (itself a ghastly misnomer) as 'the heavenly Jerusalem' (p. 40), a city where, Hebrews 12:22–3 tells us, dwell 'the spirits of just men made perfect'. (Here Hardy altered the manuscript to heighten the irony; originally he had written, 'looks as the Promised Land did to Moses from Mount Nebo,' which is unsuitable, because Jude, unlike Moses, does reach his destination.) Again, when he arrives at Christminster, he stays in a suburb called Beersheba, a name meaning 'the well of satiety', because of the covenant Abraham made there (Genesis 26:33); it was also a town inhabited by Philistines and later noted for its idol worship.[46] In Beersheba Miss Fontover worships at the church of St. Silas, a Hellenic Jew known primarily for his association with Paul and as the bearer of the Council of Jerusalem's letter to Antioch on the subject of following the laws of Moses. Jude arranges to meet Sue at the Spot of the Martyrdoms, and Sue, sensitive to the portent, refuses to see him there. Jude and Sue rehearse and Sue then marries Phillotson in the Church of St. Thomas, the apostle known for his scepticism. Two colleges of Christminster are called Sarcophagus and Rubric, their names typical of 'their four centuries of gloom, bigotry and decay' (p. 352). (Earlier Hardy had named one of the colleges 'Cloister', but he struck out the entire reference, perhaps because he considered it too benign.)

The list is impressive. Cumulatively, the formal names serve as leitmotifs, reverberating with the oppressive mood of the story – **a** mood Hardy sustains by establishing his scenes through references. Ian Gregor has noted that the characters in the novel move from place to place, but the 'world of the novel seems to be less in Wessex than at the nerves' end'.[47] To achieve this kind of tension Hardy uses allusive prisms in important scenes that refract all the complexities of emotion and in turn heighten the irony. The first such instance occurs when the young Jude, while on his way home, stops his horse and in a moment of ecstasy recites Horace's 'Carmen Saeculare', while he reverently kneels to Phoebus and Diana (p. 53). The allusion has many ramifications, for, as L. M. Findlay has pointed out, Hardy was most likely exploiting the topicality of the poem. (Findlay records the complex circumstances of the poem's popularity.) Hardy might also have been hoping that his readers would recognise the irony inherent in Jude, the orphan, reciting all of a poem which, in classical times, was sung by twenty-seven girls and twenty-seven boys, all of whose parents were living. The verses are a festival prayer for happiness and prosperity, dedicated to the fates, the earth, and the goddess of childbirth.[48] Pointedly, Jude is to pass the same sacred place again, and, under the influence of Arabella, forget his previous dedication.

When Jude is courting Arabella and the feelings involved are quite clear and elemental, there is little need for the allusive dimension. Nor are these emotions susceptible to much literary polish. Instead of allusions, a pig's penis defines the action. But after Jude meets the refined Sue, the scene heightening allusions come back, and take a different turn: all are from Scripture. The first occasion occurs when Jude is secretly watching Sue in church, and meditating on his past (p. 111). The choir sings Psalm 119, and he almost believes that God deliberately chose it. The psalmist and Jude ask, 'wherewithal shall a young man cleanse his way?' In context the rest of the psalm answers: by keeping the letter of the law − continuing the motif introduced by the novel's grim introductory quotation, 'the letter killeth'. Though the use of this psalm to enclose Jude's meditations is only subtly bleak, subsequent allusive scenes are much more piercing. As Sue and Jude, devastated by the loss of their children, await the coroner's inquest, they are taunted by what Jude recognises as the music of Psalm 75 (p. 357): 'Truly God is loving unto Israel'. The psalm ends even more derisively: 'I have put my trust in the Lord God . . .' The music is broken by the conversation of two clerics, arguing about which side of the altar is the proper one on which to celebrate communion. Jude again moans at the incongruity of such trivia, with 'all creation groaning' (Romans 8:22). God promises, only to snatch away. The Biblical hammering continues, as everything Jude holds sacred is beaten down. Jude symbolises his forced separation from Sue by throwing his pillow onto the floor, and declaring that the veil of their temple is rent (Mark 16:38; p. 374). All hope of reunion with Sue gone, Jude turns himself over to Arabella, and is led drunk through the streets, quoting the famous lines on charity from 1 Corinthians, a book of the Bible with which Hardy seems to be especially at war; it has a part in some of his most chilling scenes. And the unavoidable memorability of Jude's death is created by his recitation of Job, punctuated by the 'hurrahs' of the Remembrance games.

Given such a story, almost any humour, even among minor characters, is bound to be incongruous. Continuing the mood established in *Tess*, Hardy offers almost no allusive comic relief. There are, however, a few flashes of his old practice. A carter deflates Christminster and the academe alike by defining the curriculum as a study of foreign terms 'used in the days of the Tower of Babel' (p. 44). (Hardy conscientiously altered this allusion, which in the manuscript reads, 'foreign tongues used before the Flood'.) Vilbert's healing salve, which Jude is duped into peddling, is made from 'a particular animal which grazed on Mount Sinai' (here the allusion also serves to emphasise Jude's naïvety, shared by those who buy the salve; p. 46). One of the 'girls' in the tavern where Jude encounters the undergraduates is called 'Bower of Bliss', and sports a moral character of various depths and shades, Hardy tells us. Her Spenserian name is not in the manuscript, where she is called 'Happy Land'. Or, in the fight scene at Phillotson's resignation (p. 269), the churchwarden's head goes through Samaria when he is clouted with a map of, significantly, Palestine; and the crowd which stares at Jude is equated with the Lycaonians gaping at Paul (Acts 14:5–11; p. 344). All of these scattered references provide desperately needed, though muted, chuckles. But even the laughter rings hollow, for these allusions, attached to background characters, often serve to particularise them as naïve buffoons, or as merely curious, often insensitive commentators – not as the wise counsellors of the earlier novels. The rustic chorus does occasionally offer a flatly realistic picture, in contrast to Jude's idealism, and once even supplies a dash of humour through

ignorance of an allusion. Jude describes Christminster's silence as
'the stillness of infinite motion — the sleep of the spinning top,
to borrow the simile of a well-known writer' (probably from
D'Avenant's *The Rivals* or Congreve's *The Old Batchelour*, neither
well-known to Jude's audience). The rustic dismisses this with his
own appraisal: 'O, well, it med be all that, or it med not. As I say, I
didn't see nothing of it the hour or two I was there; so I went in and
had a pot of beer' (p. 132). But too often these characters painfully
deflate rather than entertain, and Hardy does not support their
attitude, as he had previously done by giving them the benefit of
Scripture. We smile through these few referential asides, but the
laughter is most often nervous rather than conspiratorial.

There is also little allusive treatment of the other peripheral
characters. Aunt Drusilla is helped by her only two allusions. Her
dismissal of Farmer Troutham is given the authority of Job (p. 37),
and she is described as having a 'countenance like that of
Sebastiano's Lazarus' (p. 210) just before she berates Sue for having married Phillotson. Father Time, a metaphor in himself and
seemingly ripe for elaborate allusions, is given only one direct
reference: his face is like the tragic mask of Melpomene (p. 299).
He has, however, been described by commentators as a Christ
figure, and one critic even argues that his suicide note recalls
Daniel 5 : 25: 'ME-NE, ME-NE TE-KEL.'[49] Mrs Edlen, a member
of the rustic chorus and a sympathetic critic of Sue and Jude;
Vilbert, the villain his name implies; the other children — these
are all presented without allusions, almost as if Hardy wanted to
save the whole of literature for his central figures.

Hardy's architectural training is again discernible in his pairing
of characters, and in the symmetrical structure of *Jude*, which has
been widely recognised: Phillotson and Arabella foil Sue and
Jude. Phillotson was added to the story almost as an afterthought,
and remains mostly in the shadows, with few allusions to disturb
his obscurity. None the less, he is essential to the sexual politics of
the story; he must be realistic enough to elicit both our sympathy
and our repugnance, for without both Sue becomes a grotesque
parody. Phillotson is drawn as a mild eccentric, a man with an
'unhealthy looking, old fashioned face'. His slow speech is indicative of his personality and he is the philistine his name implies.[50]
He is also sensitive, compassionate, yet basically ineffectual.
Lewis Horne correctly argues that to a certain degree he practises
Christian renunciation as it is defined by Arnold in *St. Paul and*

Protestantism − the parting with something precious. He lets Sue go to Jude at what appears to be a great personal sacrifice, but ultimately lacks the courage of his decision. He invites Sue to return to him − not for her sake, but because of the social and professional advantages which he might reap.[51] Yet, to Victorians at least, his original act of renunciation was certainly an unusually selfless one, and, regardless of Hardy's negative portrayal of him as a character − his personality, age, and physical appearance all work against him in our eyes and Sue's − Hardy supports his comprehension and sensitivity by bolstering him with secular references. We know, for example, that Phillotson profoundly understands Sue, and her relationship with Jude, when he describes them first in Shelleyan terms − comparing them to the sibling, divided-psyche, lovers in *The Revolt of Islam*[52] − and adding a dash of French romanticism by alluding to the lovers in Bernardin de St Pierre's *Paul et Virginie* (p. 252). The allusions also warn, however, of the couple's fate: the martyrdom of Laon for Cythna's sake and the death of their child; the destruction of Paul and Virginie, perpetrated in part by a society which refuses to accept their impractical love. Soon after he has explained to Gillingham why he is freeing Sue, he also writes to Jude, and again an allusion reinforces his insight. When placed in context, it also gives us a sense of his pain. He tells Jude without rancour that he and Sue are made for each other, and that Jude has always been 'the shadowy third' in their relationship (p. 260). The reference is from Browning's poem on marital communion, 'By the Fireside'. Ironically, Phillotson is closest to Sue when he lets her go, and she comes closest to loving him at that moment. But the line immediately preceding tells of the price: 'If two lives join, there is oft a scar.' Later, Sue's return to Phillotson is a grim parody of the closeness captured in the poem.

Yet in spite of his compassion at this parting, Phillotson's loneliness and irresolution − stimulated by Sue's warring personality − ultimately cause him to fall short of his potentialities, and reveal him to be, like Sue, inwardly incapable of ignoring convention, even in the interests of compassion. Sue prepares the ground for the change when she sees him at the Remembrance Day festival and draws on Luke 2:41−2, the story of Jesus coming to a Passover feast, to describe his presence. He has 'come up to Jerusalem to see the festival like the rest of us' (p. 348). Jude notes her tone, asks for assurance that she is free of Phillotson, and receives her half-hearted 'I suppose so.' She goes on, 'But I am weak. Although I know it is all right with our plans, I felt a curious dread of him; an awe, or terror, of conventions I don't believe in.' Hardy picks up the image again when Phillotson hears of the children's deaths, and muses in the mood of Christ in the garden: 'their cup of sorrow is now full.' These links, however, prove to be not with Christ the compassionate, but with Christianity as defined by the negativism of Victorian morality — a system to which, events show, Sue really does subscribe, and which, Phillotson writes to Sue, cannot be ignored with impunity: 'let crude loving-kindness take care of itself' (p. 379). Phillotson makes a poor Christ. When writing this letter, he adopts a tone of Rhadamanthine strictness. It is his last allusion, and is a fine touch: Rhadamanthus was noted for his severity, and was one of the judges in hell. The vicar supplies the final allusive word on their new relationship as he remarries them (p. 389). The grim reality mocks appearances when the vicar, as God's and society's representative, with naïve cruelty calls on 1 Corinthians 5 : 15 to assure them that they have been 'saved as by fire'. Having congratulated them for performing 'a noble, and righteous, and mutually forgiving act', he cheerily assures them that 'all's well that ends well'. The gods seem to be having their sport with Sue, too.

The relative allusive indifference Phillotson suffers is also shared by Arabella, though her amplitude alone ensures that she can never really be ignored. Hardy had trouble with Arabella from her first appearance. His readers would not tolerate a woman who could toss a pig's genitals at a man, lure him into an intimate position, hide an egg and invite its pursuit, imply pregnancy to secure a husband, and openly flirt with a man like Vilbert. All of these actions had to be expurgated from the serial. Until very recently only D. H. Lawrence and Frederick McDowell gave some measure of approval to Arabella's machinations. Sharing the Wife of Bath's disregard for propriety but lacking much of her compensatory wit, Arabella is often regarded as a villain. Margaret Oliphant sniffed: she is 'a woman so completely animal that it is at once too little and too much to call her vicious. She is a human pig.' Lascelles Abercrombie says that she is the one woman at whom Hardy directs animosity, and Pinion says she is the Venus Pandemos to the Venus Urania in Sue.[53] Even her partisans must admit that she has her flaws: she is conniving, crude, and selfish; she ensnares Jude three times, only to leave him to die alone; and, like her fourteenth-century prototype, she arranges her next marriage too hard upon the death of her previous husband. However, though she is hardly the heroine that Lawrence makes her out to be when he describes her as the embodiment of his 'female principle', she does have redeeming features: she is never deliberately evil, she is more honest and straightforward with her world than Sue, she has insight into human character, and she understands Sue's love for Jude far better than Sue does herself.

The ambiguity of Arabella's characterisation is often taken as a token of Hardy's own perplexity at such animalistic, morally empty sexuality. In a Darwinian age he could not totally degrade Arabella's behaviour, and she does survive his coarsening of her. Hardy calls her 'a complete and substantial female animal – no more, no less', and often makes her 'the flesh', the reliable figure of moral allegory. But she is flesh in a story which recognises the moral cruelty involved when just such an element is absent. Though, when she abandons the dying Jude, she is an unnatural monster, she is also the woman whose assessment of realities gives her a reliable, sensitive perceptiveness of Sue's unhappiness, and the one who speaks the novel's final, tragic words of truth.

Balanced as she is in these ways, how should Arabella finally be judged? Though sparse, the relevant allusions do tip the scales against her. For, while Hardy gives her survival tactics and thus elicits grudging respect for her common sense and resilience, he undermines her with his references. When, for example, Arabella has trapped Jude by innuendo and finally has to confess the truth, Jude is appalled at what has happened. Arabella tries to brush it all away with 'What's done can't be undone' (p. 82), unknowingly connecting herself with another destroyer of men, Lady Macbeth (III. ii. 11). Or, when she returns years later with Cartlett at the fair (p. 310), her physical appeal, her main asset, is described as 'a tale that is told', a phrase drawn directly from Psalms 90:9: 'For all our days are passed away in wrath: we spend our years as a tale *that is told.*' The reader can scarcely help taking the reference one step further to an earlier borrower and add, 'told by an idiot'. When Arabella herself quotes, the sayings are always Socratically ironic, and thus underscore her hypocrisy. She soothes Phillotson with 'a contented mind is a continual feast' (p. 337). She quotes Numbers 5:31 – reminiscent of Alec when he uses Scripture – and scoffs at what is, in the light of her history, its justice: 'then shall the man be guiltless; but the woman shall bear her iniquity'. She unwittingly points out the bitter mockery her remarriage signifies and also links her situation with the perverted one of Sue and Phillotson when she quotes her vicar: 'What God hath joined together let no man put asunder' (p. 403). The only allusive compromise allowed Arabella is in the tenuous connection between her final words and Sophocles' *Oedipus Tyrannos*.[54] Jude calls her the Whore of Babylon; the reader cannot always agree, but the allusions imply that Hardy did.

With a note of wondrous hypocrisy Arabella calls Sue Bridehead 'that strumpet'. The fact that Sue is so tragically far from even the nuances of the epithet is at the core of her personality. With Sue Hardy penetrated new depths in his study of humanity, and, unfamiliar with Freud as he was, he wrote better than he knew. In some respects Sue is obviously a female Angel Clare. Her other antecedents in Hardy are clear: like Eustacia, she romanticises; when forced into it, she can momentarily be as docile as Thomasin; and she out-Tesses Tess in her guilt. But she has nothing of Arabella in her, and for that reason she earned Lawrence's opprobrium. He calls her 'the witch type, which has no sex'.[55]

Sue has been endlessly analysed by critics, for she presents real challenges to anyone attempting to understand Hardy, the Victorian period's attitude towards women in general, and the neurotic person caught in a struggle with both history and self. Hardy himself only heightened the ambiguities. On 4 August 1895 he wrote to Florence Henniker, whom Florence Hardy identified as a source for Sue, that he was 'more interested in the Sue story than any I have written'.[56] In his autobiography he attempts to define her character:

> You are quite right; there is nothing perverted or depraved in Sue's nature. The abnormalism consists in disproportion, not in inversion, her sexual instinct being healthy as far as it goes, but unusually weak and fastidious. Her sensibilities remain painfully alert notwithstanding, as they do in nature with such women. One point illustrating this I could not dwell upon: that, though she has children, her intimacies with Jude have never been more than occasional, even when they were living together (I mention that they occupy separate rooms, except towards the end), and one of her reasons for fearing the marriage ceremony is that she fears it would be breaking faith with Jude to withhold

herself at pleasure, or altogether, after it; though while uncon-
tracted she feels at liberty to yield herself as seldom as she
chooses. This has tended to keep his passion as hot at the end as
at the beginning, and helps to break his heart. He has never
really possessed her as freely as he desired.[57]

Much has been written to enlarge upon Hardy's explanation,
and any study dealing with allusion in deference to intricate
character analysis will necessarily be reductive. A summary must
suffice, with the recommendation that one should read Robert
Heilman's and Michael Steig's fine articles and Irving Howe's and
Albert Guerard's analyses in their studies of Hardy.[58] Sue can be
most concisely explained as a woman with a twentieth-century
mind controlled by a nineteenth-century view of self. In fact,
Robert Gittings argues, she has an 1860s view of self; for Sue is not
the new woman of the 1890s, since her support of Comte and her
loss of faith date her earlier.[59] She deems herself intellectually
liberated, worships her pagan gods, lives platonically with a
student, and meets Jude as an equal. But she also marries Phillotson twice, is driven to confess her unmarried status to the landlady, cannot talk about sex to Father Time, and exceeds even
Victorian inhibitions in her horror of physical love. Howe has
called her Promethean in mind but masochist in character.[60]
There is also little doubt that the masochism stems at least in part
from vestiges of a strict Hebraic atmosphere that Sue, like Angel, is
never fully able to shed. She is an intellectual sceptic and professes
a modernist sensibility. Yet she also feels an overwhelming sense of
guilt. This duality of consciousness, so central to the drama of the
novel, reveals itself in her vacillations. Heilman has summarised
them as 'unceasing reversals, apparent changes of mind and heart,
acceptances and rejections, alternations of warmth and offishness,
of evasiveness and candour, of impulsive acts and later regrets, of
commitment and withdrawal, of freedom and constraint, unconventionality and propriety'.[61] Mary Jacobus charts a course
through this welter of contradictions: 'No longer sustained by an
enduring rural context, Sue and Jude have nothing to fall back on
but their ideas, and one by one these fail them . . . Sue's education
– her experience as a woman – bring her from clarity to compromise, from compromise to collapse.'[62] Jacobus might have
added that Sue did unfortunately have one thing to fall back on –
the Church. Sue's retreat is perhaps best described by Carlyle,

when he says in *Essays* that a noble soul, when faced with a universe from which God seems to have vanished, will fly back to his church 'as a child might to his slain mother's bosom, and cling there'. The imagery of death is particularly apt.

Sue, then, is inconsistent, a troublesome creature who teases our imagination with her contradictions, just as she did Hardy's. His allusive treatment of her gives us some definite clues to just how perplexed he was about his creation, and about his own attitude both towards her dilemmas and those of the age. That things never will be as they should be, nor are as they appear, is clear from her first entrance onwards. Aunt Drusilla sends Jude a note warning him to avoid his cousin, thereby giving him the information he needs to find her. And find her he does, while she is illuminating the word ALLELUJAH — 'praise ye the Lord' (p. 108). He next sees her in church, but again does not approach her. At the time, with more truth than he knows, he deems her 'steeped body and soul in church sentiment' (p. 112), while the narrator says that 'the atmosphere blew as distinctly from Cyprus as from Galilee'. Cyprus was the centre of the worship of Venus (Aphrodite). Sue immediately thereafter buys the statues of Venus and Apollo, ostensibly linking herself with Greek joyousness, as opposed to dour Christianity. But even here Hardy subtly forecasts that Sue's Hellenism is tenuous at best. She chooses these two statues on impulse, not because they have a special meaning for her, but because they stand out as the largest on the tray. That they are crude copies is revealed by Sue's nervous checking to make sure her Venus's arm is *not* broken; that she lacks the courage to admit to her purchase is proved by her quickly identifying them as Saints Peter and Mary Magdalen when questioned by her landlady (p. 115). In the manuscript Hardy struck out 'Paul' and substituted 'Peter', thus enunciating the historical foundation of the church. Sue then sets up her shrine, the statues on each side of her chest. But, with a fine sense of foreboding detail, Hardy places a print of Calvary between two figures. Sue tries to expunge the latter image by reading Gibbon on Julian the Apostate — a text that would display her intellectual daring to a Victorian audience — and also by reading Swinburne, another heretic. But the poem she chooses will prove, ironically, to have been prophetic: 'Thou hast conquered, O pale Galilean; the world has grown grey from thy breath.'

Sue continues in this state of suspension throughout the allusive discussion of her intellectual position. She describes her unconventionality in terms of tradition, by calling herself 'an Ishmaelite' (p. 159), an allusion that, as we shall see, has many meanings. She also inadvertently discloses that her learning, though advanced for a woman of the time, does not have the conviction of Jude's, for she has read the classics in translation rather than the original languages (p. 167). Her list of reading is also heavily laced with the satirists, both classical and contemporary. Hardy added Scarron, Brantôme, Sterne, Defoe, Smollett, and Fielding after the manuscript stage, thereby accentuating one source of her daring, and of her brittle intellectuality. Her criticism of Christminster immediately follows this catalogue, and again she draws on tradition (Matthew 9:17) to chastise the traditional, only to counter this Freudian slip with a reference from Swinburne's 'The Hymn to Proserpine' (p. 170). This rift in Sue's intellect remains allusively accurate, but fades from focus during the central section of the story, as her conflicts turn from intellectual to emotional. When she finds herself at war with the demands of the flesh (especially other people's), the references shift to define this dimension of her personality.

Sue has already told Jude that she is an Ishmaelite. In the context of Genesis 16:12 we read, 'his hand *will be* against every man, and every man's hand against him'. Sue then reveals that she longs to return to her childhood and its freedom. This desire for an escape, for a return to the womb, is a recurring motif in Victorian fiction — one only has to recall Jane Eyre, Amelia Sedley, and Catherine Earnshaw. But it is not a return to safety. For Jane it means the terrible red room; for Amelia it is the white bed where she cries on her pillow; for Catherine it is the oak-panelled bed where she wakes with a great grief, aware of sleeping alone for the first time; for Sue it is a foetal position in a closet with spiders. Perhaps this is one context Hardy had in mind when he argued that Sue was not abnormal. But to the post-Freudian world Sue seems clearly to have had an exaggerated aversion to physical contact with men, an aversion stemming not from physical frigidity, nor from lesbianism, but from a socially conditioned association of eroticism with sin — the exact association that Jude makes, and pleads with Sue to protect him against. Like Angel before her, Sue can never fully free herself from her Hebraic conscience that guards her sexuality. Hardy gives us an allusive clue to her problem when he has Sue and Jude discuss eroticism in the context

not of classical erotic poetry, but of the Hebraic Song of Solomon
6:1: 'Whither is thy beloved gone, O thou fairest among women'
(p. 172). Later, when Sue has turned to the Church, this question
is to ring mockingly in our consciousness. Sue expands on this
quotation by lamenting the ecclesiastical scholars' perversion of
'such ecstatic, natural human love' as is in Solomon, but when
Jude tries 'to apply the words profanely' to her, she quickly deflects
his intention and returns the mood to the abstract, to her vague
wish to 'ennoble some man to high aims'. Hardy further emphasises her need for asexuality when he describes her sleeping
form as 'boyish as a Ganymedes' (p. 174), the beautiful boy Zeus
chose as cupbearer to the Gods. Revealingly, Hardy had first
written the more erotic 'Cupid' in the manuscript. For Sue, then,
an applied eroticism is aligned with the sense of sin which is central
to Victorian Hebraism. Such feelings must be suppressed, so Sue
unconsciously does repress them by consistently hiding behind her
intellect and relegating desire to traditional minds. She illustrates
both when she says to Jude, in response to his confession that he is
married, that society would not have continued to let them be
friends, for 'their views of the relations of man and woman are
limited, as is proved by their expelling me from the school. Their
philosophy only recognises relations based on animal desire. The
wide field of strong attachment where desire plays, at least, only a
secondary part, is ignored by them — the part of — who is it?
Venus Urania' (p. 188). Hardy's and Sue's choice of analogy is
deliberate, for she rejects the goddess of physical love for Venus in
the aspect of spiritual love. For her, eroticism is traditional and
Biblical; her reaction to it is ultimately one of masochistic self-
denial.

   That Sue shields herself from herself in a gauze of intellect is
best illustrated in the two instances in which she must confront her
lovers: first when she asks for her freedom from Phillotson, and
then when she establishes her platonic relationship with Jude. In
the first scene she diverts the crucial discussion of her night in the
closet by quoting J. S. Mill's *On Liberty*, a book Hardy knew
almost by heart and used as one of his cures for despair (p. 244).
Sue appears unusually insensitive here, and Phillotson gains our
sympathy when he cries, 'What do I care for J. S. Mill?' But Sue's
choice of defence is crucial and subsequently ironic. After the
manuscript stage Hardy added both the quotation from Mill and,
on the next page, one from Humboldt (whom Mill quotes in *On*

Liberty).[63] Literally, Sue's argument illustrates her tendency to depersonalise emotion. It also shows her desire to see her problem only as a social one, for Mill's Chapter III is most concerned with the individual's relationship with society, not with other individuals. In context, Sue's words are to turn on her, for Mill proposes in this chapter:

> There is always need of persons not only to discover new truths, and point out when what were once truths are true no longer, but also to commence new practices, and set the example of more enlightened conduct, and better taste and sense in human life . . . exceptional individuals, instead of being deterred, should be encouraged in acting differently from the mass. . . . In this age the mere example of nonconformity, the mere refusal to bend the knee to custom, is itself a service.[64]

That Sue is incapable of divorcing herself from the mass, that she cannot, as she tragically discovers, 'be a pioneer', is adumbrated in her next letter in the strained exchange: 'No poor woman has ever wished more than I that Eve had not fallen' (p. 245).

Having escaped from Phillotson by an appeal for individual freedom from social bonds, even while Hardy hints that she is incapable of bearing such freedom, Sue next distances Jude by a similar technique, but directs her argument at private rather than public relations. Jude naturally assumes that they will sleep together; but Sue hangs up a Shelleyan curtain (p. 265), quoting 'Epipsychidion', and with coy cruelty drawing from Jude a flattering comparison. By having Sue deflect Jude's sincere passion with a reference to Shelley's celebration of a sexless woman and a love that is purely ethereal, Hardy tells us a great deal about Sue, while concomitantly exposing his antipathy to her methods.[65] Because Sue recites rather than responds, our sympathy for Jude is aroused at her expense. Jude is resigned. In the scene where she has reluctantly agreed to marry him and they are going to the clerk to make the initial arrangements, he equates her with classical beauties 'rather than a denizen of a mere Christian country', and places her in the company of Octavia, Livia, Aspasia, and Phryne (pp. 291–2). Sue does not mind the comparison, and the perceptive reader both wonders why not and questions her learning: Octavia lost her husband to Cleopatra; Livia was a notorious degenerate; Aspasia was a courtesan, first mistress and then wife of

Pericles; Phryne was another courtesan. Sue is superficially elevated by the comparison to famous women, but predominantly undermined by these associations, just as she has been by previous allusions and is to be again in the scene just mentioned. She rebels at seeing the parish clerk, and as she and Jude leave without doing so, three lines from Thomas Campbell's poem on the impossibility of sustaining married love suffice for further discussion between them. The lines are from 'How delicious is the winning', a poem which gives the reader further insight into Sue's fascination with the courtship and fear of the consummation.

Faced with confronting Phillotson, Sue quotes Mill; faced with Jude's bed, it is Shelley; faced with the banns, it is Campbell; when married, she quotes poetry again. First there is a return to Shelley – his protest against the tyranny of the Church, *The Revolt of Islam* – when she describes the plight of marrying humanity as: 'Shapes like our own selves hideously multiplied' (p. 305). Jude bridles at the desolation of the line, and at the sentiment of her next reference on the following page, an echo from Keats's 'Ode on a Grecian Urn': 'the flowers in the bride's hand are sadly like the garland which decked the heifers of sacrifice in old times'. At this point Sue refuses to be sacrificed, and we understand her need to be free. But the allusive evidence argues that her urge for freedom is an unexamined one, that her Hellenism lacks foundation, that she intellectually finesses rather than fights, that she is unknowingly fettered to the pervasive repression of the period.

Even at the time of their happiness – those largely undescribed years when Sue seems to have conquered her earlier repugnance and lived with a modicum of sexual compatibility – her inner self surfaces. She asserts Greek joyousness, but feels it is gained at the expense of truth. She realises that we 'have blinded ourselves to sickness and sorrow, and have forgotten what twenty-five centuries have taught the race since their time . . .' (p. 316). The implied reference to Arnold hints that she is never free of these shadows. Moreover, the classicism she alludes to has for her been narrowed to asexual joy, for only in that context does she really feel safe from the physical sensations she has been taught to fear. This joy, too, has gone for ever. Reality is the House of Atreus with its tradition of passion and tragedy. The death of her children, the tangible results of her plunge into sexuality, forces her to confront the profoundest parts of her instinctual self and confirms her most neurotic fears. This time the intellect offers no protection. Hardy has cautioned us, in his allusions, that this will happen: As she is looking for the fateful lodgings and just before she makes her guilty, compulsive confession to the landlady, Sue says that 'leaving Kennetbridge for this place is like coming from Caiaphas to Pilate' (p. 349). Christ was tried by both before his crucifixion, a death that is going to be visited on Sue's children.[66] After all her children, born and unborn alike, are dead, Sue, with autistic repetition, litanizes the *bête noire*, Corinthians: 'We are made a spectacle unto the world, and to angels, and to men' (1 Corinthians 4:9; pp. 357,363). In context, the next verse begins, 'we are fools for Christ's sake'. Paul goes on to say that, in spite of all hardships, he continues to be blessed. Sue's actions represent Hardy's devastating comment on such faith.

Sue returns to the Church, assuming the yoke of Hebraism. She warns Jude of her new attitude, and Hardy imagistically foreshadows her return to Phillotson by reminding us of her wish that Eve had not eaten. Now, she says, 'we should mortify the flesh — the terrible flesh — the curse of Adam' (p. 364). Jude attempts to return to the past with a quotation from Shelley (p. 365) and several pages later with references to her former reading of Gibbon, Shelley and Mill (p. 371), three allusions which Hardy added in print and which recall her early reliance on the intellect. But Sue is already on her Via Dolorosa. Only once more is her mind briefly allowed to shield her, this time when she quotes Browning to Jude in the church: 'the world and its ways have a certain worth' (p. 380). But again the quotation is brutally ironic; it is from the poet's story of two frustrated loves, 'The Statue and the Bust'. Sue admits that her mind has bowed to her conditioned emotions, seeing herself now as 'a poor wicked woman who is trying to mend'. In a scene that is surely one of Hardy's most oppressive Sue says goodbye to Jude, mouthing 1 Corinthians 13:5 — 'charity seeketh not her own' (p. 384) — and assuring him that his worldly failure is surely his triumph. Sue, her practice never as advanced as her theories, regresses to Phillotson, the only man she fears, and the 'sackcloth of Scripture' (p. 384), just as Hardy hinted she would when he put that picture between the statues. She can no longer act upon the division in her personality, and in her last meeting with Jude, cries that she will hate herself for ever for her sin (p. 409). Hardy, deliberately drawing the connection in a revision in the manuscript, tells us she looks like her name (p. 388), an appearance which derides circumstances. Susanna means 'lily' in Hebrew, and also suggests the chaste wife of the Apocrypha, a woman brought up 'according to the law of Moses' and discussed in the Book of Daniel, whose moral, ironically, is innocence vindicated. Florence was the name of the virgin saint who became an abbess; Mary the name of another virgin, whose Hebrew name denotes both rebellion and bitterness. And Bridehead speaks for itself.

Hardy's allusive pattern for Sue, then, is intricate, ironic, and an indictment of Christianity as Victorians interpreted it. His scheme for Jude follows a similar plan and is the only one that has previously received close critical attention.[67] Jude is allotted more allusions than any other character in Hardy; over fifty-five groups of them directly concern him, and there are well over a hundred references if counted singly. There are several obvious reasons for this concentration, the chief of these being Hardy's wish to outline Jude's intellectual quest in detail by means of allusions. Secondly, Hardy once again uses this technique to demonstrate his own learning; it is a particularly poignant feature of the novel that Jude's curriculum was the same as Hardy's. In Chapters 5 and 6 of the Marygreen section we are given virtually a card index of Jude's library. As he worked on the novel, Hardy very carefully revised this list and subsequent ones, demonstrating his own concern for accuracy, and perhaps his insecurity. For example, the list on p. 51 includes 'Caesar, Virgil, or Horace' – Homer and Ovid he ruled out in the manuscript as possible substitutes for Horace. On p. 54 he added Clark's Homer to the reading list after *Jude* was already in print. And the catalogue that Jude thinks about on p. 56 was very carefully worked over to make it more specific: the manuscript's 'eleven books by Homer' becomes 'two books of the *Iliad*'; 'Theocritus, Apuleius, Lucretius' becomes 'Euripides, Plato, Aristotle, Lucretius'. Later, on p. 63, Hardy even changed the Greek phrase he had ostentatiously used. And, in the final references to Jude's learning – a list of the books which stare at him from the shelf as he dies – the manuscript 'Homer' is changed to 'Horace' (p. 428). On his walk through Christminster Jude associates himself with the great dreamers of the past through a welter of allusions that read like a literary quiz (pp. 100–4). Here Hardy seems deliberately to be testing his readers, for he gives clues rather than identifications: 'the Corn Law convert' for Sir Robert Peel as Jude recalls a part of his speech before the House of Commons; 'the sly author' for Gibbon; the 'last of the optimists' for

Browning; the 'gentle-voiced' prelate for Bishop Ken; and so on through a list of almost a dozen.[68]

These clusters continue to crop up throughout the novel. Jude describes Christminster as the city of 'Newman, Pusey, Ward, Keble' (p. 123). Later Fourways is described as a place where men had 'stood and talked of Napoleon, the loss of America, the execution of King Charles, the burning of the Martyrs, the Crusades, the Norman Conquest, possibly of the arrival of Caesar' (p. 137). Or Jude and Sue are visiting the art museum at Wardour Castle: Jude stops before the devotional pictures, Sue before the secular (p. 156). Jude pauses at five specific works, all of which actually hang in this castle.[69] Each of these groups of images serves a specific purpose: Jude's early studies were classical and he must make a conscious recorded shift to theology; his naïve reverence for Christminster is made painfully clear, and it is the Christminster of theological orthodoxy and strictness, not enlightened disinterestedness; Fourways is a place of intense emotion, emotion divorced from the snobbish academe; Jude is still traditional and believing, whereas Sue considers herself secular. Because they add this richness to the novel, the reader welcomes their presence, but only to a degree. Seemingly Hardy could not resist adding four allusions when two would have sufficed.

But if Hardy indulges himself in these instances, and perhaps thereby unwittingly dulls some of the early emotional force of his story, he does create some highly successful patterns for Jude. Readers familiar with Hardy have long recognised that, structurally, *Jude* is *Tess* turned round, the sexes reversed in the triangle. Philosophically, Sue has Angel's Hebraic–Hellenic schizophrenia. Jude is also affected by this dichotomy, but its elements do not operate simultaneously within him. He is in the course of his career, first a believer, then a sceptic. Like Hardy himself, Jude reluctantly abandons formal Christianity; but once he ceases to believe in Christminster, he is willing to throw off what he recognises as its stultifying morality, and redirect his aspirations into broader, more enlightened areas, hoping in the course of his search to maintain the best of both worlds. He looks to Sue as a guide and companion in this new adventure. However, as Arabella reminds us, he is never free of his past mistakes; as Jude reminds us, he is never free of his personality, of his weaknesses for whisky and women; and, as Sue proves to us, the blight of perverted Christian morality runs deep in the society in which he must operate. All of these factors, stimulated by a universe which is at best indifferent, conspire to force Jude to curse the day he was born. He develops his consciousness, and gradually becomes aware of the intellectual turmoil around him, only to discover that his sensitivity is ground for pain; that his intellectual search is constantly thwarted by physical desires he hardly understands and economic necessities he understands only too well; that his guide is not strong enough to carry either herself or him through. As Norman Holland observes, 'the best of Hebraism and the best of Hellenism are destroyed.'[70] Jude is betrayed and abandoned by God, society, and himself, an example of the coming universal wish not to live in a world which no longer offers any stable and humane values.

Because Jude's overriding impulse, as Ward Hellstrom has pointed out, is towards Hellenic self-development rather than towards Hebraic concerns with conduct, and because he struggles successfully to let his mind explore diverse areas of learning, the allusions attached to his philosophy are not divided.[71] He relies on Biblical studies and constantly quotes Scripture even after he has formally declared that 'the church is no more to me' (p. 258), punctuating his stand with a secular quotation from Browning's 'The Statue and the Bust': 'I am not to be one of "the soldier-saints who, row on row, / Burn upward each to his point of bliss."' Later he draws on both Romans 8:22 ('all creation groaning') and a chorus in Aeschylus' *Agamemnon* (pp. 357, 359) to vent his pain after the death of his children. He is Laocoön (p. 144), he is a Spartan (p. 190), but he is also Joseph the dreamer of dreams, Don Quixote, and St Stephen (p. 226). Jude, then, fights for eclecticism, for sweetness and light, for the balance that was Arnold's ideal, for a combination of discipline and curiosity that will let him 'see things as they are, and by seeing them as they are to see them in their beauty'. Of course he fails in his quest. The allusive strands threading through his actions and describing his meditations forewarn us that the quest is always futile and underscore Hardy's deep personal despair at the chances for happiness on this planet.

The quotation from 'The Statue and the Bust' is just one example of how Hardy allusively portends Jude's failure. It occurs when Sue has just left Phillotson and joined Jude. He announces his renunciation, and thereby his plans for their union, through a poem which, though iconoclastically approving of adultery, tells of futile loves. Nor is this the earliest example of allusions ironically preparing for the fall. The child Jude is bathed in Wordsworthian optimism − which Hardy even labels a 'flattering fancy' (p. 488) − just before he realises that his innocence has let him be duped by Vilbert. Heaven is supposed to lie around Jude, but he cries bitterly. The process is repeated when Jude tries another step forward, after Arabella has left him. He starts off for Christminster, spurred on by Spinoza (p. 94) 'to do good cheerfully'. He is neither happy nor helpful there. He arrives as a kind of Dick Whittington (p. 97), the poor boy who became a Lord Mayor; the city coldly rejects his attempts to better himself. Later, when his spirits flag during his first short stay in Christminster, he looks at the tall cathedral spires and consoles himself with Ecclesiastes 7:12: 'For wisdom is a defence, and money is a defence; but the excellency of knowledge is, that wisdom giveth life to them that have it' (p. 107). That the consolation is more salt than salve is apparent in the narrator's next line: 'his desire absorbed him, and left no part of him to weigh its practicability.' Jude is soon forced to weigh practicability, and the painful enlightenment is emphasised by two juxtaposed allusions, the before and after (p. 135). Initially he was like the fatuous Robinson Crusoe, who built a boat too big to drag to the water. Reality is forced upon him as the narrator draws on Heine's 'Götterdämmerung' to fix his disillusionment: 'Above the youth's inspired and flashing eyes / I see the motley mocking fool's-cap rise!'

Diverse allusions, then, consistently push Jude's rock up the hill, only to make the downward roll more painful. More overtly, Hardy also emphasises Jude's plight by repeating an image, by connecting Jude with the same familiar figures to give both structure to his narrative and poignancy to his hero's situation. The most obvious and simplistic of these clusters is the sequence from the story of Samson and Delilah, that infamous tool of the Philistines. In three instances Jude is aligned with the Biblical hero: as one who looks at the picture on the wall in the tavern when he first drinks with Arabella (p. 66); on his return to the same inn after he has just been spared from his suicide attempt (p. 91); and as a 'shorn Sampson' (p. 398), who so attracts Arabella again when, with remarriage on her mind, she plies him with liquor. All three of these references connect him with Arabella, identify his weakness for destructive women and alcohol, and predict his fate. The conjunction is intentional: in the manuscript Hardy first wrote

'Susanna and the Elders' for two of the three references (the manuscript page for the third is missing). But Susanna was reserved for someone else.

A second series of images makes Jude a Christ figure. Again the pattern is overt, but it is more intricate, for here Hardy is dealing with the complexities of Jude's mind rather than the simplicities of his physical desires. Once more the comparison is bleak; the shorn Samson also makes a 'poor Christ' (p. 144), though now the fault is not in the individual. The first comparison comes from Jude himself, and the juxtaposition with setting is illuminating: Jude says, 'Christminster shall be my Alma Mater; and I'll be her beloved son, in whom she shall be well pleased' (p. 58). The second reference pairs Christ–Jude with Sue (p. 112) – the wind blows from both Cyprus and Galilee. And the third connects him with both Sue and Phillotson (p. 127): Jude's face is hidden from view by the Mount of Olives, the scene of much of Christ's teaching, as he looks at the Valley of Jehosaphat, the place of judgment for the heathen. All three references define Jude's tragedy. His aspirations lead him to search for the spirit of Christianity – or Christ the teacher: 'he considered that he might so mark out his coming years as to begin his ministry at the age of thirty – an age which much attracted him as being that of his exemplar when he first began to teach in Galilee' (p. 149). The 'in Galilee' was added post-manuscript. His circumstances and associates – Christminster, Sue, Phillotson – make him Christ-the-Crucified. Thematically, the attack is more than a personal one, for as Jude becomes victim, Hardy exposes the source of his oppression (p. 228). On Easter Eve he writes a note to Sue, saying that he supposes he must learn the lesson of renunciation, of self-denial, the Hebraic element that is the curse of Christminster and at the centre of Sue's masochism. The remaining elements of the cluster continue the message: we remember that Jude signifies his divorce from Sue with the words from Mark used to describe the effect of Christ's death; Jude refuses to mention Sue in Arabella's house, calling it 'this Capharnaum' (p. 401), the town with which Jesus remonstrates. For ignoring His teaching, He warns, it will be brought down to hell. Jude dies in his 'new Jerusalem', calling for his Susanna, who in Luke 8:3 ministers to Jesus,[72] and begging for water; as with his predecessor, no water comes. Sue has returned to Phillotson the philistine; Delilah has gone to the games.

If Jude makes a poor Christ, and fares the way Hardy believes

Jesus has fared in the harsh Victorian atmosphere, he does make a good Job. It is through these images that Hardy expresses the full strength of his rancour, and gives readers some of the most unforgettable scenes in fiction. Surprisingly, there are fewer references to Job in the text than a casual reader would suppose, because the few are so central and memorable. It is the idiom of Job that Jude uses for his rebellion, drawing forth our admiration, and our sense of futility. Jude writes his challenge on the wall of a college, quoting Job 12:3: 'I have understanding as well as you; I am not inferior to you: yea, who knoweth not such things as these?' (p. 138). The next verse in Job reads, 'I am *as* one mocked of his neighbour, who calleth upon God, and he answereth him: the just upright *man is* laughed to scorn.' Later he challenges Sue's unbending chastity with a reference to the 'patience of Job'.

But the crucial allusion comes from Job 3:3, and Hardy integrates it brilliantly. Jude first uses the verse, 'Let the day perish wherein I was born', to outline the future of Little Father Time if they do not take him in. They do take him, and Father Time, Age masquerading as Juvenility, with his fixed ideas and constant stare at the worst, is a metaphor for the perverted spirit of the times, for all that is wrong with Jude's world. Willingly sacrificed by Arabella to save the expenses of a Christian funeral, he arrives unchristened, symbolically doomed under the same strictures which relegated Tess's Sorrow to a plot of weeds. Sue sees him as the one shadow on their Greek joyousness. Time, as tradition, crucifies the fruits of this joy. He is the present, and portends the future. He is 'the universal wish not to live' (p. 357) in such a world. The Job reference links him to his father. Jude dies quoting long portions of the same chapter, all added in a post-manuscript revision. He curses the day he was born, but rebels to the last. The Christian images here mingle with Job, and, just as in the scene of Father Time's death, the Crucifixion is a travesty of justice. Self-denial does not bring redemption. 'The letter killeth', Jude had said. The rest of the verse, from 2 Corinthians 3:6 − 'but the spirit giveth life' − is withheld. Samson dies, Christ dies, only Job lives. In this bleakest of novels, even that is impossible. Jude endures, but he cannot survive. Jude's name has proved to be his destiny: in the New Testament he is the writer who asks that the Christians remember the old laws, and apply them with compassion. He is also the patron saint of craftsmen and lost causes. At one point in the manuscript he was 'Jude England'.

Ian Gregor has called Jude's death a triumph, in that he goes down fighting; if so, it is indeed a Pyrrhic one. But his death is high tragedy, in that by what he loses we get an understanding of our own loss. Certainly Hardy has rejected Browning's 'success in failure', for Jude's resilience, so evident throughout the novel, only prolongs his agony. Not only is there no longer an appetite for joy; there is no appetite for life — unless it is a craving for self-punishment, such as drives Sue back to Phillotson's bed. It is the tragic predicament of individuals caught in the fret and fever of Victorian orthodoxy on the one hand, and of an insentient universe on the other. The old order fights change, the new is valueless chaos. Jude's final allusion in the novel reduces everything to dust. Sitting on the shelf as he dies, 'the old superseded, Delphin editions of Virgil and Horace, and the dog-eared Greek Testament on the neighbouring shelf, and the few other volumes of the sort that he had not parted with, roughened with stone-dust where he had been in the habit of catching them up for a few minutes between his labours, seemed to pale to a sickly cast . . .' (p. 428). Sue lives in agony, Jude smiles in death, at last released from the letter into obscurity.

Hardy once said of his writing, 'my art is to intensify the expression of things, as is done by Crivelli, Bellini, etc., so that the heart and inner meaning is made vividly visible'.[73] That he uses allusions even as he examines his own method is emblematic of how rewardingly dependent he was on this device. References drawn from his vast and varied learning permeate his style from his earliest to his last novel, and as he constructed his allusive technique he gradually became a master craftsman.

Hardy's reliance on allusions in his fiction is of course not unique in itself, and his art is deeply rooted in tradition. Starting with his title-page, where he quotes Juvenal, Sterne used the device in *Tristram Shandy* to such excess that he drew charges of plagiarism, and Hippolyte Taine says of the novel, 'son livre est comme un grand magasin de bric à brac où les curiosités de tout siècle, de toute espèce et de tout pays gisent entassées pêle-mêle'. Even Sterne's diatribe against borrowings is itself pieced together out of Burton's own assembled allusions as he rails on the same subject in *The Anatomy of Melancholy*.[74] Sterne's method is thus obviously intentional, and is used for a more sophisticated purpose than to fill in for his own creative lapses. George Eliot also relies on the technique, having in her work, for example, 226 epigraphs alone, 130 of which are drawn from works by 56 identifiable authors, ranging from Shakespeare to Heine and covering the literatures of at least seven countries. And, as in Hardy, many of these references help to control plots, distinguish tones, and establish ironies.[75] Then there is Meredith, whose practice is suggested by *The Ordeal of Richard Feverel*, where, as noted by Lionel Stevenson, he relies heavily on references to Ferdinand, Miranda, and the magic island, while the novel itself distinctly resembles *Romeo and Juliet* in both plot and characterisation.[76] On the Continent we have Cervantes, who in *Don Quixote* uses his quotations to help develop the thematic contrast between high and low, delusion and reality. Rabelais makes his erudition a primary means of shaping his humour; and later Thomas Mann, in *The Magic Mountain*, was to use many obvious literary quotations which contribute to the contextual and formal structure of the work.[77] Then in Ireland there was to be James Joyce, the master quoter of them all.

The catalogue, both in England and on the Continent, could be extended well beyond such a list. Hardy obviously learned much from and expanded upon his predecessors and contemporaries, but none the less had to feel his own way with his own method. In *Desperate Remedies* we see a novice author, who, caught up in the mysteries of his work, drops allusive clues to both plot and character which also inadvertently reveal his own inexperience. Hardy changed his approach in *Under the Greenwood Tree*, as he was to do in each of his next four novels; but rather than omitting them, he retained allusions to help establish and record each new experiment. In his bucolic novelette they begin to inform the reader of tone, and aid in executing the subtle shifts between the comic and the serious. *A Pair of Blue Eyes* illustrates the allusive technique in an extravagant form, but even in this smothering surfeit of references there is a pattern of allusive character enlargement, humorous observation, and foreshadowing of events. With *Far From the Madding Crowd* Hardy hit his allusive stride, and skilfully uses his method as one way in which to control our responses to the major figures, to sketch his setting, and to give authority to his choric rustics. He momentarily stumbled over *The Hand of Ethelberta*, but more than regained his stylistic balance with *The Return of the Native*, coming of artistic age and gaining a confidence in the technique that was well rewarded in his last two important novels, *Tess of the d'Urbervilles* and *Jude the Obscure*. It is generally recognised that in them Hardy is more profound, and consistently more didactic, than ever before, sternly lecturing his public on the ills of society, and the Immanent Will on the injustice of things. His allusions continue increasingly to be a carefully ordered supporting device as he gives a new dimension to themes broached in *The Return*: the Hebraic-Hellenic conflict so central to the Victorian frame of mind; the darkling mood of the turn of the century; and the profound problems of the human pair caught between Arnold's two worlds.

Hardy's work, then, is artistic proof of Herman Meyer's observation that 'the charm of the quotation emanates from a unique tension between assimilation and dissimulation; it links itself closely with its new environment, but at the same time detaches itself from it, thus permitting another world to radiate into the self-contained world of the novel'.[78] Hardy drew from many worlds to enlarge his own novelistic universe, making allusions serve his audience as avenues into his fiction. Once inside his world, the reader is manipulated into the desired responses as Hardy undermines or ennobles his characters, foreshadows events, injects his humour, and projects his irony — all through his masterful choice of what Coleridge called 'sovereign fragments'. He requires of his readers that they bring to his novels an imaginative effort, that they read as connoisseurs. He directs his allusions to the gourmets, and their good taste is well rewarded: Wessex and its people are made vividly visible.

List of Abbreviations Used in the Notes and Bibliography

AN&Q	*American Notes and Queries* (New Haven, Conn.)
BUSE	*Boston University Studies in English*
CLQ	*Colby Library Quarterly*
EIC	*Essays in Criticism: A Quarterly Journal of Literary Criticism* (Oxford)
ELH	*Journal of English Literary History*
ELN	*English Language Notes* (University of Colorado)
ELT	*English Literature in Transition (1880–1920)*
K–SJ	*Keats–Shelley Journal: Keats, Shelley, Byron, Hunt, and Their Circles*
MFS	*Modern Fiction Studies*
MLN	*Modern Language Notes*
MSE	*Massachusetts Studies in English*
N&Q	*Notes and Queries*
NCF	*Nineteenth-Century Fiction*
PMLA	*Publications of the Modern Language Association of America*
PQ	*Philological Quarterly* (Iowa City)
PULC	*Princeton University Library Chronicle*
RES	*Review of English Studies: A Quarterly Journal of English Literature and the English Language*
SAQ	*South Atlantic Quarterly*
SNNTS	*Studies in the Novel* (North Texas State University)
SoR	*Southern Review* (Louisiana State University)
SP	*Studies in Philology*
SR	*Sewanee Review*
TSE	*Tulane Studies in English*
TSL	*Tennessee Studies in Literature*
TSLL	*Texas Studies in Literature and Language: A Journal of the Humanities*
VN	*Victorian Newsletter*
VS	*Victorian Studies* (Indiana University)

Notes and References

INTRODUCTORY TEXTUAL NOTE

1. There are no extant manuscripts of *Desperate Remedies* or *The Hand of Ethelberta*. Manuscripts of *A Pair of Blue Eyes* and *Far From the Madding Crowd* are in the Berg and Thorne collections respectively in New York. *Under the Greenwood Tree* is in the Dorset County Museum in England, and *The Return of the Native* is in the library of University College, Dublin. Of the later novels the manuscript of *Tess of the d'Urbervilles* is in the British Library and *Jude the Obscure* in the Fitzwilliam Museum, Cambridge.

CHAPTER ONE: STYLE AND THOMAS HARDY

1. Robert B. Heilman, 'Hardy's *Mayor*: Notes on Style', *NCF*, XVIII (March 1964) 328.
2. For a discussion of Hardy's interest in the gothic, see James F. Scott, 'Thomas Hardy's Use of the Gothic: An Examination of Five Representative Works', *NCF*, XVII (March 1963) 363–80.
3. Richard C. Carpenter, 'Thomas Hardy and the Old Masters', *BUSE*, V (spring 1961) 18–28, discusses effects in Hardy's fiction which suggest painting techniques.
4. The *Academy*, for example, revealed that Hardy appropriated material for *The Trumpet Major* from Gifford's *History* and for *A Laodicean* from Charles Apperly's article in the 1833 *Quarterly Review*. See C. J. Weber, 'Plagiarism and Thomas Hardy', *The Colophon*, n.s., II (July 1937) 443–50.
5. W. R. Rutland, *Thomas Hardy: A Study of his Writings and their Background* (Oxford, 1938) pp. 1, 18–20.
6. Lennart A. Björk (ed.), *The Literary Notes of Thomas Hardy* (Göteborg, Sweden, 1974).
7. Phyliss Bartlett, 'Hardy's Shelley', *K-SJ*, IV (1955) 16.
8. See Carl J. Weber, *Hardy of Wessex* (New York, 1940).
9. Ernest Brennecke, Jr., *The Life of Thomas Hardy* (New York, 1925) p. 180.
10. S. F. Johnson, 'Hardy and Burke's Sublime', in Harold C. Martin (ed.), *Style in Prose Fiction: English Institute Essays 1958* (New York, 1959) p. 70; Michael Millgate, *Thomas Hardy: His Career as a Novelist* (New York, 1971) pp. 131 and *passim*.
11. Norman Friedman, 'Point of View in Fiction: The Development of a Critical Concept', *PLMA*, LXX (December 1955) 1174.
12. Florence Emily Hardy, *The Life of Thomas Hardy: 1840–1928* (London, 1962) p. 252.

176

13. Stephen Ullman, *Style in French Fiction* (Cambridge, 1957) p. 25.
14. Robert C. Slack, 'Some Characteristics of Hardy's Novels', in William Schutte (ed.), *Six Novelists; Carnegie Studies in English, no. 5.* (Pittsburg, 1959) pp. 45–6.
15. Miss Lois Deacon attempts to prove the existence of an illegitimate child, but her case is tenuous. See Lois Deacon and Terry Coleman, *Providence and Mr. Hardy* (London, 1966). For a discussion of the personal upheavals which led to Hardy's loss of faith see Robert Gittings, *Young Thomas Hardy* (London, 1975) ch. 9.
16. Nathan Scott, 'The Literary Imagination and the Victorian Crisis of Faith: The Example of Thomas Hardy', *Journal of Religion*, XL (October 1960) 274.
17. Florence Hardy, op. cit., p. 218.
18. Rutland, op. cit., p. 93.
19. Carl J. Weber, 'Hardy's Copy of Schopenhauer', *Colby Library Quarterly*, IV (November 1957) 221.
20. Harold Orel, *The Final Years of Thomas Hardy: 1912–28* (London, 1976) p. 118.
21. Harold Orel (ed.), *Thomas Hardy's Personal Writings* (Lawrence, Kansas, 1966) p. 39.
22. For a detailed history of this progression see Albert P. Elliott, *Fatalism in the Works of Thomas Hardy* (Philadelphia, 1935), especially pp. 41–2, 47.
23. Florence Hardy, op. cit., p. 311.
24. Orel, *The Final Years of Thomas Hardy*, p. 122.
25. Herbert J. Muller, *Modern Fiction* (New York, 1957) p. 143.
26. Ibid., p. 425.
27. John Holloway, *The Victorian Sage: Studies in Argument* (New York, 1965) p. 252.
28. Mary Caroline Richards, 'Thomas Hardy's Ironic Vision', *NCF*, III (March 1949) 269.
29. See Norman Knox, *The Word Irony and Its Context, 1500–1755* (Durham, 1961); Alan R. Thompson, *The Dry Mock, a Study of Irony in Drama* (Berkeley, 1948); G. G. Sedgewick, *Of Irony: Especially in Drama* (Toronto, 1935).
30. Clearly the philosophically ironic situation has existed in literature for centuries, but the term 'irony' was not applied to the condition until the mid-seventeenth century, and even then its associations were primarily comic. The word was not applied specifically to tragedy until early in the nineteenth century, when Bishop Thirlwall's essay, either explicitly or by implication, added some important terms to the vocabulary of literary criticism. Irony of fate or circumstance, and tragic, Sophoclean or dramatic irony were considered in the essay under the general topic of 'practical irony' and what had heretofore been primarily a 'sense of irony' was now given a reliable, transferable meaning. See J. J. Stewart Perowne (ed.), *Remains: Literary and Theological of Connop Thirlwall, Vol.* III (London, 1878) pp. 1, 11.
31. Elizabeth Drew, *The Novel: A Modern Guide to Fifteen English Masterpieces* (New York, 1963) p. 144.
32. Haakon Chevalier, *The Ironic Temper* (New York, 1932) pp. 11–12.
33. Northrop Frye, *Anatomy of Criticism* (Princeton, 1957) p. 237.

34. S. F. Johnson (op. cit., pp. 58, 61) conclusively proves that Hardy thoroughly digested Burke's *A Philosophical Enquiry into the Origin of our Ideas of the Sublime and Beautiful*. He argues that from Burke, Hardy could have learned the literary effectiveness of injecting into his novels pity and terror, as well as obscurity, power, vastness and infinity, and privation or solitude as elements in a plot. Evidence indicates that Hardy read Burke shortly before or during his work on *Far From the Madding Crowd*, and he paraphrases Burke's unusual definition of 'delight' in this novel. However, most of Burke's influence on Hardy is revealed in *The Return of the Native*, where he not only develops terror, but also intensifies the emotion by masterfully applying subtle ironic touches, as, for example, when the snake causes Mrs Yeobright's death on a heath that is anything but a paradise. This is not to imply that Burke was a 'source' for Hardy, or that Hardy deliberately attempted to write a fictional *Enquiry*; but his reading of Burke certainly reinforced a number of his literary concepts. And Hardy's injection of the ironic into his acquired notions of the sublime yielded rich stylistic rewards.

35. Leslie H. Palmer has written an interesting study of several instances where Hardy employs verbal irony. Palmer discusses Hardy's use of both connotative and denotative irony in his choice of particular words, and agrees, in passing, that Hardy's ironic use of allusion, metaphor, simile, image and naming becomes increasingly refined. See Palmer, 'The Ironic Word in Hardy's Novels', *TSL*, xx (1975) 109–23.

CHAPTER TWO: THREE EXPERIMENTS IN FORM

1. Walter Scott, *The Monastery* (Boston, 1880) p. xiii. In the 1871 (first) edition Hardy misquotes Scott: 'Though a course of adventures which are only connected with each other by having happened to the same individual is what most frequently occurs in nature, yet the province of the romance-writer being artificial, there is more required from him than a mere compliance with the simplicity of reality.'

2. For a discussion of Hardy's debt here see Joseph Warren Beach, *The Technique of Thomas Hardy* (Chicago, 1922) p. 23.

3. W. R. Rutland, *Thomas Hardy: A Study of his Writings and their Background* (Oxford, 1938) p. 141.

4. The painting has now been attributed to one of Greuze's followers. See Alastair Smart, 'Pictorial Imagery in the Novels of Thomas Hardy', *RES*, n.s., XII (August 1961) 264–5.

5. Here Hardy is most likely using Tennyson's poem 'Lilian', whose heroine shows a similar frivolity.

6. See Albert J. Guerard, *Thomas Hardy: The Novels and Stories* (Cambridge, 1949) p. 36. An interesting aside on this subject is found in Elaine Showalter, 'Desperate Remedies: Sensation Novels of the 1860's', *VN*, no. 49 (spring 1976) 1–5. Though Showalter does not deal with Hardy at all, she provocatively argues that the popularity of this type of sensation fiction 'came from its exploitation of repressed sexual fantasy and covert protest against the restrictions of domestic sensibility'.

7. Evelyn Hardy, in *Thomas Hardy: A Critical Biography* (London, 1954) p. 104, cites this passage as 'clever', but 'not pleasing writing'.

8. For a history of Hardy's choice of the title, see Michael Millgate, *Thomas Hardy: His Career as a Novelist* (New York, 1971) pp. 44–6. Millgate also notes, accurately I believe, that it is unlikely that Hardy attempted any detailed correspondences between his story and Shakespeare's play.

9. Carl J. Weber, *Hardy of Wessex* (New York, 1940) p. 53.

10. For a discussion of Hardy's admiration of the Dutch school, see Evelyn Hardy, op. cit., pp. 124–5.

11. Kenneth and Miriam Allott (eds), *Introduction to Victorian Prose: 1830–1880* (London, 1956) p. xii.

12. This is not to say, however, that the novel is pure fantasy. Robert Draffan has convincingly argued ('Hardy's *Under the Greenwood Tree*', *English*, XXII (1973) 55–60) that the felicities of the Mellstock milieu are often overstated. The background material here, he notes, does contain appropriate Hardian tragedy: families have lost infants, one brother drowns, a friend dies of consumption, several people are maimed, and so on. But these incidents remain peripheral to the central tale of love and languishment.

13. For a detailed textual history of the punctuation changes and their possible effects on meaning in both *Under the Greenwood Tree* and *Tess* see Simon Gatrell, 'Hardy, House-Style, and the Aesthetics of Punctuation', in Anne Smith (ed.), *The Novels of Thomas Hardy* (London, 1979) pp. 169–92.

14. George Wing makes the rather bizarre statement that the entire book is comic, contending that Elfride's death is more ludicrous than tragic, that her method of rescuing Knight at the cliff is prudery reduced to intentional hilarity, and so on. See George Wing, *Thomas Hardy* (New York, 1963) p. 30.

15. Michael Steig goes so far as to argue that the book is even superior to *Far From the Madding Crowd* because it enables us to see through our fantasies, and 'refuses to employ quasi-mythic appeals as an alternative to its own acerbic vision'. See his 'The Problem of Literary Value in Two Early Hardy Novels', *TSLL*, XII (1970) 55–62. For a good discussion of the novel as a failure, see Millgate, op. cit., pp. 66–76.

16. Florence Emily Hardy, *The Life of Thomas Hardy: 1840–1928* (London, 1962) pp. 104–5.

17. H. C. Webster, *On a Darkling Plain: The Art and Thought of Thomas Hardy* (Chicago, 1947) p. 104.

18. Hardy later much improved his use of introductory quotations, and by the time he was writing *Jude the Obscure* had disciplined himself into using such epigraphs only for the major divisions of the novel.

19. Another such evasive chapter title comes in Chapter 22, the famous cliff chapter. The title in the Wessex Edition reads 'A woman's way'. Here Hardy revised for the worse, since the manuscript is more definitive. The manuscript reads 'Love will find out the way', the titular line from a song found in Percy's *Reliques*.

20. Millgate (op. cit., p. 69) notes that this epigraph also suggests that Hardy saw Knight 'as the romantic intellectual whose essential nobility of soul cannot prevent him from bringing disaster upon himself and others'.

21. Hardy uses the *Psalmster* version, rather than the Authorized Version.

22. Hardy again uses the *Psalmster* version.

23. Smart, op. cit., p. 266.

24. Hardy has been criticised by Edmund Blunden and others for his unwillingness to control several figures simultaneously, and for his consequent artifice of having one depart as the second enters.
25. See Guerard, op. cit., p. 135.

CHAPTER THREE: THE DIMENSIONS OF SUCCESS AND FAILURE

1. Thomas Hardy, *Far From the Madding Crowd*, ed. Carl J. Weber (New York, 1937) p. xvii. I am also indebted to the valuable notes Mr Weber has included in this edition.
2. Robert C. Schweik, 'The Early Development of Hardy's *Far From the Madding Crowd*', *TSLL*, IX (1967) 415–28.
3. For the revision of Fanny's wake, see *The A. E. Newton Collection of Books and Manuscripts*, sale catalogue, Parke-Bernet Galleries, Inc., II (1941) 67–9.
4. Thomas Hardy, *Far From the Madding Crowd*, *Eclectic Magazine*, 82–84 (March 1874–February 1875).
5. One critic has counted eighty-two such revisions of geography. See Janice Nyman Keefe, 'The Textual Revisions in *Far From the Madding Crowd*', *MSE*, V (fall 1975) 10–24.
6. For a detailed comparison of the changes from serial to Wessex Edition, see Keefe, op. cit.
7. Elizabeth Drew, *The Novel: A Modern Guide for Fifteen English Masterpieces* (New York, 1963) p. 43.
8. Carl J. Weber, *Hardy of Wessex* (New York, 1940) pp. 62–3.
9. And, as Keefe, op. cit., points out, in the serial version she remains saucy and coquettish.
10. Howard Babb, 'Setting and Theme in *Far From the Madding Crowd*', *ELH*, XXX (June 1963) 148.
11. In fact, Beach goes so far as to say that in this novel Hardy started with setting and then added plot. See Joseph Warren Beach, *The Technique of Thomas Hardy* (Chicago, 1922) p. 50.
12. For a discussion of the eroticism here, see Richard C. Carpenter, 'The Mirror and the Sword: Imagery in *Far From the Madding Crowd*', *NCF*, XVIII (March 1964) 341.
13. William Dean Howells, *Heroines of Fiction* (New York, 1901) p. 194.
14. Albert J. Guerard, *Thomas Hardy: The Novels and Stories* (Cambridge, 1949) p. 137.
15. Schweik, op. cit., p. 420 notes that Hardy was careful with his effects here, for he added the Fanny–Oak meeting as a manuscript revision.
16. *Newton Collection*, sale catalogue, p. 67.
17. For a Freudian interpretation see Carpenter, 'The Mirror and the Sword', 331–45.
18. J. R. Moore contends that Troy's entire personality is an opprobrious allusion, asserting that Troy is obviously taken from Sergeant Bothwell, a dragoon in the Life Guards in Scott's *Old Mortality*; 'but almost every quality of Bothwell was copied in Troy only to be degraded'. See John Robert Moore, 'Two Notes on Thomas Hardy', *NCF*, V (September 1950) 162–3.

19. Richard C. Carpenter, 'Hardy's "Gargoyles"', *MFS*, VI (autumn 1960) 227.
20. See, for example, Herbert B. Grimsditch's discussion in *Character and Environment in the Novels of Thomas Hardy* (London, 1925) p. 62.
21. Again Hardy is making a careful choice here, for Oak was given another surname in the manuscript, which was heavily crossed out and replaced by 'Oak'. See Schweik, op. cit., 422.
22. Carpenter, 'The Mirror and the Sword', 340–1.
23. Alan Friedman, *The Turn of the Novel* (New York, 1966) p. 51.
24. See Henry C. Duffin, *Thomas Hardy: A Study of the Wessex Novels* (Manchester, 1937) p. 14; Drew, op. cit., p. 148.
25. Millgate, for example, defends the novel as an often successful 'experiment with techniques and areas of subject matter which he had not previously exploited in print' (Michael Millgate, *Thomas Hardy: His Career as a Novelist* (New York, 1971) p. 115). Millgate notes as especially important Hardy's decision to angle his point of view from below stairs.
26. The revisions Hardy made between the first edition (there is no extant manuscript) and the Wessex Edition reflect his lackadaisical approach to its deficiencies. He did, however, make some judicious changes: the Wessex Edition is two chapters shorter than the first. As Hardy condensed the novel from fifty to forty-eight chapters, he excised much of Chapters 9 and 12, adding the remainder to Chapters 8 and 11. The section cut from Chapter 9 concerns, first, a visit by Ladywell and Christopher Julian to Rookington Park in a vain attempt to see Ethelberta just one more time, and then a conversation between Faith and Christopher wherein she senses that he still loves Ethelberta. Omitted from Chapter 12 is another visit, this time by Faith and Christopher to town, during which Faith meets Picotee and learns of her secret love for Christopher. The novel does not suffer from any of this cutting; the Rookington Park visit is an extraneous episode in a story already surfeited with social calls, and Faith's multiple discoveries give her an insight that her personality and position in the plot render useless.
    Hardy made some other minor improvements. He tended to urbanise in his revisions in an attempt to fit his characters and their speech to his setting. A tedious story Ethelberta tells to her younger brothers and sisters is reduced to the exciting essentials. Names are changed, and once again some Wessex locales are substituted for random place names. Finally, in keeping with his usual practice, the early long paragraphs are cut into manageable sections in the Wessex Edition.
27. The Latin references are: the title page epigraph from Lucretius' *De Rerum Natura*, IV, 1182, and Neigh's companion's use of a phrase from Horace's *Odes*, III, i, 4 (p. 92). Sol and Dan are compared to the Zamzummims [sic] (p. 192), a giant race mentioned once in the Bible, and then in parenthesis (Deuteronomy 2:20); Ethelberta wishes herself in Kamtschatka, the German spelling for the Russian peninsula, Kamchatka (p. 205); and the little known Welby Pugin, the architect who fostered the Gothic revival, is called upon in a description of the bad taste displayed by Mountclere's mansion (p. 304).
28. See, for example, pp. 75–80, where her meter is described as Anacreontic; Romeo and Juliet, Othello, Shakespeare, and Sappho are all mentioned in the discussion; and reviews from the *Seven Days Review* and *London Lights*

are quoted, though here Hardy was twitting his own audience's memory, for the usually authentic Hardy this time chose two imaginary journals.

29. His art is pompously inscribed with a quotation from Shakespeare (p. 191), and he is 'blind as Bartimeus' (p. 214) in insight, never to receive a healing touch as did his Biblical namesake (Mark 10:46).

30. This reference to Hawthorne also calls to mind another Faith, who, in 'Young Goodman Brown', plays much the same Cassandrian role.

CHAPTER FOUR: THE RUSTIC CHORUS

1. 'Dialect in the Novels', Harold Orel, *Thomas Hardy's Personal Writings* (Lawrence, Kansas, 1966) p. 92.

2. Robert Heilman, 'Hardy's *Mayor*: Notes on Style', *NCF*, xviii (March 1964) 325.

3. John Paterson, '*The Return of the Native* as Antichristian Document', *NCF*, xiv (September 1959) 123.

4. Henry C. Duffin, *Thomas Hardy: A Study of the Wessex Novels* (Manchester, 1937) p. 4.

5. Northrop Frye, *Anatomy of Criticism* (Princeton, 1957) p. 218.

6. Harold E. Toliver, 'The Dance Under the Greenwood Tree: Hardy's Bucolics', *NCF*, xvii (June 1962) 60.

7. Henri Bergson, *Laughter: An Essay on the Meaning of the Comic*, trans. Cloudesley Brereton and Fred Rothwell (New York, 1914) p. 123.

8. Joseph Warren Beach, *The Technique of Thomas Hardy* (Chicago, 1922) p. 68.

9. Carl Weber, 'Hardy: Twin Voices of Shakespeare', *Shakespeare Association Bulletin*, ix (April 1934) 97.

10. Lascelles Abercombie, *Thomas Hardy: A Critical Study* (New York, 1927) p. 79. For a detailed analysis of Victorian uses of comedy see also Donald J. Gray, 'The Uses of Victorian Laughter', *VS*, x (December 1966) 145–76.

CHAPTER FIVE: STYLISTIC MATURITY IN 'THE RETURN OF THE NATIVE'

1. Hardy's revisions are broadly summarised in Otis B. Wheeler, 'Four Versions of *The Return of the Native*', *NCF*, xiv (June 1959) 27–44. Also relevant here, but more open to question, is John Paterson, *The Making of* THE RETURN OF THE NATIVE, University of California English Studies, no. 19 (Berkeley, 1960).

2. In spite of his attempt to obey this unity, Hardy does make minor errors in his time scheme. For a discussion of these mistakes see A. A. Murphee and C. F Strauch, 'The Chronology of *The Return of the Native*', *MLN*, liv (November 1939) 491–7.

3. George Wing (*Thomas Hardy* (New York, 1963) pp. 54–5) criticises Hardy's technique here, contending that the personification of the heath is an artistic flaw, for a heath cannot be a player.

4. Eugene Goodheart, 'Thomas Hardy and the Lyrical Novel', *NCF*, xii (December 1957) 220–2.

5. Benjamin Sankey, *The Major Novels of Thomas Hardy* (Denver, 1965) p. 53.
6. Blacklock, an eighteenth-century Scottish divine and poet, and Sanderson, a professor of mathematics at Cambridge, were probably not well known even to Hardy's contemporaries. Hardy in all likelihood borrowed his references from Burke's *A Philosophical Inquiry into the Origin of Our Ideas of the Sublime and Beautiful*. For a discussion of Burke's influence on Hardy's choice of allusion see William R. Orwen, 'Hardy and Burke', *AN&Q*, III (April 1965) 116–17.
7. For a summary of these views, see John Hagan, 'A Note on the Significance of Diggory Venn', *NCF*, XVI (September 1961) 146–51.
8. Louis Crompton, 'The Sunburnt God: Ritual and Tragic Myth in *The Return of the Native*', in John Vickery (ed.), *Myth and Literature: Contemporary Theory and Practice* (Lincoln, Nebraska, 1966) p. 293.
9. Paterson (*The Making of 'The Return of the Native'*, pp. 9, 41) contends that Hardy originally intended, in an *Ur* version of the novel, that Diggory should be a nephew of Christian Cantle. But Paterson has misread a manuscript 'whom' for 'who was'. See ms. f. 89.
10. J. O. Bailey's excellent article mentions representatives of this type in several of Hardy's novels. See his 'Hardy's "Mephistophelian Visitants"', *PMLA*, LXI (December 1946) 1146–84.
11. Richard C. Carpenter, 'Thomas Hardy and the Old Masters', *BUSE*, V (spring 1961) 23.
12. John Paterson's contention here (see *The Making of 'The Return of the Native'*) – that Hardy, in an *Ur* version of the novel, intended Eustacia to be a purely satanic villain – is, however, an overstatement. He rests much of his theory on the deletion from the manuscript of a passage in which the peasant chorus calls 'Avice Vye a witch'. In the manuscript these words are legible, but the clauses immediately preceding them – clauses that might modify Hardy's meaning – are illegible. Moreover, the next line in the manuscript reads, 'That's true, said Fairway.'
13. For a fine discussion of the influence of Arnold on Hardy see David J. De Laura, '"The Ache of Modernism" in Hardy's Later Novels', *ELH*, XXXIV (1967) 380–99.
14. Crompton, op. cit., p. 293.
15. J. I. M. Stewart, *Thomas Hardy: A Critical Biography* (New York, 1971) p. 103.
16. Ibid., p. 296.
17. This distinction also supports John Paterson's contention that the novel is subversively anti-Christian. See his edition of *The Return of the Native* (New York, 1966) pp. xxvii–xxviii.
18. As with his previous reference to Napoleon and Saul, Hardy added these two after the manuscript stage.
19. J. I. M. Stewart, op. cit., p. 105. However, Ken Zellenfrow ('*The Return of the Native*: Hardy's Map and Eustacia's Suicide', *NCF*, XXVIII (September 1973) 214–20) argues persuasively for suicide, using manuscript revisions and a map of Egdon Heath to support his thesis.
20. See Robert C. Schweik, 'Theme, Character, and Perspective in Hardy's *The Return of the Native*', *PQ*, XLI (October 1962) 757–67; and Leonard

W. Deen, 'Heroism and Pathos in Hardy's *The Return of the Native*', *NCF*, xv (December 1960) 207–19.

21. The manuscript calls Clym an 'assistant to a Paris jeweller'. The reviewer for the *Athenaeum* (23 November 1878) criticised Hardy for the 'low social position' of his characters, and Hardy presumably revised his text in the light of this comment.

22. De Laura, op. cit., p. 383.

23. Schweik, op. cit., p. 766.

24. D. H. Lawrence, 'Study of Thomas Hardy', in Edward D. McDonald (ed.), *Phoenix: The Posthumous Papers of D. H. Lawrence* (New York, 1972) p. 414.

25. George Wing goes so far as to contend, with sensitive accuracy, that Clym is an early, masculine attempt at Sue Bridehead. See Wing, op. cit., pp. 53–4.

26. Clym himself is later to quote Job, and again Hardy injects irony. Clym answers Humphrey's contention that he could still win Thomasin from Diggory Venn with: 'In the words of Job [31:1], "I have made a covenant with mine eyes; why then should I think upon a maid."'

27. That Hardy deliberately emphasises Clym's circumstantial similarities to the Greek tragic figure is supported by his revisions of the manuscript: the manuscript allusion here reads 'Laocoon', an irrelevant figure in Hardy's pattern for Clym.

28. Michael Millgate (*Thomas Hardy: His Career as a Novelist* (New York, 1971) p. 143) adds an interesting speculation concerning a possible echo of Matthew 13:54–8 in the novel's title. Louis Crompton also notes the use of Oedipus with regard to Clym, rightly contending that the entire mood of 'Aftercourses' is that of *Oedipus at Colonus*.

29. The irony of the situation becomes even more intense with the realisation that the woman in the quotation, Solomon's mother, is Bathsheba, certainly the most notorious mother in the Bible.

CHAPTER SIX: AFTERCOURSES: 'TESS OF THE D'URBERVILLES' AND 'JUDE THE OBSCURE'

1. After he had first failed to get a publisher for *Tess*, Hardy dashed off a minor tale, *The Well-Beloved*, which appeared in the periodical press in 1892. F. B. Pinion says of the novel that it was 'for Hardy largely a divertissement between two serious works of fiction'. See his *A Hardy Companion* (New York, 1968) p. 51.

2. J. T. Laird, *The Shaping of 'Tess of the d'Urbervilles'* (London, 1975). See especially 190 ff. See also Mary Jacobus, 'Tess's Purity', *EIC*, xxvi (October 1976) 318–38.

3. For example, in 1895, after T. H. Huxley had died, Hardy returned to his novel to add *Huxley's Essays*, written in 1892, to a narrative description of Tess's discussion of Angel's philosophy.

4. Florence Emily Hardy, *The Life of Thomas Hardy: 1840–1928* (London, 1962) p. 240.

5. W. R. Rutland, *Thomas Hardy: A Study of his Writings and their Background* (Oxford, 1938) p. 240.

6. Roy Morrell, *Thomas Hardy: The Will and the Way* (Singapore, 1965) p. 32.

7. See Philip Mahone Griffith, 'The Image of the Trapped Animal in Hardy's *Tess of the d'Urbervilles*', *TSE*, XIII (1963) 88.

8. For further discussion of this allusion in context, and of Hardy's probable source, see Jeremy V. Steele, 'Which Ovid in the Hay-Shed? A Note on *Tess of the d'Urbervilles*', *N&Q*, n.s. XXIV (October 1977) 430–2.

9. Hardy had not attributed the quotation to Taylor in the manuscript, so he, too, must have been concerned about its obscurity.

10. Irving Howe, *Thomas Hardy* (London, 1967) p. 112.

11. See Benjamin Sankey, *The Major Novels of Thomas Hardy* (Denver, 1965) p. 51.

12. Dorothy Van Ghent, *The English Novel: Form and Function* (New York, 1953) pp. 208–9.

13. F. B. Pinion, *Thomas Hardy: Art and Thought* (London, 1977) p. 116.

14. Rutland, op. cit., p. 237.

15. Varley Lang, 'Crabbe and *Tess of the d'Urbervilles*', *MLN*, LIII (May 1938) 369–70.

16. Howe, op. cit., p. 122.

17. David J. De Laura, '"The Ache of Modernism" in Hardy's Later Novels', *ELH*, XXXIV (1967), especially 392 ff.

18. See Robert Gittings, *The Older Hardy* (London, 1978), and Peter Casagrande, *Unity in Hardy's Novels: 'Repetitive Symmetries'* (London, 1982).

19. For a review of Hardy's attitude towards Shelley and a list of criticism on the topic see Lennart A. Björk (ed.), *The Literary Notes of Thomas Hardy*, 2 vols (Göteborg, 1974) pp. 357–8. Of the other four allusions to modern poetry, two are appropriately from Swinburne, another poet of ambiguous sexuality, while two are taken from Browning and used ironically. There is no discernable pattern to these clusters.

20. See his introduction to the Riverside Edition of *Tess* (Boston, 1960). Robert Heilman also has a helpful article on Angel entitled '*Gulliver* and Hardy's *Tess*: Houyhnhnms, Yahoos, and Ambiguities', *SR*, VI (spring 1970) 277–301. Pages 296–9 are especially helpful.

21. The two exceptions here, both minor references, are drawn from *As You Like It*. Hardy tells us (p. 183) that he is adopting 'the safe phrase of evasive controversialists' to say that Angel preferred 'sermons in stones to sermons in churches' (II. i. 17). The second reference appears when Angel encounters Mercy Chant (p. 339) and draws on III. ii. 44 to banter with her. He is obviously quoting Touchstone's line, 'Thou art in a parlous state, shepherd,' in jest.

22. For further discussion of Hardy's use of St. Paul in *The Dynasts*, for example, see Björk, op. cit., p. 293.

23. Björk, ibid., suggests that Hardy's own attitude towards Marcus Aurelius' saying is also ambiguous. See p. 289.

24. See R. G. Cox, *Thomas Hardy: The Critical Heritage* (New York, 1970) p. 236.

25. D. H. Lawrence, 'Study of Thomas Hardy', in Edward McDonald (ed.), *Phoenix: The Posthumous Papers of D. H. Lawrence* (New York, 1972) p. 486.

26. Howe, op. cit., p. 128. See also James Hazen, 'The Tragedy of Tess Durbeyfield', *TSLL*, XI (spring 1969) 779–94; Michael Murray, 'The Patterns of Biblical and Classical Myth in the Novels of Thomas Hardy', unpublished dissertation, New York University, 1972, p. 88; Michael Millgate, *Thomas Hardy: His Career as a Novelist* (New York, 1971) p. 272; James Hazen, '*Tess of the d'Urbervilles* and *Antigone*', *ELT*, XIV (1971) 207–15; Arnold Kettle, *An Introduction to the English Novel, Vol. II* (New York: Harper & Row Torchbooks Edition, 1960) pp. 49–62; and Douglas Brown, *Thomas Hardy* (London, 1954) pp. 89–98.

27. See Jacobus, 'Tess's Purity', for an analysis of Hardy's ennobling of Tess.

28. Bernard J. Paris, '"A Confusion of Many Standards": Conflicting Value Systems in *Tess of the d'Urbervilles*', *NCF*, XXIV (June 1969) 76.

29. M. D. Faber, '*Tess* and *The Rape of Lucrece*', *ELN*, V (June 1968) 292–3.

30. Jacobus, 'Tess's Purity', pp. 324–5.

31. Sankey, op. cit., 47.

32. Van Ghent, op. cit., pp. 203–4.

33. In the manuscript Hardy had also used the 'Two Apostles' allusion to describe Marian and Tess, but revised it to 'two Marys' (p. 364). The painting is now attributed to Spinello Aretino.

34. For a full explanation of this law see Judy Weissman, 'The Deceased Wife's Sister Marriage Act and the Ending of *Tess*', *AN&Q*, XIV (May 1976) 132–4.

35. Florence Hardy, op. cit., p. 271.

36. For a full discussion see Rutland, op. cit., pp. 23–40. Mary Ellen Chase, *Thomas Hardy from Serial to Novel* (Minneapolis, 1927) also has a perceptive chapter on Hardy's changes here; see pp. 113–80.

37. For a full discussion of Hardy's revisions see John Paterson, 'The Genesis of *Jude the Obscure*', *SP*, LVII (1960) 87–98, and Patricia Ingham, 'The Evolution of *Jude the Obscure*', *RES*, XXVII (February 1976) 27–37. I am also indebted to Robert O. Slack's unpublished dissertation, 'Variorum Edition of *Jude the Obscure*', University of Pittsburg, 1954, though I have made a study of the manuscript myself.

38. Slack, op. cit., p. xxx.

39. Florence Hardy, op. cit., p. 269.

40. Ibid., p. 325.

41. Rutland, op. cit., pp. 256–7.

42. J. I. M. Stewart, *Thomas Hardy: A Critical Biography* (New York, 1971) p. 191.

43. F. R. Southerington, *Hardy's Vision of Man* (New York, 1971) p. 144.

44. Howe, op. cit., pp. 134–5.

45. Florence Hardy, op. cit., pp. 272–3.

46. As is also recognised by Murray, op. cit., p. 202.

47. Ian Gregor, *The Great Web: The Form of Hardy's Major Fiction* (London, 1974) p. 209.

48. For a thorough discussion of this allusion, see L. M. Findlay, 'Horace's "Carmen Saeculare" and *Jude the Obscure*', *N&Q*, XXIV (October 1977) 428–30.

49. See Norman Holland's fine article, '"Jude the Obscure": Hardy's Symbolic Indictment of Christianity', *NCF*, IX (June 1954) 54. See also Walter Gordon, 'Father Time's Suicide Note in *Jude the Obscure*', *NCF*, XXII (December 1967) 299.

50. Sankey, op. cit., pp. 51–2.
51. See Lewis Horne, '"The Art of Renunciation" in Hardy's Novels', *SNNTS*, IV (winter 1972) 556–67.
52. Hardy marked his copy of this poem heavily at a time in his life when, Robert Gittings proposes, he was experiencing his final loss of faith, due in part to his love for an unknown woman, a kindred spirit with whom he felt in complete sympathy. See his *Young Thomas Hardy* (London, 1975) p. 91.
53. See Frederick McDowell, 'In Defense of Arabella: A Note on *Jude the Obscure*', *ELN*, I (June 1964) 274–80; Lascelles Abercrombie, *Thomas Hardy: A Critical Study* (New York, 1927) p. 31; Pinion, *A Hardy Companion*, p. 300.
54. For a brief discussion of this reference see Millgate, op. cit., p. 324.
55. Lawrence, op. cit., p. 496.
56. However, Lois Deacon, op. cit., F. R. Southerington, op. cit., and F. E. Halliday, *Thomas Hardy: His Life and Work* (Adams, 1972), argue that she was drawn from Tryphena Sparks.
57. Florence Hardy, op. cit., p. 272.
58. See Robert Heilman, 'Hardy's Sue Bridehead', *NCF*, XX (March 1966) 307–23; Michael Steig, 'Sue Bridehead', *Novel*, I (spring 1968) 260–6; the book-length studies of Hardy by Albert J. Guerard (*Thomas Hardy: The Novels and Stories*, Cambridge, 1949) and Howe (op. cit.). For a treatment of Sue in historical perspective see also my essay in *What Manner of Woman* (New York, 1977) pp. 124–59.
59. Robert Gittings, *Young Thomas Hardy*, p. 94.
60. Howe, op. cit., p. 138.
61. Heilman, 'Hardy's Sue Bridehead', 310.
62. See Mary Jacobus, 'Sue the Obscure', *EIC*, XXV (July 1975) 320.
63. It is worth noting that Hardy does not have Sue mention Mill's *The Subjection of Women* here. Apparently Hardy was not as familiar with this more appropriate work. In September 1895 he wrote to Mrs Henniker, 'I am going to get Mill's *Subjection of Women* – which I do not remember ever reading.'
64. Jacobus, 'Sue the Obscure', 312–13.
65. For further discussion of the parallels between Jude's and Sue's relationship and the couple in '*Epipsychidion*', see Michael E. Hassett, 'Compromised Romanticism in *Jude the Obscure*', *NCF*, XXV (March 1971) 440–2.
66. For a discussion of this scene and a comparison with the death of Tess's baby see Penelope Vigar, *The Novels of Thomas Hardy* (London, 1974) p. 207.
67. The following discussion was stimulated by Norman Holland's study (op. cit.) of Hardy's indictment of Christianity, and David De Laura's (op. cit.) of the 'ache of modernism'.
68. Hardy has Jude falling asleep quoting Ken's hymn, ending the quotation with 'teach me to die . . .' The line continues, 'That so I may / Rise glorious at the awful day', a hope he denied both to Jude and to himself.
69. Millgate, op. cit., p. 331.
70. Norman Holland, op. cit., 58.
71. See Ward Hellstrom, 'Hardy's Scholar-Gypsy', in George Goode (ed.), *The English Novel in the Nineteenth Century*, 'Illinois Studies in Language and Literature', no. 63 (Urbana, 1972) p. 204.
72. Murray's dissertation (op. cit., p. 202) drew my attention to this parallel.

73. Florence Hardy, op. cit., p. 177.
74. Herman Meyer, *The Poetics of Quotation in the European Novel*, trans. Theodore and Yetta Ziolkowski (Princeton, 1968) pp. 73, 89.
75. See David Leon Higdon, 'The Sovereign Fragments: A Study of George Eliot's Epigraphs', unpublished dissertation, University of Kansas, 1968, pp. 1–2, 115.
76. Lionel Stevenson, *The Ordeal of George Meredith* (New York, 1953) pp. 322, 62.
77. Meyer, op. cit., pp. 76, 32, 253.
78. Ibid., p. 6.

Bibliography

Abercrombie, Lascelles, *Thomas Hardy: A Critical Study* (New York, 1927).
Academy, review of *The Hand of Ethelberta*, 13 May 1876, 453—4.
Alexander, B. J., 'Criticism and Thomas Hardy's Novels: A Selected Checklist', *SNNTS* (1972) 630—54.
Allott, Kenneth and Miriam (eds), *Introduction to Victorian Prose: 1830—1880* (London, 1956).
Athenaeum, review of *Desperate Remedies*, 1 April 1871, 399.
————, review of *Under the Greenwood Tree*, 15 June 1872, 748.
————, review of *A Pair of Blue Eyes*, 28 June 1873, 820.
————, review of *Far From the Madding Crowd*, 5 December 1874, 747.
————, review of *The Hand of Ethelberta*, 15 April 1876, 523.
————, review of *The Return of the Native*, 23 November 1878, 654.
————, review of *Tess of the d'Urbervilles*, 9 January 1892, 49—50.
Babb, Howard, 'Setting and Theme in *Far From the Madding Crowd*', *ELH*, xxx (June 1963) 147—61.
Bailey, J. O., 'Hardy's "Mephistophelian Visitants"', *PMLA*, LXI (December 1946) 1146—84.
Bartlett, Phyliss, 'Hardy's Shelley', *Keats—Shelley Journal*, IV (1955) 15—29.
Beach, Joseph Warren, *The Technique of Thomas Hardy* (Chicago, 1922).
Beebe, M., B. Culotta, and E. Marcus, 'Criticism of Thomas Hardy: A Selected Checklist', *MFS*, VI (autumn 1960) 258—79.
Bergson, Henri, *Laughter: An Essay on the Meaning of the Comic*, trans. Cloudesley Brereton and Fred Rothwell (New York, 1914).
Björk, Lennart A. (ed.), *The Literary Notes of Thomas Hardy*, 2 vols (Göteborg, Sweden, 1974).
Brennecke, Ernest, Jr., *The Life of Thomas Hardy* (New York, 1925).
Brown, Douglas, *Thomas Hardy* (London, 1954).
Carpenter, Richard C., 'Hardy's "Gargoyles"', *MFS*, VI (autumn 1960) 223—32.
————, 'Thomas Hardy and the Old Masters', *BUSE*, V (spring 1961) 18—28.
————, 'The Mirror and the Sword: Imagery in *Far From the Madding Crowd*', *NCF*, XVIII (March 1964) 331—45.
Casagrande, Peter, *Unity in Hardy's Novels: 'Repetitive Symmetries'* (London, 1982).
Chappell, William, *Old English Popular Music*, rev. H. Ellis Wooldridge (London, 1893).
Chase, Mary Ellen, *Thomas Hardy from Serial to Novel* (Minneapolis, 1927).
Chevalier, Haakon, *The Ironic Temper* (New York, 1932).
Chew, Samuel, *Thomas Hardy: Poet and Novelist* (New York, 1921).
Christensen, Glenn J., 'The Thomas Hardy Collection', *PULC*, VIII (November 1946) 24—7.

Cox, R. G., *Thomas Hardy: The Critical Heritage* (New York, 1970).

Crompton, Louis, 'The Sunburnt God: Ritual and Tragic Myth in *The Return of the Native*', in John Vickery (ed.), *Myth and Literature: Contemporary Theory and Practice* (Lincoln, Nebraska, 1966).

Davidson, Donald, 'The Traditional Basis of Thomas Hardy's Fiction', *Southern Review*, VI (summer 1940) 162–78.

Deacon, Lois, and Terry Coleman, *Providence and Mr. Hardy* (London, 1966).

Deen, Leonard W., 'Heroism and Pathos in Hardy's *The Return of the Native*', *NCF*, XV (December 1960) 207–19.

De Laura, David J., '"The Ache of Modernism" in Hardy's Later Novels', *ELH*, XXXIV (1967) 380–99.

Draffan, Robert, 'Hardy's *Under the Greenwood Tree*', *English*, XXII (1973) 55–60.

Drew, Elizabeth, *The Novel: A Modern Guide to Fifteen English Masterpieces* (New York, 1963).

Duffin, Henry C., *Thomas Hardy: A Study of the Wessex Novels* (Manchester, 1937).

Elliott, Albert P., *Fatalism in the Works of Thomas Hardy* (Philadelphia, 1935).

Examiner, W. Minto, review of *Far From the Madding Crowd*, 5 December 1874, 1329.

Faber, M. D., '*Tess* and *The Rape of Lucrece*', *ELN*, V (June 1968) 292–3.

Findlay, L. M., 'Horace's "Carmen Saeculare" and *Jude the Obscure*', *N&Q*, XXIV (October 1977) 428–30.

Firor, Ruth A., *Folkways in Thomas Hardy* (Philadelphia, 1931).

Friedman, Alan, *The Turn of the Novel* (New York, 1966).

Friedman, Norman, 'Point of View in Fiction: The Development of a Critical Concept', *PMLA*, LXX (December 1955) 1160–84.

Frye, Northrop, *Anatomy of Criticism* (Princeton, 1957).

Gatrell, Simon, 'Hardy, House-Style, and the Aesthetics of Punctuation', in Anne Smith (ed.), *The Novels of Thomas Hardy* (London, 1979).

Gittings, Robert, *Young Thomas Hardy* (London, 1975).

———, *The Older Hardy* (London, 1978).

Goodheart, Eugene, 'Thomas Hardy and the Lyrical Novel', *NCF*, XII (December 1957) 215–25.

Gordon, Walter, 'Father Time's Suicide Note in *Jude the Obscure*', *NCF*, XXII (December 1967) 298–300.

Gray, Donald J., 'The Uses of Victorian Laughter', *VS*, X (December 1966) 145–76.

Gregor, Ian, *The Great Web: The Form of Hardy's Major Fiction* (London, 1974).

Griffith, Philip Mahone, 'The Image of the Trapped Animal in Hardy's *Tess of the d'Urbervilles*', *TSE*, XIII (1963) 85–94.

Grimsditch, Herbert B., *Character and Environment in the Novels of Thomas Hardy* (London, 1925).

Guerard, Albert J., *Thomas Hardy: The Novels and Stories* (Cambridge, 1949).

Hagan, John, 'A Note on the Significance of Diggory Venn', *NCF*, XVI (September 1961) 146–55.

Halliday, F. E., *Thomas Hardy: His Life and Work* (Bath, 1972).

Hardy, Evelyn, *Thomas Hardy: A Critical Biography* (London, 1954).

Hardy, Florence Emily, *The Life of Thomas Hardy: 1840–1928* (London, 1962).

Hardy, Thomas, *Desperate Remedies* (London: Tinsley Brothers, 1871).

————, *Desperate Remedies*, New Wessex Edition, paperback (London: Macmillan, 1975).

————, *Far From the Madding Crowd*, *Eclectic Magazine*, March 1874–February 1875.

————, *Far From the Madding Crowd* (London: Smith, Elder, and Co., 1874).

————, *Far From the Madding Crowd*, ed. Carl J. Weber (New York: Oxford University Press, 1937).

————, *Far From the Madding Crowd*, New Wessex Edition, paperback (London: Macmillan, 1974).

————, *The Hand of Ethelberta* (London: Smith, Elder, and Co., 1876).

————, *The Hand of Ethelberta*, New Wessex Edition, paperback (London: Macmillan, 1975).

————, *Jude the Obscure*, author's manuscript, 377 leaves.

————, *Jude the Obscure*, New Wessex Edition, paperback (London: Macmillan, 1974).

————, *A Pair of Blue Eyes*, author's partial manuscript, 115 leaves.

————, *A Pair of Blue Eyes*, New Wessex Edition, paperback (London: Macmillan, 1975).

————, *The Return of the Native*, author's manuscript, 439 leaves.

————, *The Return of the Native*, *Belgravia Magazine*, January–December 1878.

————, *The Return of the Native*, ed. Cyril Aldred, 'The Scholar's Library' (London: Macmillan, 1935).

————, *The Return of the Native*, New Wessex Edition, paperback (London: Macmillan, 1974).

————, *Tess of the d'Urbervilles*, author's manuscript, 525 leaves.

————, *Tess of the d'Urbervilles*, ed. William Buckler, Riverside Edition (Boston: Houghton Mifflin, 1960).

————, *Tess of the d'Urbervilles*, New Wessex Edition, paperback (London: Macmillan, 1974).

————, *Tess of the d'Urbervilles*, ed. Scott Elledge, Norton Critical Edition (New York: W. W. Norton, 1979).

————, *Under the Greenwood Tree*, author's manuscript, 194 leaves.

————, *Under the Greenwood Tree*, ed. Adrian Alington, 'The Scholar's Library' (London: Macmillan, 1935).

————, *Under the Greenwood Tree*, New Wessex Edition, paperback (London: Macmillan, 1974).

Hassett, Michael E., 'Compromised Romanticism in *Jude the Obscure*', *NCF*, xxv (March 1971) 432–43.

Hawkins, Desmond, *Thomas Hardy* (London, 1950).

Hazen, James, 'The Tragedy of Tess Durbeyfield', *TSLL*, xi (spring 1969) 779–94.

————, '*Tess of the d'Urbervilles* and *Antigone*', *ELT*, xiv (1971) 207–15.

Heilman, Robert, 'Hardy's *Mayor*: Notes on Style', *NCF*, xviii (March 1964) 307–29.

————, 'Hardy's Sue Bridehead', *NCF*, xx (March 1966) 307–23.

———, '*Gulliver* and Hardy's *Tess*: Houyhnhnms, Yahoos, and Ambiguities', *SR*, VI (spring 1970) 277–301.

Hellstrom, Ward, 'Hardy's Scholar-Gypsy', in George Goode (ed.), *The English Novel in the Nineteenth Century*, *Illinois Studies in Language and Literature*, no. 63 (Urbana, 1972).

Higdon, David Leon, 'The Sovereign Fragments: A Study of George Eliot's Epigraphs', unpublished dissertation, University of Kansas, 1968.

Holland, Norman, '"Jude the Obscure": Hardy's Symbolic Indictment of Christianity', *NCF*, IX (June 1954) 50–60.

Holloway, John, *The Victorian Sage: Studies in Argument* (New York, 1965).

Horne, Lewis, '"The Art of Renunciation" in Hardy's Novels', *SNNTS*, IV (winter 1972) 556–67.

Howe, Irving, *Thomas Hardy* (London, 1967).

Howells, William Dean, *Heroines of Fiction* (New York, 1901).

Ingham, Patricia, 'The Evolution of *Jude the Obscure*', *RES*, XXVII (February 1976) 27–37.

Jacobus, Mary, 'Sue the Obscure', *EIC*, XXV (July 1975) 304–28.

———, 'Tess's Purity', *EIC*, XXVI (October 1976) 318–38.

James, Henry, review of *Far From the Madding Crowd*, *Nation*, XIX, 24 December 1874, 423–4.

Johnson, S. F., 'Hardy and Burke's Sublime', in Harold C. Martin (ed.), *Style in Prose Fiction: English Institute Essays 1958* (New York, 1959).

Keefe, Janice Nyman, 'The Textual Revisions in *Far From the Madding Crowd*', *MSE*, V (fall 1975) 10–24.

Kettle, Arnold, *An Introduction to the English Novel*, vol. II (New York: Harper & Row Torchbooks Edition, 1960).

Knox, Norman, *The Word Irony and its Context, 1500–1755* (Durham, 1961).

Laird, J. T., *The Shaping of 'Tess of the d'Urbervilles'* (London, 1975).

Lang, Varley, 'Crabbe and *Tess of the d'Urbervilles*', *MLN*, LIII (May 1938) 369–70.

Lawrence, D. H., 'Study of Thomas Hardy', in Edward D. McDonald (ed.), *Phoenix: The Posthumous Papers of D. H. Lawrence* (New York, 1972).

Lea, Herman, *Thomas Hardy's Wessex* (London, 1913).

Lerner, Laurence, and John Holmstrom (eds), *Thomas Hardy and his Readers: A Selection of Contemporary Reviews* (New York, 1968).

McDowell, Frederick, 'In Defense of Arabella: A Note on *Jude the Obscure*', *ELN*, I (June 1964) 274–80.

Meyer, Herman, *The Poetics of Quotation in the European Novel*, trans. Theodore and Yetta Ziolkowski (Princeton, 1968).

Millgate, Michael, *Thomas Hardy: His Career as a Novelist* (New York, 1971).

Moore, John Robert, 'Two Notes on Thomas Hardy', *NCF*, V (September 1950) 159–63.

Morrell, Roy, *Thomas Hardy: The Will and the Way* (Singapore, 1965).

Morris, Mowbray, review of *Tess of the d'Urbervilles*, *Quarterly Review*, April 1892, 319–26.

Muller, Herbert J., *Modern Fiction* (New York, 1937).

Murphee, A. A., and C. F. Strauch, 'The Chronology of *The Return of the Native*', *MLN*, LIV (November 1939) 491–7.

Murray, Michael, 'The Patterns of Biblical and Classical Myth in the Novels of Thomas Hardy', unpublished dissertation, New York University, 1972.

Myers, Henry, 'Style and the Man', *SAQ*, XL (July 1941) 259–68.

Newton, The Edward A., Collection of Books and Manuscripts (sale catalogue of Parke-Bernet Galleries, Inc.), vol. II, 1941.

Ohmann, Richard, 'Methods in the Study of Victorian Style', *Victorian Newsletter*, no. 27 (spring 1965) 1–4.

Oliphant, Margaret, review of *Tess of the d'Urbervilles*, *Blackwood's Magazine*, March 1892, 464–74.

———, review of *Jude the Obscure*, *Blackwood's Magazine*, January 1896, 135–49.

Orel, Harold, *Thomas Hardy's Personal Writings* (Lawrence, Kansas, 1966).

———, *The Final Years of Thomas Hardy: 1912–28* (London, 1976).

Orwen, William R., 'Hardy and Burke', *AN&Q*, III (April 1965) 116–17.

Palmer, Leslie H., 'The Ironic Word in Hardy's Novels', *TSL*, XX (1975) 109–23.

Paris, Bernard J., '"A Confusion of Many Standards": Conflicting Value Systems in *Tess of the d'Urbervilles*', *NCF*, XXIV (June 1969) 57–79.

Paterson, John, '*The Return of the Native* as Antichristian Document', *NCF*, XIV (September 1959) 111–27.

———, 'The Genesis of *Jude the Obscure*', *SP*, LVII (1960) 87–98.

———, *The Making of 'The Return of the Native'*, *University of California English Studies*, no. 19 (Berkeley, 1960).

———, 'Introduction', *The Return of the Native* (New York: Harper & Row, 1966).

Paul, Herbert, 'The Apotheosis of the Novel under Queen Victoria', *Nineteenth-century*, XLI (May 1897) 769–92.

Pinion, F. B., *A Hardy Companion* (New York, 1968).

———, *Thomas Hardy: Art and Thought* (London, 1977).

Purdy, Richard L., *Thomas Hardy: A Bibliographical Study* (New York, 1954).

Ray, Gordon N., Carl Weber, and John Carter, *Nineteenth-century English Books: Some Problems in Bibliography* (Urbana, 1952).

Richards, Mary Caroline, 'Thomas Hardy's Ironic Vision', *NCF*, III (March 1949) 265–79, and IV (June 1949) 21–35.

Rutland, W. R., *Thomas Hardy: A Study of his Writings and their Background* (Oxford, 1938).

Sankey, Benjamin, *The Major Novels of Thomas Hardy* (Denver, 1965).

Saturday Review, review of *Under the Greenwood Tree*, by H. Moule, 28 September 1872, 417.

———, review of *A Pair of Blue Eyes*, 2 August 1873, 158.

———, review of *Far From the Madding Crowd*, 9 January 1875, 57–8.

Schweik, Robert C., 'Theme, Character and Perspective in Hardy's *The Return of the Native*', *PQ*, XLI (October 1962) 757–67.

———, 'The Early Development of Hardy's *Far From the Madding Crowd*', *TSLL*, IX (1967) 415–28.

Scott, James F., 'Thomas Hardy's Use of the Gothic: An Examination of Five Representative Works', *NCF*, XVII (March 1963) 363–80.

Scott, Nathan, 'The Literary Imagination and the Victorian Crisis of Faith: The Example of Thomas Hardy', *Journal of Religion*, XL (October 1960) 267–81.

Scott, Sir Walter, *The Monastery* (Boston, 1880).

Sedgewick G. G., *Of Irony: Especially in Drama, University of Toronto Studies in Philology and Literature Series*, no. 10 (Toronto, 1935).

Short, Clarice, 'In Defense of Ethelberta', *NCF*, XIII (June 1958) 48–57.

Showalter, Elaine, 'Desperate Remedies: Sensation Novels of the 1860's', *VN*, no. 49 (spring 1976) 1–5.

Slack, Robert C., 'Variorum Edition of *Jude the Obscure*', unpublished dissertation, University of Pittsburgh, 1954.

————, 'Some Characteristics of Hardy's Novels', in William Schutte and others, *Six Novelists; Carnegie Studies in English*, no. 5 (Pittsburgh, 1959) 41–52.

Smart, Alastair, 'Pictorial Imagery in the Novels of Thomas Hardy', *RES*, n.s., XII (August 1961) 262–80.

Southerington, F. R., *Hardy's Vision of Man* (New York, 1971).

Spectator, review of *Desperate Remedies*, 22 April 1871, 481.

————, review of *A Pair of Blue Eyes*, 28 June 1873, 831–2.

————, review of *Far From the Madding Crowd*, 19 December 1874, 1597.

Springer, Marlene (ed.), *What Manner of Woman* (New York, 1977).

Steele, Jeremy V., 'Which Ovid in the Hay-Shed? A Note on *Tess of the d'Urbervilles*', *N&Q*, n.s., XXIV (October 1977) 430–2.

Steig, Michael, 'Sue Bridehead', *Novel*, I (spring 1968) 260–6.

————, 'The Problem of Literary Value in Two Early Hardy Novels', *TSLL*, XII (1970) 55–62.

Stevenson, Lionel, *The Ordeal of George Meredith* (New York, 1953).

Stewart, J. I. M., *Thomas Hardy: A Critical Biography* (New York, 1971).

Tate, Allen, 'Hardy's Philosophic Metaphors', *SoR*, VI (summer 1940) 99–108.

Thirlwall, Connop, ed. J. J. Stewart Perowne, *Remains: Literary and Theological of Connop Thirlwall*, 3 vols (London, 1878).

Thompson, Alan R., *The Dry Mock: A Study of Irony in Drama* (Berkeley, 1948).

Thorpe, James, 'The Aesthetics of Textual Criticism', *PMLA*, LXXX (December 1965) 465–82.

Toliver, Harold E., 'The Dance Under the Greenwood Tree: Hardy's Bucolics', *NCF*, XVII (June 1962) 57–68.

Ullman, Stephen, *Style in French Fiction* (Cambridge, 1957).

Vandiver, Edward P., 'Hardy and Shakespeare Again', *Shakespeare Association Bulletin*, XIII (April 1938) 87–95.

Van Ghent, Dorothy, *The English Novel: Form and Function* (New York, 1953).

Vigar, Penelope, *The Novels of Thomas Hardy* (London, 1974).

Weber, Carl J., 'Hardy: Twin Voices of Shakespeare', *Shakespeare Association Bulletin*, IX (April 1934) 91–7.

————, 'Plagiarism and Thomas Hardy', *The Colophon*, n.s., II (July 1937) 443–54.

————, *Hardy of Wessex* (New York, 1940).

————, *The First Hundred Years of Thomas Hardy 1840–1940: A Centenary Bibliography of Hardiana* (Waterville, Maine, 1942).

————, 'Hardy's Copy of Schopenhauer', *CLQ*, IV (November 1957) 217–24.

Webster, H. C., *On a Darkling Plain: The Art and Thought of Thomas Hardy* (Chicago, 1947).

Weissman, Judy, 'The Deceased Wife's Sister Marriage Act and the Ending of *Tess*', *AN&Q*, XIV (May 1976) 132–4.

Wheeler, Otis B., 'Four Versions of *The Return of the Native*', *NCF*, XIV (June 1959) 27–44.

Wing, George, *Thomas Hardy* (New York, 1963).
Zellenfrow, Ken, '*The Return of the Native*: Hardy's Map and Eustacia's Suicide', *NCF*, xxviii (September 1973) 214–20.

Index